The Endangered Species Act

The Endangered Species Act

A Stanford Environmental Law Society Handbook

STANFORD UNIVERSITY PRESS
STANFORD, CALIFORNIA

Stanford University Press
Stanford, California

© 2001 by the Board of Trustees of the
Leland Stanford Junior University

Printed in the United States of America

Library of Congress Cataloging-in-Publication Data

The Endangered Species Act
by the Stanford Environmental Law Society
    p. cm. – (A Stanford Environmental Law Society handbook)
  Includes bibliographical references and index
  ISBN 0-8047-3842-4 (alk. paper)
ISBN 0-8047-3843-2 (paper: alk. paper)
    1. United States. Endangered Species Act of 1973. 2. Endangered species – Law and
legislation – United States. I. Stanford Environmental Law Society. II. Series.

KF5640 .E48 2001
346.7304'69522 – dc21   00-0562091

This book is printed on acid-free, archival quality paper.

Original printing 2001
Last figure below indicates year of this printing:
10   09   08   07   06   05   04   03   02   01

Typeset by Mary Ann Rundell in 10 Book Antiqua

To Paul Brest

Staff

Editors-in-Chief

P. Stephanie Easley
Jason P. Holtman
Janine Scancarelli
Brian A. Schmidt

Author

Stanford Environmental Law Society

Author Team Members (completed chapters)

Josh Eagle
P. Stephanie Easley
Jason Holtman
Kristina Emanuels Phipps

Ana Rowena Mallari
Janine Scancarelli
Brian Schmidt
Shannon Petersen

Editing/Writing Staff

Michelle Friedland
Ryan Harris
Kara Moran
Janette Schue
Janelle Kellman
Mallory Stewart
Valerie Burman
Leslie Barnhorn
Julie Willoughby
Mie Lewis
Lynn Fischer
Clay Samford
Lincoln Davies
Dan Chiplock
Brian Fonville
Andrea Kendrick

Jessica Gonzalez
Kyle Lonergan
Amy Wepsic
Annie Mbote
Ethan Schutt
Michael Strauss
Deborah Bardwick
Stig Colberg
Alicia Thesing
Sanjay Ranchod
Paul Logan
Juge Gregg
Tom Ballantine
Angela Chabot
Brian Johnson
Kol Medina

Cover photo by Galen Rowell
Reprinted with permission

Contents

PREFACE

The law pertaining to endangered species protection is complex and dynamic. The goal of this book is to enable both lawyers and lay people to understand the impetus for and the implementation of the Endangered Species Act. This book is also intended to assist members of local, state, and federal governments who are frequently confronted with complicated legal, science, and policy decisions involving endangered or threatened species and their habitat. As with most legal frameworks governing environmental and natural resource protection, controversy and change are regular features of the legal landscape relating to endangered species. For example, as this book goes to print, competing proposals to weaken and strengthen the Act (in the form of reauthorization bills) make their way through congressional offices. Consequently, this book cannot and should not be a substitute for the guidance and advice of an attorney.

While we cannot possibly thank everyone involved with developing this book, there are some people we would like to give special mention. The following people associated with Stanford Law School were essential to this project: Dan Olincy, Yvonne Yazzie, Frank Brucato, Buzz Thompson, Paul Brest, Rinnie Nardone, Marina Sleeper, Josh Eagle, Debbie Sivas, Paul Lomio, Andy Eisenberg, and the incredible Stanford Law School Library staff. The following people provided invaluable guidance by reading and commenting on chapters, or by supplying information used in writing and editing the book: J. B. Ruhl, Linus Masouredis, Kristen Boyles, Sybil Ackerman, Jim Moose, Mike Sherwood, Murray D. Feldman, William Snape, Susan Jacobsen, Irene James, Dan Licht, Susan Lieberman, Mark Albert, Kristein Nelson, Eileen Sobeck, Susan Jacobsen, Connie Heller, Tara L. Mueller, Herb Raffel, the U.S. Fish and Wildlife Service Office of International Affairs, and Alison Willy. All errors and omissions are, of course, the sole responsibility of the author, the Stanford Environmental Law Society.

The original steering committee members provided the initial impetus for this book in the spring of 1997: Meg Caldwell, Susan Cleveland, Jason Holtman, Janine Scancarelli, Kristina Phipps, Jessica Gonzales, Julie Willoughby, Lynn Fisher, Ana Mallari, Brian Schmidt, and Noah Sachs. Special thanks are due to both Stanford Law School, for all the assistance the school provided, and Stanford University Press, for taking on this project.

We are enormously grateful for the careful and expert advice of Laura Comay, Kate Warne, and Harrison Shaffer at Stanford University Press. Laura and Kate were unfailing in their belief in the importance of this project and were stalwart in supporting ELS through completion of this book.

We would also like to thank the superbly competent Mary Ann Rundell, who always kept a sense of humor while converting mere text to finished pages.

The one person who falls in a category all by herself is Meg Caldwell, Director of Environmental and Natural Resources Law and Policy Program at Stanford Law School. Her unwavering enthusiasm and support carried this book through all the tightest spots.

The Endangered Species Act

The Modern Extinction Crisis and the Endangered Species Act

I would be in favor of undertaking tremendous costs to preserve the bald eagle, and other major species, but that kind of effort is out of proportion to the value of the woundfin minnow, or the snail darter, or the lousewort, or the waterbug, or many others that we are attempting to protect.

SENATOR JAKE GARN (R-UT)
Committee on Environment and Public Works
Legislative History of the Endangered Species Act of 1973 (1982)

The last word of ignorance is the man who says of an animal or plant: what good is it?. . . If the biota, in the course of aeons, has built something we like but do not understand, then who but a fool would discard seemingly useless parts? To keep every cog and wheel is the first precaution of intelligent tinkering.

ALDO LEOPOLD
A Sand County Almanac (1949)

Life began on this planet about four billion years ago. It is estimated that there are now between ten million and one hundred million species on earth.[1]

In between, the world has seen several very significant extinction events, each of which resulted in temporary decreases in biodiversity.[2] Scientists have identified five periods of mass extinction within the last

---

1. *See* Thomas Lovejoy, *Biodiversity: What is It?, in* Biodiversity II: Understanding and Protecting Our Biological Resources 7 (Marjorie L. Reaka-Kudla et al. eds., 1997).

2. According to the Convention on Biological Diversity (1992), "'Biological diversity' [or biodiversity] means the variability among living organisms from all sources including, inter alia, terrestrial, marine and other aquatic ecosystems and the ecological complexes of which they are part; this includes diversity within species, between species and of ecosystems."

five hundred million years. The best known are the Permian-Triassic extinctions 245 million years ago, the Cretaceous-Tertiary extinctions 65 million years ago, and the Pleistocene-Holocene extinctions only eleven thousand years ago. Approximately 65 percent of terrestrial species perished during the Permian-Triassic, while 90 percent of terrestrial and marine reptiles, including the dinosaurs, disappeared during the Cretaceous-Tertiary.[3] During the Pleistocene-Holocene, some combination of climate change and prehistoric human over-hunting killed off many large mammal genera and species, such as the giant ground sloth, the mastodon, and the sabertooth tiger.[4] Now, as E. O. Wilson puts it, "[t]he sixth great extinction spasm of geological time is upon us, grace of mankind."[5]

Our species, *Homo sapiens*, emerged only about one hundred thousand years ago, at a time when biodiversity was at what is believed to have been its all-time high. Since the arrival of humans, however, the total number of species on earth has declined, with the most dramatic decrease occurring over the last few centuries. Most important, the current rate of extinctions far exceeds the so-called background rate.[6]

Humans have been and continue to be the chief cause of many of these extinctions. Because of human activity, including over-hunting, the introduction of non-native (exotic) species, and habitat degradation, biodiversity today has fallen to its lowest level in 65 million years, about the time the dinosaurs died out.[7]

The modern extinction crisis differs in important ways from earlier events. With the possible exception of the Pleistocene-Holocene extinc-

---

3. *See* National Research Council, Science and the Endangered Species Act viii (1995).

4. *See id.* at 27-9. *See generally* Paul S. Martin, *Prehistoric Overkill, in* Quaternary Extinctions 354 (Paul S. Martin & Richard G. Klein eds., 1984).

5. E. O. Wilson *quoted in* Biodiversity and the Law 33 (William J. Snape III ed.) (1996).

6. The continual extinction of species is part of evolution. Geological records have allowed scientists to estimate a "normal" or "background" rate of extinction. Some research estimates that, in the absence of catastrophic events, species go extinct at the rate of about eight per million years. *See* David M. Raup and J. John Sepkoski, Jr., *Mass Extinctions in the Marine Fossil Record*, 215 Science 1501 (1982). The precise rate of modern extinctions is difficult to estimate. The U.S. Fish and Wildlife Service (FWS) lists 1036 animals and 722 plants worldwide as either endangered or threatened under the Endangered Species Act. *See* U.S. Fish & Wildlife Service, *Box Score Listing and Recovery Plans as of November 30, 1999* (visited May 21, 2000) <http://endangered.fws.gov/boxscore.html>. Scientists believe that 60 species of mammals have died out in the recent past, and that close to 40 species of freshwater fishes in the United States have become extinct over the last century. *See* National Research Council, *supra* note 3, at 33. One estimate places the current global extinction rate somewhere between one hundred and one thousand times the pre-human level. *See* F. Stuart Chapin et al., *Biotic Control over the Functioning of Ecosystems*, 277 Science 500 (1997).

7. E. O. Wilson, The Diversity of Life 280, 330 (1992).

tions, major physical events like climate change precipitated earlier mass extinctions, while the activities of one species alone have caused the current crisis. In addition, modern extinctions threaten all groups of organisms, not just particular groups, like dinosaurs or large mammals.[8]

A. Economic and Direct Human Health Benefits of Saving Species

Man should be concerned about the scope and rate of modern extinctions of plant and other animal species for many reasons. To begin with, many of our modern drugs derive from plants and animals. The rosy periwinkle, a tropical flower, supplies compounds necessary for a chemotherapy treatment that has dramatically increased the remission rates of certain cancers. The Pacific yew tree, native to the United States, yielded another cancer drug. Marketed as Taxol, it is used to treat breast and ovarian cancers that have not responded to other treatments. With 1997 sales of nearly $1 billion, it is the largest selling cancer drug in the world.[9] Provir, a promising new drug based on latex from the South African croton tree,[10] was developed to treat symptoms associated with AIDS.[11] Scientists have studied only a small fraction of species for their potential medical uses, but the overall economic value of plant-derived pharmaceuticals tops tens of billions of dollars annually.[12]

Plants and animals are not only useful for directly extracted agents, but also as scientific models. The cheetah, for example, is a living cardiovascular model. It can accelerate to speeds over 70 miles per hour and maintain that pace for several hundred meters. Cheetahs can withstand sudden and severe oxygen debt, which may harbor vital clues for the treatment of heart disease, blood pressure, and circulatory disorders in humans.

Biodiversity also preserves genetic diversity, essential to protecting and improving our food supply. Currently, most of the world's food supply comes from fewer than 20 species of plants.[13] Modern agriculture

---

8. *See* National Research Council, *supra* note 3, at 25.

9. *See* Carol Smith, *Researchers Pin Hopes on New Cancer Treatment*, Seattle Post-Intelligencer, Aug. 11, 1998, at B1, *available in* 1998 WL 4302143 (August 11, 1998).

10. *See Chemical Market Reporter: A Growing Market for Botanicals Broadens the Reach of Global Sourcing*, Chemical Business Newsbase, July 28, 1998, *available in* 1998 WL 14751796 (July 28, 1998).

11. *See id.*

12. *See* Norman Myers, A Wealth of Wild Species 90-91 (1983). *See generally* Ruth Patrick, *Biodiversity: Why is it Important?*, *in* Biodiversity II 15 (Marjorie L. Reaka-Kudla et al. eds., 1997); Stephen R. Kellert, The Value of Life (1996); A. Randall, *What Mainstream Economists Have to Say About the Value of Biodiversity*, *in* Biodiversity (Edward O. Wilson ed., 1988).

13. P. Ehrlich & A. Ehrlich, Extinction: The Causes and Consequences of the

has achieved unprecedented productivity among these crops, in part because of the uniformity of crop strains. But this uniformity has left modern crops vulnerable to pests and blights. Genetic diversity supplied by the wild cousins of commercial crops helps protect these crops, thus safeguarding the human food supply. In 1970, about 15 percent of the U.S. corn crop was lost to a leaf blight, resulting in a two billion dollar cost to farmers and consumers.[14] This epidemic was halted only with the aid of blight-resistant germ plasm of unique genetic ancestry that originated in Mexico. Right now genes from a wild Ethiopian barley plant protect the entire $160 million California barley crop from yellow dwarf virus.[15]

Humans value biodiversity for nonutilitarian reasons as well. Many people simply enjoy plants and animals, and believe extinction causes irreparable loss. A compelling case can be made that species should be conserved "because they exist and because this existence is itself . . . the present expression of a continuing historical process of immense antiquity and majesty. Long-standing existence in Nature is deemed to carry with it the unimpeachable right to continued existence."[16] Less poetically, Congress declared that species of fish, wildlife, and plants possess "esthetic . . . educational, historical [and] recreational" value.[17] Even for those who do not take direct pleasure from contact with endangered species, knowing that wild things thrive in faraway places can provide sufficient reason for preservation.

Many people believe that species should be protected for their own sake. Religions often teach that life has inherent value and that humans are stewards for the earth and the living things upon it.[18] For many, the human-caused loss of a species is both incalculable and immoral.[19]

Disappearance of Species 62 (1981).

14. N. Myers, The Sinking Ark: A New Look at the Problem of Disappearing Species 63-64 (1979).

15. See Al Gore, Earth in the Balance 139 (1992). See generally Cary Fowler & Pat Mooney, Shattering: Food, Politics, and the Loss of Genetic Diversity (1990).

16. D. Ehrenfeld, The Arrogance of Humanism (1978), quoted in P. Ehrlich & A. Ehrlich, supra note 13, at 48.

17. See 16 U.S.C. § 1531(a)(3).

18. Some organized religious groups, such as the Evangelical Environmental Network (EEN), have used TV, radio, and print ads to speak out against amendments that would weaken the Endangered Species Act. The Washington Post reprinted the EEN's "Evangelical Declaration on the Care of Creation," which quoted from the Bible to argue that humans had an obligation to preserve and protect all species. See Bill Broadway, Tending God's Garden: Evangelical Group Embraces Environment, Washington Post, Feb. 17, 1996, at C8.

19. See generally Environmental Philosophy (Michael E. Zimmerman et al. eds., 1993).

Nevertheless, to many people the need to preserve biodiversity seems less obvious than the need to safeguard other resources, like clean air and water. In part, this is because scientists often cannot fully characterize or quantify the economic loss to humans of any particular species extinction. No one knows exactly the worth of the Houston toad or the spotted owl, or the effect their disappearance may have on human welfare. Congress passed the Endangered Species Act[20] in part to compensate for this scientific uncertainty and to remove the fate of species from the free market.

B. Ecological Benefits of Saving Species

Biodiversity is also important to humans in more subtle ways. It contributes to ecosystem stability, sustaining natural resources and energy flows upon which we all depend. Plants supply oxygen to the air we breathe through photosynthesis. Forests reduce evaporation, limit erosion, and protect our water supplies. Invertebrates decompose plant and animal wastes, supplying nutrients to the soil. Species extinctions erode the ecological foundation for our existence.[21] If enough species die out, our planetary ecosystem may collapse to the point where it can no longer support human life.[22]

A change in the composition of the earth's natural systems can have a far-reaching effect. Tropical forest depletion illustrates this problem. Destruction of these forests reduces the recycling of water from plant to atmosphere, increases the reflectivity of the earth's surface, and decreases the earth's capacity to store "greenhouse gases" like carbon dioxide. The vast majority of scientists and political communities agree that human activity is causing a warming of the earth's climate.[23] While increasing global emissions cause the warming, the loss of tropical forests and the species that depend on tropical rainforest habitat exacerbates the problem.

Human activities can also affect natural systems on a more local scale. A well-known example involves the effect of the commercial taking of sea otters for their pelts. The North Pacific sea otter was hunted to near extinction in the 1800s. The otter's primary food source is the sea

---

20. 16 U.S.C. §§ 1531-1544, hereinafter "ESA."

21. *See* Donella Meadows, *Preserving Biodiversity is Protecting Life on Earth,* Los Angeles Times, May 13, 1990, at 4.

22. *See generally* Paul R. Ehrlich & Jonathan Roughgarden, The Science of Ecology (1987); Chapin, *supra* note 6.

23. *See* Jay Michaelson, *Geoengineering: A Climate Change Manhattan Project,* 17 Stan. Envtl. L.J. 73, 74 (1998).

urchin, which in turn depends on kelp for food. As hunters eradicated otters from certain regions, sea urchin populations swelled and foraged on kelp to such an extent that whole areas were swept clean of kelp. This systemic change led to local depopulation of kelp-dependent species.[24]

C. *Homo sapiens* and the Extinction of Species

In recent history, human activities have increased the rate of species extinctions. The precise rate of modern extinctions, however, is difficult to calculate. One estimate places the current global extinction rate some-where between one hundred to one thousand times the pre-human level.[25] Biology professor E. O. Wilson predicts that "a fifth or more of the species of plants and animals could vanish or be doomed to early extinction by the year 2020 unless better efforts are made to save them."[26] These extinctions are primarily caused by human actions, including hunting, introduction of exotic species, pollution and atmospheric change, and, most important, habitat destruction.[27] Wilson estimates that there are between ten and one hundred million species existing on earth today.[28] Only about 1.5 million species have actually been identified.[29] Given these statistics, it is likely that we do not even know what we are losing.

C.1. Species Decline Directly Caused by Human Activity

Consumer tastes have caused many species to decline to the point where they would not survive without human assistance. From elephant tusks, rhinoceros horn, sea otter pelts, tiger bones, exotic bird feathers, and sea turtle shells, all the way to rare orchids sought by collectors, hu-man fancies have caused the decline or extinction of some of the earth's most charismatic species.

Because of our ability to design and manufacture powerful tools, *Homo sapiens* have become the most effective and efficient predators the world has ever seen. It is not difficult for humans to hunt a species to extinction, and it is becoming easier. For example, from prehistoric times

---

24. W. J. Bond, *Keystone Species, in* Biodiversity and Ecosystem Function, 237 (E. D. Schulze and H. A. Moody, eds., 1993).

25. *See* F. Stuart Chapin, et al., "Biotic Control over the Functioning of Ecosystems," 277 *Science* (1997): 500.

26. E. O. Wilson, *supra* note 7, at 346.

27. *See id.*

28. *See id.* at 132.

29. P. Ehrlich & A. Ehrlich, *supra* note 13, at 17.

until about sixty years ago, man hunted giant bluefin tuna exclusively with harpoons and primitive traps. Consumption was local due to rapid spoilage of the fish. Today, bluefin tuna—highly sought after because of its high market price in Japan—is caught using specially designed gear, spotter aircraft, and satellite technology. Once captured, the fish can be moved, on ice, from the Atlantic Ocean to Japan in less than 24 hours. Equipped with such efficient capture and delivery systems and rewarded with nearly inelastic market demand, humans have hunted bluefin to barely sustainable populations in a very short period of time. From 1975 to 1998, market-driven fishing reduced western Atlantic bluefin populations by more than 80 percent.[30]

The demise of the North American bison provides another example of the speed at which we can reduce the population of a hunted species. At the time of westward expansion in the United States, there were about 30 million bison.[31] By 1894, only about 25 wild bison remained in the west, protected in Yellowstone National Park.[32]

C.2. Species Decline Indirectly Caused by Human Activity
C.2.a. Non-Native Species Introductions

In addition to hunting wild species, humans can affect other species by changing or destroying the landscapes in which they exist. The introduction of non-native species, both deliberately and inadvertently, has caused the displacement and extirpation of species throughout the United States. Pollution and atmospheric changes are affecting species in many ways, some of which we do not fully comprehend yet.

Exotic species introductions disrupt ecological and economic systems. Scientists have identified more than 4,500 introduced species in the United States.[33] Some of these species do enormous ecological damage and cost millions of dollars annually. The zebra mussel, a small freshwater mollusk native to eastern Europe and western Asia, for example, has spread from the Great Lakes down the Mississippi, across the entire eastern United States. Scientists believe that the zebra mussel was acci-

---

30. *Report of the Standing Committee on Research and Statistics,* International Commission for the Conservation of Atlantic Tunas (1998).

31. T. McHugh, The Time of the Buffalo 17 (1972).

32. *Id.* at 294.

33. *See National Invasive Species Act of 1996: Hearings on S.1660 Before the Subcomm. on Drinking Water, Fisheries, and Wildlife, of the Senate Comm. on Env't and Pub. Works,* 104th Cong. 19 (statement of Rowan Gould, Deputy Assistant Dir. Fisheries, U.S. FWS, (citing Congressional Office of Technology Assessment, Harmful Nonindigenous Species in The United States (1993)).

dentally introduced to North America from ship ballast water. The mussel's high reproductive rate and ability to attach to hard surfaces have caused havoc along the inland waterways of the eastern United States.[34] It is estimated this tiny mollusk will cost water users at least $120 million per year because zebra mussel colonies invade and clog water diversion and conveyance systems.[35] The zebra mussel has also contributed to the disappearance of native fresh-water mussels in the Great Lakes and the Mississippi.[36]

Aquatic plants, many released from home aquariums and ponds, are choking waterways in the south, displacing native aquatic plants and the wildlife that utilizes them. Eurasian water milfoil is wrecking native systems from Louisiana bayous to the Lake Tahoe Basin. Water hyacinth and hydrilla are other examples of highly invasive species. Non-native predatory sport fishes like brown trout and northern pike are out-competing and damaging native fish communities.[37]

Non-native species also threaten terrestrial plants and animals. Spotted knapweed is increasing soil erosion and decreasing biodiversity on millions of acres in the western United States.[38] Kudzu is smothering native forests in the eastern United States. Exotic animals such as the nutria and the gypsy moth have significantly affected native species throughout the United States. Altogether, competition with and predation by non-native species is cited as a factor in the threatened or endangered status of half the species listed under the ESA.[39]

C.2.b. Pollution and Atmospheric Change

Scientists do not yet know exactly how pollution and climate change affect species diversity. In effect, we are conducting a global experiment. One alarming omen is the worldwide crash in amphibian populations. Amphibians are disappearing from all parts of the world,

---

34. *See generally* U.S. Geological Survey, *Zebra Mussel Information* (visited May 21, 2000) <http://nas.er.usgs.gov/zebra.mussel/>.

35. *See National Invasive Species Act of 1996: Hearings on S.1660 Before the Subcomm. on Drinking Water, Fisheries, and Wildlife, of the Senate Comm. on Env't and Pub. Works, supra* note 33.

36. *See id.* at 8 (statement of Sen. Glenn).

37. *See* U.S. Geological Survey, *Nonindigenous Aquatic Species* (visited May 21, 2000) <http://nas.er.usgs.gov/>.

38. *See* Roger L. Sheley & James S. Jacobs, *Response of Spotted Knapweed and Grass to Picloram and Fertilizer Combinations*, 50 Journal of Range Management 263 (1997).

39. Curtis H. Flather, Linda A. Joyce, Carol A. Bloomgarden, *Species Endangerment Patterns in the United States*, U.S. Department of Agriculture, General Technical Report RM-241 (1994).

including Yosemite National Park, the Rocky Mountains, and throughout South America, the United Kingdom, and the Australian rainforests.[40] A well-known example is the Costa Rican golden toad. The golden toad was noted for its beauty; the males were bright, glossy orange and the females were black, red, and yellow. In 1987, more than 1,500 toads were recorded at breeding ponds in Monteverde Cloud Forest Reserve in Costa Rica. In 1989, one golden toad was sighted at these ponds. Despite intensive searching, no one has seen a golden toad since 1989, and the species is assumed to be extinct.[41]

No one is sure what has caused amphibians such as the golden toad to decline. One possibility is that the thinning ozone layer allows more ultraviolet radiation to penetrate their eggs.[42] Alternately, some researchers have suggested that acid rain lowers the pH of breeding pools, killing the eggs and larvae.[43] Another possibility is that an environmental change has enabled a ubiquitous fungus, previously harmless, to attack amphibians.[44] Some scientists suspect that rising global temperatures and declining rainfall may stress amphibians enough so that this fungus can kill them.[45]

C.2.c. Habitat Alteration

Habitat modification, fragmentation, and destruction are the leading causes of human-induced extinctions, playing a part in the endangered status of about 95 percent of ESA listed species.[46] It is easy to see how habitat destruction, for example, paving an area, harms a species. Species that formerly lived in a now clear-cut forest will have to move elsewhere. The ability to move may be limited by the species' physiological or behavioral characteristics, or by the lack of other nearby available habitat.

The effects of habitat modification, for instance, the removal of all large trees from a given forest, while less obvious, are often no less harmful. Certain owl species will only nest in trees of a certain age, and thus

---

40. Timothy R. Halliday & W. Ronald Heyer, *The Case of the Vanishing Frogs,* 100 Tech. Review 56 (1997), *available in* 1997 WL 9803408 (May 15, 1997).

41. *See id.; see also,* John Tuxill, *The Latest News on the Missing Frogs,* 11 World Watch 9 (1998) (*available in* 1998 WL 15229390).

42. *See* John Tuxill, *supra* note 41.

43. *See* Timothy R. Halliday & W. Ronald Heyer, *supra* note 40.

44. *See* John Tuxill, *supra* note 41.

45. *Id.*

46. *See* Curtis H. Flather, Linda A. Joyce, Carol A. Bloomgarden, *supra* note 39, at 9.

removal of these trees results in *de facto* habitat destruction, even though the forest still exists.

Habitat fragmentation, for example, the construction of a road through a given forest, can also have significant impacts. In such cases, the amount of habitat lost to a species can far exceed the area that has been cleared to make way for the road. Some animals cannot or will not live near cleared spaces, such as the new road. The reduction in habitat caused by the building of the road will equal the area that the road occupies plus some amount of "edge" habitat on either side. Some species need a large, contiguous area. In that case, the construction of the road may render the entire previously occupied area unsuitable.

C.2.d. Costs of Species Protection

ESA critics point to the direct and indirect costs borne by private landowners associated with ESA implementation as grounds for reforming the law. Direct costs to landowners include the costs of habitat conservation plan (HCP) preparation and development design alteration. Indirect costs are more difficult to accurately gauge. These include the opportunity costs of foregone development that might have been approved in the absence of the Act, including lost labor income, and changes in general economic growth for the affected community or region.[47]

Comparing costs and benefits of species protection is a difficult task and may be futile given the incommensurate time scales, many uncertainties, and incalculable price tags on both sides of the ledger.

C.2.e.   Taking Stock

The ESA is nearly three decades old. It remains the "broadest and most powerful law" in the world for the protection of species.[48] However, the ESA has not saved all listed species from extinction. A recent report by the National Research Council found that the ESA has "prevented the extinction of some species and slowed the declines of others," but that "the ESA by itself cannot prevent the loss of many species and their habitats."[49]

Critics of the law argue, among other things, that it has failed in its primary goal; they point to the fact that very few species have been de-

---

47. See, *e.g.*, National Endangered Species Act Reform Coalition (visited May 21, 2000) <www.nesarc.org>.

48. National Research Council, *supra* note 3, at 1.

49. *Id.* at 4.

listed, that is, recovered to a population level where they are no longer considered threatened or endangered. There are many factors that limit the potential recovery of listed species. For one thing, full implementation of the law has never been possible due to severe deficiencies in funding. And it is doubtful that even a fully funded ESA would result in the de-listing of many species. As noted, loss of habitat is the reason that 95 percent of species become threatened or endangered. Unless we devise a method for manufacturing new habitat, which seems unlikely, these species will probably never recover. It is worth noting that species that have been de-listed were not habitat constrained. For example, the peregrine falcon and bald eagle were endangered primarily because pesticides constrained their ability to reproduce. Gray whales were threatened by over-hunting.

Clearly though, endangered and threatened species are better off with the ESA than without it.[50] When originally listed, virtually all threatened and endangered species were declining in numbers, but after listing, many species stabilized and improved.[51] Slowly, the ESA is making a difference in the rate of extinctions.

It is hard to argue that slowing the rate of human caused extinctions is not an admirable objective. Some argue that the financial cost of merely allowing a species to exist for a limited period of time is not justified. Others feel that resources would be better spent on protecting species not yet in jeopardy. While few people would advocate the elimination of a species, some do defend taking action that will result in species decline or extinction,[52] citing, for example, beliefs that the potential danger to the species is overstated or that the loss of a species is a small price to pay for "progress."

As the ESA enters the 21st century, its fate remains as uncertain as many of the species it protects. As the extent of the extinction problem has become clearer, the widespread, unqualified support the law enjoyed in its early years has diminished. It is not just a few large, beautiful species that are going extinct. Many smaller, less aesthetically pleasing ones are disappearing as well. While it is easy to justify the cost of protecting

50. Jeffrey J. Rachlinski, *Noah by the Numbers: An Empirical Evaluation of the Endangered Species Act*, 82 Cornell L. Rev. 356, 383 (1997) (book review).

51. *See id.*

52. Not long after the FWS listed the northern spotted owl as threatened, the timber industry sponsored rallies in the Pacific Northwest against the decision to list. At one such rally, a journalist observed t-shirts and bumper stickers emblazoned with slogans like "Save a Logger—Eat an Owl" and "I Love Spotted Owls—Fried." *See* Paul Taylor, *Spotted Owl Creates Flap in Governor's Campaign*, Washington Post, July 6, 1990, at A6.

the eagle in the court of public opinion, it is hard for some to understand why the Delhi Sands flower-loving fly ought to be protected as well.

C.2.f. Overview of the ESA and this Handbook

This handbook explains how the ESA works — what the law says and how the implementing agencies, the U.S. Fish and Wildlife Service and the National Marine Fisheries Service, have interpreted and applied the law.[53]

Chapter One provides a brief history of the Act and its goal, "to provide a means whereby the ecosystems upon which endangered species and threatened species depend may be conserved. . . ."[54]

The ESA aims at reaching those goals in a variety of ways, described in the remaining chapters of this handbook. First, in Sections 4 (*see* Chapter Two), 7 (*see* Chapter Three), and 9 (*see* Chapter Four),[55] the ESA mandates that certain activities be undertaken by federal agencies. The law requires the Secretary to (1) list endangered species; (2) designate critical habitat for listed species; (3) evaluate the impact of other federal agencies' activities on listed species; (4) formulate recovery plans for listed species; (5) monitor the recovery of listed species; and (6) enforce the law's prohibition on harming listed species.

Other federal agencies are required to consult with the Secretary regarding the impact of their activities on listed species. All federal agencies must "utilize their authorities in furtherance of the purposes of" the ESA.[56] The ESA also encourages the Secretary to work with other nations in their efforts to protect listed species.[57]

In addition to requiring that federal agencies do certain things, the ESA also requires that federal agencies not do certain things. It places restrictions, through the provisions of Section 7, on activities "authorized, funded, or carried out by" all federal agencies.[58] With one significant exception, the ESA prohibits such federal activities to the extent that they "jeopardize the continued existence of any endangered species or threatened species."[59]

---

53. The full text of the ESA, 16 U.S.C. §§ 1531-1544, appears in the Appendix.
54. 16 U.S.C. §1531(b).
55. 16 U.S.C. §§1533, 1536 and 1538, respectively.
56. 16 U.S.C. §1536(a)(1).
57. 16 U.S.C. §1537.
58. 16 U.S.C. §1536(a)(2).
59. *Id.*

Through Sections 9 and 11 (*see* Chapters Four and Seven), the law protects individual listed organisms by prohibiting the wrongful take of those organisms by private or government actors. Under the law and regulations, "taking" covers a wide range of acts, from actually killing the organism to harassing it to modifying or destroying its habitat.

Chapter Five of the handbook explains how the FWS has implemented the incidental take permit and HCP process under Section 10 of the Act, including discussion of the controversial "no surprises" policy. The HCP process was developed to give incentives to non-federal land managers and private landowners to help protect listed and unlisted species while allowing some development that may harm listed species.

Chapter Six of the handbook describes ESA provisions relating to international cooperation for endangered and threatened species protection.

Finally, Chapter Seven explains how Section 11 of the Act provides for citizen enforcement of the law. Section 11 gives private parties the right, through a civil lawsuit, to stop other private parties or government agencies from violating provisions of the law, and, in the case of the Secretary, to bring suit for government's failure to perform non-discretionary duties under the ESA.

When Congress passed the ESA in 1973, it did so nearly unanimously, with little discussion and no debate. Over the last three decades, the Act has become one of the most controversial environmental laws yet enacted. Although attempts to repeal or weaken the ESA have so far failed, since the early 1990s Congress has deadlocked over the ESA, failing to either amend or reauthorize appropriations for the Act. As this handbook goes to print, proposed amendments to the Act wait to be considered by Congress, while the ESA outsurvives many of the species it was designed to protect.

CHAPTER ONE

A Brief History of the
Endangered Species Act

A. Introduction

Late in 1973, Congress passed the ESA, alarmed that "various species of
fish, wildlife, and plants in the United States have been rendered extinct
as a consequence of economic growth and development untempered by
adequate concern and conservation."[1] The Senate supported the ESA
unanimously, while only four members of the House of Representatives
voted against it.[2] On December 28, 1973, President Richard Nixon signed
the ESA into law, declaring that "[t]his legislation provides the federal
government with the needed authority to protect an irreplaceable part of
our national heritage — threatened wildlife."[3] The ESA was not the first
attempt to deal with the national problem of species extinction. It
represented the culmination of a long history of federal involvement in
wildlife management.

B. Federal Wildlife Law Before 1966

Prior to the twentieth century, the federal government played a minor
role in wildlife management, limiting its efforts to the conservation of
natural resources outside of state jurisdiction. In 1868, for example,
Congress passed a law prohibiting the killing of certain fur-bearing
animals in the territory of Alaska.[4] Three years later, it created the Office
of the U.S. Commissioner of Fish and Fisheries to conserve fisheries
along the coasts and navigable waterways, areas of traditional federal
jurisdiction.[5] Congress also took steps that indirectly secured wildlife
habitat, for example when it passed the Forest Reserve Act of 1891
authorizing the President to establish forest reserves out of the public

---

1. *See* The Endangered Species Act of 1973, Pub. L. No. 93-205, 87 Stat. 884 (1973) (codified
at 16 U.S.C. §§ 1531–1544).

2. *See* SENATE COMM. ON ENV'T AND PUB. WORKS, LEGISLATIVE HISTORY OF THE
ENDANGERED SPECIES ACT OF 1973, at 409, 483 (1982) [hereinafter LEGISLATIVE HISTORY].

3. Richard Nixon, Public Papers of the Presidents of the United States, 1973, at 1027-1028
(1975).

4. Act of July 27, 1868, ch. 273, 15 Stat. 240 (repealed 1944).

5. Act of February 9, 1871, 16 Stat. 593 (repealed 1964).

domain.[6] For the most part, these early federal efforts were motivated by economic concerns rather than a conservation ethic.[7]

The disturbing spectacle of bison annihilation on the Great Plains during the 1870s, however, aroused different concerns. To prevent that species' extinction and to preserve a remnant of frontier heritage, Congress passed a bill in 1874 to outlaw hunting of buffalo in federal territories.[8] President Grant pocket-vetoed the bill.[9] Two years later, the House passed a similar bill, but it died in Senate Committee.[10] In 1894, in part to protect the remaining herds of bison, Congress prohibited hunting within Yellowstone National Park.[11] With these few exceptions, federal involvement in the conservation and preservation of wildlife remained minimal throughout the nineteenth century.

During this time the states assumed primary responsibility for wildlife management. State laws of this period were aimed at conserving wildlife for the purpose of supporting recreational hunting activities.[12] In 1896, the Supreme Court validated the states' power to regulate wildlife in *Geer v. Connecticut*.[13] In that decision, the Supreme Court quoted with approval the following statement of the Supreme Court of California:

> The wild game within a state belongs to the people in their collective sovereign capacity. It is not the subject of private ownership, except in so far as the people may elect to make it so; and they may, if they see fit, absolutely prohibit the taking of it, or traffic and commerce in it, if it is deemed necessary for the protection or preservation of the public good.[14]

Federal regulation soon began to replace the so-called "state ownership doctrine," as progressive conservationists began to wrest control of wildlife management from the states. The first significant step toward national wildlife regulation came when Congress passed the Lacey Act of 1900.[15] The inability of states alone to prevent species extinctions moti-

---

6. Forest Reserve Act of March 3, ch. 561, § 24, 26 Stat. 1103 (1891) (repealed 1976).

7. *See generally* Samuel Hays, Conservation and the Gospel of Efficiency (1959).

8. *See* 1874 Cong. Rec. H2105 (daily ed. Mar. 10, 1874).

9. *See id.*

10. *See* 1876 Cong. Rec. H1237 (daily ed. Feb. 23, 1876).

11. Act of May 7, 1894, ch. 72, 28 Stat. 73. *See generally* Alfred Runte, National Parks (2d ed. 1987).

12. *See generally* John Reiger, American Sportsmen and the Origins of Conservation (1975); James Tober, Who Owns the Wildlife? (1982).

13. Geer v. Connecticut, 161 U.S. 519 (1896).

14. *Id.* at 529.

15. *See* Lacey Act, ch. 553 § 2, 16 U.S.C. § 3372.

vated the Act's sponsor, Representative John Lacey.[16] The Lacey Act prohibited interstate commerce in animals and birds killed in violation of state law, and required the Secretary of Agriculture to take measures to ensure the preservation, introduction, and restoration of game animals and birds. The Act recognized the national scope of species protection problems and marked the beginning of significant federal involvement in addressing those problems.

Three years after passage of the Lacey Act, President Roosevelt created the first national refuge explicitly for the protection of wildlife on Florida's Pelican Island. In addition, by greatly expanding U.S. forest reserves, Roosevelt created the potential for expanded federal involvement in wildlife management. Gifford Pinchot, the first chief of the U.S. Forest Service and a close friend of President Roosevelt, aimed to manage these reserves for "multiple uses" beyond timber harvesting, including the preservation of wildlife habitat.[17]

As the demise of the bison had done 40 years before, the fate of the passenger pigeon brought national attention to the potential for human eradication of a species. Throughout the nineteenth century, enormous flocks of this diminutive bird had moved across American skies. An easy target for sport hunters, and an ingredient in the popular meal of "pigeon on toast," the passenger pigeon fell victim to over-hunting, and the last survivor died in the Cincinnati Zoo in 1914.[18] Partly in response to this extinction, Congress passed the Migratory Bird Treaty Act of 1918, which made it illegal to hunt migratory birds without a federally issued permit.[19] That act implemented the United States-Canada Migratory Bird Treaty of 1916, which explicitly recognized that international efforts were necessary to protect species that moved across national boundaries.[20]

The state of Missouri promptly challenged the constitutionality of the Migratory Bird Treaty Act, arguing that the state ownership doctrine and the Tenth Amendment of the U.S. Constitution gave it the exclusive power to regulate wildlife in Missouri. In the landmark decision of *Missouri v. Holland,* the U.S. Supreme Court upheld the Act on the basis of constitutional treaty-making power and rejected outright the contention that the state ownership doctrine precluded federal regulation.[21] In

---

16. *See* 33 Cong. Rec. H4871 (daily ed. 1900) (statement of Representative Lacey).

17. *See* Michael Bean, The Evolution of National Wildlife Law 138 (1983).

18. *See* James Trefethen, An American Crusade for Wildlife 65 (1975).

19. *See* Migratory Bird Treaty Act of 1918, ch. 128, 40 Stat. 755 (1918) (codified as amended at 16 U.S.C. §§ 703-711).

20. *See* Convention for the Protection of Migratory Birds, Aug. 16, 1916, United States-Gr. Brit. (on behalf of Can.), 39 Stat. 1702.

21. Missouri v. Holland, 252 U.S. 416, 434-435 (1920).

1929, Congress extended bird protection with the Migratory Bird Conservation Act.[22]

New Deal conservationists expanded federal efforts to protect wildlife. In 1934, Congress passed the Fish and Wildlife Coordination Act.[23] The Act directed the Secretary of the Interior to investigate the effects of "domestic sewage, trade wastes, and other polluting substances on wild life. . . ."[24] It also encouraged dam-building agencies to consult with the Bureau of Fisheries about the potential impact on fish before starting on a dam.[25] Finally, it called for federal and state cooperation to conserve and rehabilitate wildlife[26] and proposed that federal lands be set aside to protect wildlife habitat.[27] The voluntary nature of the first two provisions rendered them largely ineffective, but the third met with some success through the expansion of national forest reserves, national wildlife refuges, and the national park system.

During the first half of the twentieth century, ecology emerged as an independent discipline, and scientific appreciation for species diversity grew. Aldo Leopold, the father of modern wildlife management, helped popularize this knowledge, teaching Americans to care about the land and the "wild things" that live on it. About the passenger pigeon, he eulogized: "Our grandfathers were less well-housed, well-fed, well-clothed than we are. The strivings by which they bettered their lot are also those which deprived us of pigeons. Perhaps we now grieve because we are not sure, in our hearts, that we have gained by the exchange."[28] In 1940, Congress passed the Bald Eagle Protection Act, which aimed to save the nation's symbol from extinction.[29]

By the 1960s, a growing awareness of environmental problems, including an increasing rate of species extinction, fostered a national environmental movement. In 1962, Rachel Carson, a biologist who had worked for the Department of the Interior, wrote the book "Silent Spring." A bestseller, Carson's work described how the growing use of pesticides, herbicides, and insecticides poisoned wildlife and threatened human health.[30] The chilling image of songbirds falling dead from sub-

---

22. Migratory Bird Conservation Act of 1929, ch. 257, 45 Stat. 1222 (codified at 16 U.S.C. §§ 715-715r (1985)).

23. Act of March 10, 1934, ch. 55, 48 Stat. 401 (codified at 16 U.S.C. §§ 661-667e).

24. *Id.* § 2.

25. *See id.* § 3.

26. *See id.* § 1.

27. *See id.* § 3.

28. Aldo Leopold, A Sand County Almanac 109 (commemorative ed. 1989).

29. Bald Eagle Protection Act, Pub. L. No. 567, 54 Stat. 278 (codified at 16 U.S.C. § 668).

30. *See* Rachel Carson, Silent Spring (1962).

urban trees brought home the disturbing implications of environmental degradation.[31] As much as any other single factor, Carson's book acted as a catalyst for the modern environmental movement.[32]

That movement raised public awareness of the effect of human activities on other species and prompted the passage of more legislation aimed at mitigating those impacts. In 1964, Congress created the National Wilderness Preservation System, which provided crucial habitat for wildlife.[33] That same year, the Department of the Interior's Bureau of Sport Fisheries and Wildlife, later renamed the U.S. Fish and Wildlife Service, created a Committee on Rare and Endangered Species. Composed of nine biologists, the committee published the first federal list of species known to be threatened with extinction. It was called the "Redbook"; the first edition included 63 plants and animals.[34]

C. The 1966 Endangered Species Preservation Act

In 1966, Congress passed the Endangered Species Preservation Act (1966 Act), the first comprehensive legislative attempt to prevent human-caused extinctions.[35] The 1966 Act directed the Departments of the Interior, Agriculture, and Defense to protect threatened species "insofar as is practicable and consistent" with the primary purposes of the services, bureaus, and agencies within their departments.[36] It required the Department of the Interior to consult with and "encourage" all other federal agencies to conform to the purposes of the Act "where practicable."[37] It also instructed the Department of the Interior to continue compiling lists of endangered species.[38] Most important, the 1966 Act created the National Wildlife Refuge System out of a hodgepodge of federal lands and authorized funds for the maintenance and expansion of this system.[39] Finally, the 1966 Act prohibited the "taking" of any species within these wildlife refuges without a permit.[40]

---

31. *See generally* Steven Yaffee, Prohibitive Policy 37-38 (1982) (discussing the catalyzing effect of charismatic endangered species on environmental activism in general).

32. *See generally* Samuel Hays, Beauty, Health, and Permanence (1987).

33. *See* Wilderness Act of 1964, Pub. L. No. 88-577, 78 Stat. 890 (1964) (codified as 16 U.S.C. § 1131 (1985)).

34. *See* Yaffee, *supra* note 31, at 35.

35. Pub. L. No. 89-669, 80 Stat. 926 (1966).

36. *See id.* § 1(b).

37. *See id.* § 2(d).

38. *See id.* § 1(c).

39. *See id.* § 4.

40. *See id.* § 4(c).

But the 1966 Act suffered from several serious weaknesses. First, the language of the Act made agency cooperation purely voluntary. Second, the 1966 Act applied only to domestic, vertebrate species of fish and wildlife, and did not extend to plants. Most important, the restriction against the taking of species applied only within the National Wildlife Refuge System. Nevertheless, the 1966 Act laid the foundation for more significant legislation.

D. The 1969 Endangered Species Conservation Act

Three years later, Congress supplemented the 1966 Act with the Endangered Species Conservation Act of 1969 (1969 Act).[41] The 1969 Act explicitly recognized the international scope of the extinction crisis, authorizing the expansion of the Redbook to include threatened species worldwide.[42] Most important, it banned the importation of members of listed species and products made from those organisms.[43] This prohibition significantly curtailed the trade in declining species. For example, trade between 1968 and 1970, prior to the prohibition, accounted for 18,456 leopard skins, 31,105 jaguar skins, and 249,680 ocelot skins to be used in fur coats.[44] The 1969 Act eliminated the legal trade in these skins. Furthermore, the 1969 Act extended the Lacey Act by prohibiting the selling or transporting of any listed species or its product taken in violation of state, national, or foreign law.[45] Finally, the 1969 Act expanded the definition of "fish or wildlife" to include amphibians, reptiles, and invertebrates,[46] and called for an international convention to protect endangered species from extinction.[47]

E. The Demand for Stronger Wildlife Protection

Other species protection acts followed in the wake of the first Earth Day, April 22, 1970. In 1971, Congress passed the Wild Free-Roaming Horses and Burros Act to preserve what Congress called "living symbols of the historic and pioneering spirit of the West."[48] A year later, Congress ap-

---

41. Pub. L. No. 91-135, 83 Stat. 275 (1969).

42. *See id.* § 3(a).

43. *See id.* § 2.

44. *See* Tom Garrett, *Wildlife, in* Nixon and the Environment 131 (1972).

45. *See* Pub. L. No. 91-135, § 7(a), 83 Stat. 275 (1969).

46. *Id.* § 1.

47. *See id.* § 2.

48. Pub. L. No. 92-195, 85 Stat. 649 (1971) (codified as 16 U.S.C. §§ 1331-1340 (1985)).

proved the Marine Mammal Protection Act, which prohibited the taking or importation of endangered marine mammals.[49]

In the spring of 1973, an international body, the Convention on International Trade in Endangered Species of Wild Flora and Fauna (CITES), established an elaborate scheme of import-export restrictions for endangered species.[50] Significantly, both the Marine Mammal Protection Act and CITES recognized a management classification for species threatened with endangerment but not yet depleted enough to be called endangered, a system later adopted by the ESA. These actions, the inadequacy of the 1966 and 1969 Acts, and a growing appreciation for the scope of the extinction crisis, led many to push for more potent species protection legislation.

Early in 1972, President Nixon called for the adoption of "a stronger law to protect endangered species of wildlife." Nixon stated that "even the most recent Act to protect endangered species, which dates only from 1969, simply does not provide the kind of management tools needed to act early enough to save a vanishing species."[51] In this address, Nixon also announced the promulgation of Executive Order 11643, which barred the use of poisons to control predators, like grizzly bears and gray wolves, on all public lands. On the day of the President's address, Representative John Dingell (D-MI) introduced endangered species legislation endorsed by the Nixon administration. Ten days later, Senator Mark Hatfield (R-OR) submitted identical legislation to the Senate.[52]

F. The Endangered Species Act of 1973

Congress did not pass new species legislation in 1972, but reconsidered the issue in 1973. Following his reelection, in his State of the Union Address, Nixon renewed his call for a stronger endangered species act and recommended that the Senate ratify the CITES treaty.[53] Congress then considered two new endangered species act bills; one in the House, sponsored by Representative Dingell,[54] and one in the Senate, sponsored by Senator Harrison Williams (D-NJ).[55] The bills were very similar.

---

49. Pub. L. No. 92-552, 86 Stat. 1027 (1972) (codified as 16 U.S.C. §§ 1361-1407).

50. Convention on International Trade in Endangered Species of Wild Fauna and Flora, March 3, 1973, 27 U.S.T. 1087.

51. Richard Nixon, Public Papers of the Presidents of the United States, 1972, at 183 (1974). *See generally* John Flippen, *The Nixon Administration, Timber, and the Call of the Wild*, 19 Envtl. Hist. Rev. 37 (1995).

52. *See generally* Yaffee, *supra* note 31, at 49.

53. Nixon, *supra* note 3, at 94, 101, 285-286.

54. H.R. 37, 93rd Cong. (1973).

55. S. 1983, 93rd Cong. (1973).

Congress debated relatively little over the bills, and public support was widespread and enthusiastic. Representative Dingell remarked that in the month after the committee report on the bill was available for review,[56] he did not "hear a whisper of opposition to its passage at the earliest opportunity."[57] No special interest group came forward to oppose the ESA, no commercial interest testified in either House or Senate hearings, and no organized lobby countered the environmental supporters of the ESA.

Each house overwhelmingly passed its respective bill.[58] The conference committee debated only one relatively minor issue: the division of administrative duties between the Department of Commerce, which was assigned responsibility for marine species, and the Department of the Interior, which was assigned responsibility for terrestrial and avian species.[59] Significantly, the conference committee strengthened the ESA by adding the term "harm" to the definition of what it meant to "take" a species.[60] The Senate, including Republican leaders Bob Dole (R-KS) and Jesse Helms (R-NC), as well as future ESA critics Howard Baker (R-TN), Bob Packwood (R-OR), and Mark Hatfield (R-OR), supported the bill unanimously. Only four members of the House of Representatives voted against it.[61]

President Nixon signed the ESA into law on December 28, 1973. During the signing ceremony, Nixon remarked: "This legislation provides the Federal Government with the needed authority to protect an irreplaceable part of our national heritage—threatened wildlife."[62] Just before signing the ESA into law, he concluded that "[n]othing is more priceless and more worthy of preservation than the rich array of animal life with which our country has been blessed."[63]

For several years after 1973, the scope of the ESA remained untested, and the ESA enjoyed almost unqualified support.[64] In 1975, however, FWS listed as endangered the snail darter, a three-inch perch, which had

---

56. H.R. Rep. No. 93-412 (1973).

57. *See* Legislative History, *supra* note 2, at 196.

58. *See id.* at 205, 410.

59. *See id.* at 480.

60. H.R. Conf. Rep. No. 93-740 at 4.

61. *See* Legislative History, *supra* note 2, at 409, 483.

62. Nixon, *supra* note 3, at 1027-1028.

63. *Id.*

64. *See* Pub. L. No. 94-325, 90 Stat. 724 (1976) (increasing appropriations seven million dollars beyond what the Secretary of the Interior requested); *see also* Legislative History, *supra* note 2, at 505-511.

no known commercial or recreational value.[65] Soon after the listing, a local conservation group brought a suit against the Tennessee Valley Authority (TVA) to halt the completion of Tellico Dam on the Little Tennessee River, the only known habitat of the darter. The suit asserted that the dam would jeopardize the survival of the snail darter species and that Section 7 therefore prevented the TVA from completing the dam.[66] TVA argued that Section 7 could not stop the dam because: (1) it had followed the law and consulted with the Fish and Wildlife Service; (2) it had begun construction of the dam before the ESA was enacted; and (3) Congress had demonstrated its support for the dam by repeatedly allocating money for its completion. TVA also argued that the dam was vital for the economic rehabilitation of the entire region.[67] In 1978, in its landmark decision of *TVA v. Hill,* the Supreme Court interpreted Section 7 as strictly prohibiting any activity by any federal agency that might jeopardize a species listed as threatened or endangered.[68] The Supreme Court relied on the plain language of Section 7 to reach this conclusion.

The Supreme Court's decision outraged some in Congress. The industrial lobby, too, proved to be a growing counterweight to the environmental movement, pressuring many in Congress to revise the ESA. In 1978, the Senate voted to amend the ESA 94 to 3, while the House approved the amendments with a vote of 384 to 12.[69]

G. The 1978 ESA Amendments

The 1978 amendments did address the situation in *TVA.* However, instead of discarding Section 7 or making consultations non-binding on agencies, Congress created a committee with the power to grant exemptions to Section 7. A newly created Endangered Species Committee (ESC) was given the power to grant exemptions to federal projects halted by the ESA, but only if it first found that the economic benefits of those projects outweighed the benefits of conserving the endangered species. Informally dubbed the "God Squad" or "God Committee," the committee consists of the Secretary of the Interior, the Secretary of Agriculture, the Secretary of the Army, the Chairman of the Council of Economic Advisors, the Administrator of the EPA, the Administrator of National Oceanic and Atmospheric Administration, and an individual nominated

---

65. *See* 40 Fed. Reg. 47,505-06 (1975); *see also* 50 C.F.R. § 17.11(I) (1976).

66. *See* Tennessee Valley Auth. v. Hill, 437 U.S. 153, 161 (1978).

67. *See Endangered Species Act Oversight: Hearing Before the Subcomm. on Resource Protection of the Senate Comm. on Env't and Pub. Works,* 95th Cong. 279 (1977) (statement of Lynn Seeber, General Manager of the TVA).

68. *See* 437 U.S. at 173.

69. *See* Legislative History, *supra* note 2, at 895-898, 1167-68.

by the governor of the state where the project is located and appointed by the President.

Congress anticipated that in the wake of the 1978 amendments, the ESC would promptly exempt Tellico Dam. Under the amended law, the ESC could grant an exemption if five out of its seven members determined that no reasonable and prudent alternatives to the proposed agency action existed, and that the proposal's benefits clearly outweighed the conservation of the species in question.[70] After consideration of the Tellico Dam matter, however the ESC refused to grant an exemption, opting instead to protect the darter.

Frustrated, Congress approved a non-germane rider to the Energy and Water Development Appropriations Act of 1980, which granted a legislative exemption from Section 7 for the Tellico Dam project.[71] TVA finally finished its dam. Ironically, soon after the dam's completion, the Fish and Wildlife Service discovered healthy populations of snail darters in other Tennessee rivers and down-listed the species from endangered to threatened.

One result of the snail darter controversy was that the Fish and Wildlife Service became more cautious about listing species. Changes in the ESA wrought by the 1978 amendments allowed the agency to exercise more caution.[72] For example, Congress dramatically changed the listing procedure by requiring designation of a species' critical habitat concurrent with its listing. The original ESA had considered threats to a species' critical habitat relevant to listing decisions, but had not required the Fish and Wildlife Service to specifically identify critical habitat at the time a species was listed. In the 1978 amendments, attempting to relieve fears that critical habitat designations would impose land use restrictions on both private and public land, Congress not only linked critical habitat designation to listing, but also permitted the Secretary to consider the economic impacts of critical habitat designation.[73] Further, the Secretary could delay or withdraw the proposed listing if he or she found that critical habitat was not yet determinable.

Linking the listing procedure to critical habitat designation and economic considerations almost completely halted new ESA listings. Approximately 2,000 species proposed for listing were withdrawn from consideration in 1978.

---

70. 16 U.S.C. § 1536(h).

71. *See* Pub. L. No. 96-69 (1979).

72. *See* Bean, *supra* note 17, at 335-36.

73. *See* 16 U.S.C. § 1533(b)(1)(B)(2).

The snail darter controversy altered public perception of the ESA. It became clear that protecting species would not in all cases be a cost-free proposition. The controversy helped fuel organized opposition to the environmental movement in the late 1970s and early 1980s.[74] In 1980, widespread anti-regulatory sentiment helped elect Ronald Reagan to the presidency. Reagan rode into the White House as part of the sagebrush rebellion, an anti-environmental movement originating in the West. Reagan called himself a "Sagebrush Rebel" and pledged "to work toward a Sagebrush solution" for the nation's environmental problems.[75]

Reagan appointed James Watt, known for his opposition to the environmental movement, as Secretary of the Interior. Watt led, in the words of historian Sam Hays, "a massive assault on environmental policies."[76] Spearheading the sagebrush rebellion in the early eighties, Watt profoundly influenced the Fish and Wildlife Service, virtually halting ESA implementation and enforcement. During the first year of the Reagan presidency, not one new species was proposed for listing.[77] Although Watt did not last long as Secretary of the Interior, his imprimatur lingered and the Fish and Wildlife Service refrained from aggressively implementing and enforcing the ESA throughout the 1980s.

H. The 1982 ESA Amendments

Despite the frustration it evidenced in response to the Tellico Dam situation, Congress continued to support the Act. In 1982, it passed additional amendments intended to eliminate the listing roadblock created by the 1978 amendments. The 1982 amendments required critical habitat designation concurrent with listing a species, but only to "the maximum extent prudent and determinable."[78] Congress also stressed that listings themselves should be made solely on the basis of biological criteria, and allowed listings to proceed even if a corresponding critical habitat determination would be delayed for up to a year.[79] Other 1982 changes were designed to speed up the listing process, including a requirement that the Secretary make a preliminary finding within 90 days of the receipt of a petition to list a species or to revise critical habitat.[80]

---

74. *See* Hays, *supra* note 32, at 60.
75. Ronald Reagan, *quoted in* William Graf, Wilderness Preservation and the Sagebrush Rebellions 231 (1990).
76. Hays, *supra* note 32, at 59-60.
77. *See Endangered Species Act Oversight: Hearing Before the Subcomm. on Envtl. Pollution of the Senate Comm. on Env't and Pub. Works,* 97th Cong. 53 (1982).
78. 16 U.S.C. § 1533(a)(3).
79. *See id.* §§ 1533(b)(1)(A), (b)(6)(C).
80. *See id.* § 1533(b)(3)(A).

While the pace of species listings accelerated after 1982, the huge backlog of species considered candidates for listing often prevented quick action. Several species suffered serious population declines or became extinct before they could be listed.[81]

The 1982 amendments also evidenced congressional concern with respect to the ESA's impact on non-federal property. This concern stemmed in part from a 1979 federal court decision, *Palila v. Hawaii Department of Land and Natural Resources*.[82] In that case, the court held that the Hawaii Department of Land and Natural Resources had violated the Section 9 prohibition against "takes" when it allowed feral goats onto state lands for hunting purposes. The court determined that grazing by these animals degraded the habitat of an endangered bird, the palila, and therefore constituted an illegal take of an endangered species.[83] In 1981, the Ninth Circuit affirmed *Palila*, using even stronger language to affirm an expansive interpretation of "take" under Section 9.[84]

Soon after this decision, the Fish and Wildlife Service narrowed its regulatory definition of Section 9 "harm" to include only any action that "kills or injures wildlife."[85] Congress also attempted to address the issue in the 1982 ESA amendments, authorizing the Secretary to issue permits for the taking of listed species, but only "if such taking is incidental to, and not the purpose of, the carrying out of an otherwise lawful activity."[86] Between 1982 and 1994, few landowners applied for these permits and the Secretary granted only 21.[87]

In 1988, President Reagan issued an executive order directing all federal agencies to promulgate regulations, including those implementing Section 9, in such a way as to limit their impact on private property use.[88]

I. The 1988 ESA Amendments

In 1988, Congress again amended the ESA, in the process reaffirming its intent to protect all species. The 1988 amendments specifically addressed the plight of candidate species, unprotected while they waited for listing

81. Congress attempted to remedy this problem in the 1988 ESA amendments.
82. 471 F. Supp. 985 (D. Haw. 1979).
83. *See id.* at 995.
84. *See* Palila v. Hawaii Dept. of Land & Natural Resources, 639 F.2d 495, 497 (9th Cir. 1981).
85. *See* 46 Fed. Reg. 54,748, 54,750 (1981); *see also* 50 C.F.R. § 17.3.
86. *See* Endangered Species Act Amendments of 1982, Pub. L. No. 97-304, 96 Stat. 1423, § 6(1)(B) (1982); *see also*, 16 U.S.C. § 1539(a).
87. *See* Robert Meltz, *Where the Wild Things Are: The Endangered Species Act and Private Property*, 24 Envtl. L. 369 (1994).
88. *See* Exec. Order No. 12,630, 53 Fed. Reg. 8859 (1988).

determinations. In an effort to protect these species, the Secretary was required to establish a system to monitor the status of candidate species.[89] Further, the amendments directed the Secretary to use the emergency listing powers to prevent "a significant risk to the well-being of any [candidate] species."[90]

The 1988 Amendments also address Section 4 recovery plans. The Secretary was prohibited from considering a species' taxonomic classification in establishing recovery plan preparation priorities.[91] In other words, the Secretary may not prepare a recovery plan for a well-known mammal before a plan for an uncharismatic invertebrate merely because of the mammal's greater visibility and appeal. Congress also established specific content requirements for recovery plans, provided for public input in plan formulation, and added a provision which requires the Secretary to report to Congress at least once every two years on the status of efforts to implement recovery plans.[92]

J.   The Spotted Owl

Disputes over Section 9 re-emerged in the 1980s during the controversy over the northern spotted owl. The owl controversy provides the most notorious example of the abuse of administrative discretion with regard to Section 4. Despite scientific evidence of its endangered status by the early 1980s, FWS refused to list the northern spotted owl out of concern for the impact that listing might have on the timber industry in the Pacific Northwest.[93] In the face of administrative foot-dragging, environmental organizations again turned to the courts.

Following their experience with Tellico Dam, however, they did so reluctantly. Throughout the 1980s, these organizations had avoided suing to force the Fish and Wildlife Service to list the owl because they feared a political backlash like the one that followed *TVA*. In 1986, however, Green World, a tiny environmental group working out of a phone booth in Massachusetts, submitted a petition to the Fish and Wildlife Service to list the owl. Soon after, thirty major environmental groups filed a similar petition. Despite scientific arguments in favor of listing by

---

89. *See* 16 U.S.C. § 1533(b)(3)(C)(iii).

90. *Id.*

91. *See id.*

92. *See id.*

93. *See generally* Victor M. Sher, *Travels with Strix: The Spotted Owl's Journey Through The Federal Courts*, 14 Pub. Land L. Rev. 41, 42-43 (1993).

its own chief biologists, the Fish and Wildlife Service denied the petitions late in 1987.[94]

On May 6, 1988, acting on behalf of 25 environmental organizations, the Sierra Club Legal Defense Fund filed suit in federal district court in Seattle. They contested the decision not to list the spotted owl, claiming that the decision was based on economics, not scientific evidence, and therefore violated Section 4. The court found in favor of the environmental organizations and ordered the Fish and Wildlife Service to reconsider the listing of the owl, this time taking into account only biological factors.[95] In June of 1990, the Fish and Wildlife Service finally listed the owl, claiming that the "biological evidence says that the northern spotted owl is in trouble. We will not and, by law, cannot, ignore that evidence. . . . But [we] strongly believe there is room in the world to protect both owls and loggers. Our intent now . . . is to find ways to protect the owl with the least possible disruption to the timber economy of the Northwest."[96]

Environmental groups did not wholeheartedly celebrate their victory. According to Yaffee, "[f]or many environmental groups, listing meant having to live with their great fear that they may win the owl battle but lose the endangered species war."[97]

Nonetheless, environmental organizations continued to fight, arguing that although the Fish and Wildlife Service had finally listed the owl, it had illegally failed to designate critical habitat. The court ordered the agency to designate critical habitat in *Northern Spotted Owl v. Lujan*.[98] Pursuant to this order, the Fish and Wildlife Service identified a total of 11.6 million acres of critical habitat—6.5 million acres of it on U.S. Forest Service land, 1.4 million acres on Bureau of Land Management (BLM) land, .7 million acres on state and tribal lands, and 3 million acres on private lands. The agency found that as a result of critical habitat designation "there may be significant impacts on private and other non-Federal lands."[99]

Following this legal victory over the Fish and Wildlife Service, environmental lawyers went after the BLM. Responding to complaints that the BLM had violated Section 7 by failing to consult with the Fish and Wildlife Service on certain timber sales, the Ninth Circuit enjoined a

---

94. *See* Steven Yaffee, The Wisdom of the Spotted Owl 109-111 (1994).

95. *See* Northern Spotted Owl v. Hodel, 716 F. Supp. 479, 483 (W.D. Wash. 1988).

96. *See* John Lancaster, *Northern Spotted Owl is "Threatened,"* Wash. Post, June 23, 1990, at A1.

97. Yaffee, *supra* note 94, at 116.

98. 758 F. Supp. 621 (W.D. Wash. 1991).

99. 56 Fed. Reg. 20,821 (1991).

number of BLM timber sales likely to damage critical owl habitat.[100] The
George H.W. Bush administration responded by convening the "God
Squad," which voted for only the second time ever to grant an exemption
from the ESA, releasing 13 BLM timber sales enjoined by the court. The
administration planned to pursue additional ESA exemptions, if
necessary, in order to free the sale of timber on public lands throughout
the areas designated as protected critical habitat for the spotted owl.[101]
On the legislative front, Bush's Secretary of the Interior, Manuel Lujan,
lobbied hard for significant ESA amendments, claiming that the ESA was
"just too tough an act. . . . We've got to change it."[102]

But the courts foiled the Bush administration's attempt to weaken the
ESA. In his zeal to obtain the Section 7 exemptions, President George
H.W. Bush had summoned three members of the Endangered Species
Committee to the White House, where he lobbied them personally. In
Portland Audubon Society v. Oregon Lands Coalition, the Ninth Circuit
found that this ex parte contact between the President and members of
the God Squad violated the Administrative Procedure Act.[103] The Ninth
Circuit overturned the God Squad's Section 7 exemptions for the BLM
timber sales. By this time, Bush had lost the presidential election of 1992,
leaving the owl crisis to President Clinton.

During his election campaign, Clinton promised to convene a bipar-
tisan working group to resolve the owl controversy within the first one
hundred days of his administration. Although Clinton had an unremark-
able environmental record while governor of Arkansas, his administration promised a new, environmentally proactive future. The selection of
Al Gore for Vice President and the appointment of Bruce Babbitt, former
president of the League of Conservation Voters, as Secretary of the Interior boded well for environmentalists and the ESA. On April 2, 1993, true
to his promise, President Clinton convened a forest conference in Portland to resolve the owl crisis. Vice President Gore and three cabinet
members, including Secretary Babbitt, chaired the conference, which
consisted of representatives from the timber industry, the scientific
community, and the major environmental organizations.[104]

Despite high expectations, the conference produced a forest plan that
disappointed the environmental community. However, environmental
organizations recognized that the Clinton administration was the most

100. *See* Lane County Audubon Soc'y v. Jamison, 985 F.2d 290, 294 (9th Cir. 1992).
101. *See* Yaffee, *supra* note 94, at 139-42, 246.
102. Manuel Lujan, *quoted in id.* at 128.
103. 988 F.2d 121 (9th Cir. 1993).
104. *See* Yaffee, *supra* note 94, at 208-11.

environmentally sympathetic in years, and initiated efforts to form a closer working relationship with the administration. In part, this was a strategic decision aimed at staving off the inevitable reaction against environmentalism and the ESA because of the owl crisis.

The owl controversy, however, did not end with President Clinton's forest conference. Debate over the scope of Section 9 emerged yet again when Sweet Home Chapter of Communities for a Great Oregon, a coalition of small landowners, logging companies, and forest products industries in the Pacific Northwest, brought a suit against the Secretary of the Interior challenging his regulatory interpretation of Section 9. In 1995, however, the U.S. Supreme Court disagreed, holding that the Secretary of the Interior reasonably construed congressional intent when he defined "harm" to include habitat modification.[105]

K. Conflict and Deadlock

The controversy over the northern spotted owl eventually subsided. But like the snail darter, the spotted owl fueled a backlash against the ESA. In particular, the potential of Section 9 to limit the use of private property contributed to the rise of an organized property rights movement, closely related to the anti-environmental "wise-use" movement. In 1994, Bruce Babbitt wrote that the ESA stood "at the top of the list" of environmental legislation that the wise-use movement hoped the courts would declare unconstitutional.[106] The Supreme Court failed to fulfill wise-use hopes in *Babbitt v. Sweet Home Chapter of Communities for a Great Oregon* (hereinafter *Sweet Home*). The movement changed its tactics, and began to lobby some in Congress to weaken the ESA. However, their lobbying has not produced results; Congress has deadlocked over ESA reauthorization since 1992.

In 1994, property rights groups and wise-users contributed to the election of a conservative Congress hostile to the nation's environmental laws. In 1995, the Speaker of the House, Newt Gingrich, pledged to "rethink, not repair" environmental laws and said that it made little sense to spend money on species protection because extinction is "the way life is."[107] Gingrich outlined more than a dozen proposals for changes in existing environmental laws, including amendments to eliminate key provisions of the ESA. That same year, the Republican Congress suc-

---

105. Babbitt v. Sweet Home Chapter of Communities for a Great Oregon, 515 U.S. 687, 704 (1995).

106. Bruce Babbitt, *The Endangered Species Act and Takings: A Call for Innovation Within the Terms of the Act*, 24 Envtl. L. 355, 357 (1994).

107. Newt Gingrich, *quoted in* Heather Dewar, *Gingrich is Going for the Green*, Wis. St. J., Apr. 25, 1996, at 3A.

ceeded in passing an amendment to a defense appropriation bill that precluded ESA listings and critical habitat designations.[108] The bill had one exception: the Service could use funds to determine if a species should be downlisted from endangered to threatened. Congress went further, mandating that court orders requiring a species be listed were not valid as long as funds were unavailable.

These anti-conservation, anti-wildlife measures created a backlash of their own. Environmental groups filed a petition under the Environmental Side Agreement of the North American Free Trade Agreement (NAFTA). Under the Agreement, a multilateral treaty between the United States, Canada, and Mexico, parties are required to enforce their domestic environmental laws. The environmentalists' petition did not result in enforcement actions against the United States, but it did focus international attention on the moratorium. There was also much opposition domestically. The moratorium's opponents argued that Congress had implicitly repealed the ESA and without providing any alternative. As one commentator stated, "[d]espite all the frustration engendered by America's health care crisis, no one has suggested locking the hospital doors until we have a better health care system."[109] In response to increasing public pressure, the moratorium was repealed in April 1996.[110]

Despite numerous bills and proposals for change, Congress has not as of this writing agreed on how and whether to amend the ESA. Many people accept that the ESA is not a perfect law, but few want to do away entirely with endangered species protections. The future of the ESA will depend on the ongoing interplay of administrative implementation, legislative proposals, judicial interpretation, and public opinion in the face of the continuing extinction crisis.

---

108. *See* Emergency Supplemental Appropriations and Recissions for the Department of Defense to Preserve and Enhance Military Readiness Act of 1995, Pub. L. No. 104-6, 109 Stat. 73, 86 (including a rider withdrawing all funding from FWS for listing new species as endangered or threatened during the remainder of the fiscal year 1995).

109. Margaret McMillan, *Effects of the Moratorium on Listings Under the Endangered Species Act*, Endangered Species Update, Vol. 13 No. 1, 1996, at 6.

110. *See* Omnibus Consolidated Rescissions and Appropriations Act of 1996, Pub. L. No. 104-134 (1996).

CHAPTER TWO

Section 4: Listing, Critical Habitat Designation, and Recovery Plans

A. Introduction

The ESA only protects "listed" species. Section 4, which governs the why and how of listing, is therefore the threshold provision of the law.[1] A species that crosses the listing threshold, becoming officially "endangered" or "threatened," will receive a wide array of benefits and protections until such time as it is no longer imperiled. Because they are at the threshold of protection, listing decisions are extremely important and tend to be closely scrutinized by the public.

At the time a species is listed, the Service normally must also designate the species' "critical habitat." Critical habitat gives added protection to species with respect to federal actions.[2] Occasions where critical habitat designations affect private landowners are rare.

Section 4(f) mandates the development and implementation of recovery plans for listed species. The Service considers recovery plans to be guidance documents that do not have the force of regulations. However, the plans provide a basis for species management decisions and a blueprint for agencies and private parties to work together to recover listed species.

B. Legal and Scientific Definitions of "Species"

The ESA protects listed "species," a term which has a particular meaning in the context of the law. In the scientific realm, the meaning of the word species is not yet entirely settled. The rules for grouping sets of like organisms are still evolving. The four general categories of possible rules are morphological rules (similarity of appearance), biological rules (ability to interbreed), evolutionary rules (distinct evolutionary lineage), and genetic rules (genetic similarities). By applying one or more of these rules to a group of organisms, biologists determine whether or not that group constitutes a species.

---

1. See generally 16 U.S.C. § 1533.
2. Federal actions are those "authorized, funded, or carried out by" any federal agency. 16 U.S.C. § 1536(a)(2).

In the ESA context, the term *species* includes those scientifically de-fined groupings and two other important groups of organisms: the subspecies and the distinct population segment. In other words, groups of organisms classified as subspecies or distinct population segments can be listed as threatened or endangered "species" under the ESA. As listed "species," these groups receive the same protection as listed species.

To make matters more confusing, the line between what constitutes a subspecies and what constitutes a distinct population segment is not al-together clear. Generally speaking, distinct population segments are groups of organisms from the same species that occupy geographically discrete areas, for example, the Alaskan bald eagle and the bald eagle in the lower 48 states. Subspecies, on the other hand, are groups that may occupy the same geographic region as the species to which they belong, but are characterized by enough genetic or evolutionary difference from other members of the species so as to require separate protection. As dis-cussed further below, NMFS protects various groups of northwest salmon under a regime—the evolutionarily significant unit—that consid-ers both geographical separation and genetic differences between popu-lations. These groups are not exactly subspecies, nor distinct population segments. They are, however, protected under the ESA once listed.[3] The reasons Congress wrote the ESA so that it would protect subspecies and distinct population segments are straightforward. Two of the main pur-poses of endangered species protection are to conserve ecosystems and to protect the integrity of the evolutionary processes that are taking place in those ecosystems. Granting ESA protection to a distinct population segment serves the first purpose. For example, there may be enough grizzly bears in Alaska to make us feel comfortable that the grizzly bear species will never go extinct. However, the grizzly bear population in the Yellowstone ecosystem is dwindling and the grizzly bear is an integral part of that system. As a top predator in that system, it provides an im-portant function in maintaining the natural balance of species there. If the goal is to protect the Yellowstone ecosystem, it is important to protect the distinct population segment of Yellowstone grizzlies. Granting ESA protection to subspecies helps to protect the natural trajectory of evolu-tion. A subspecies contains genetic information that distinguishes it from other members of the species. It may be that the subspecies will eventu-ally evolve to become a new species: its genetic make-up may prove to make it more successful in persisting. Genetic diversity is the catalyst of evolution.

---

3. Technically, evolutionarily significant units are listed under the ESA as distinct popula-tion segments.

The National Research Council's View of Subspecies

Although the NRC does not recommend doing away with the concept of subspecies within the ESA context, it has advocated that, in order to help mitigate taxonomic confusion, the concept of the "evolutionary unit (EU) be applied when considering groups of organisms proposed for listing.

The NRC defines an EU as "a group of organisms that represents a segment of biological diversity that shares evolutionary lineage and contains the potential for a unique evolutionary future."

The NRC suggests that the evolutionary future of an organism be estimated by inquiring into its *distinctiveness*. This exercise may draw in many disciplines and cover many fields:

Estimates of distinctiveness are based on genetic, molecular, behavioral, morphological, or ecological information. But a single kind of information will fail to provide compelling evidence of distinctiveness. Determination of distinctiveness and the associated inference of an independent evolutionary future usually requires the careful integration of several lines of evidence.

Although the NRC recommends assembling evidence from a variety of sources and acknowledging the role of both science and policy in reaching a conclusion, it is careful to point out that the only currently valid evidence for listing decisions under the ESA is scientific evidence.

Distinctiveness is measured by looking at the isolation level of five population characteristics of an organism. The five salient population characteristics are *genetic isolation*, *geographic isolation*, *temporal isolation*, *behavioral isolation*, and *reproductive isolation*. All of these levels are to be considered holistically with no one level to be dispositive of the determination of a population's qualification as an EU.

In many ways the concept of the EU is similar to the Fish and Wildlife Service's Distinct Population Segment Policy (see text below).

For details see NATIONAL RESEARCH COUNCIL, SCIENCE AND THE ENDANGERED SPECIES ACT, Ch. 3 (1995).

B.1. Species

The legal definition of "species" covers "fish or wildlife or plants." Congress defined the terms "fish or wildlife" and "plants" very broadly[4]; however, prokaryotes (for example, bacteria), single-celled eukaryotes (for instance, paramecia and amoeba), and fungi are not included under either definition and therefore cannot be listed and do not receive protections under the Act.

B.2. Subspecies

"[A]ny subspecies of fish or wildlife or plants" can be listed as a threatened or endangered species, if it meets the listing criteria described below in this chapter.[5] The concept of "subspecies" has proven slippery for both lawyers and scientists. Primarily, the concept of subspecies is difficult for biologists because there are no hard and fast rules for when a taxon qualifies as a subspecies.[6] The National Research Council (NRC) notes that there is "a crucially important recognition that different concepts of species, subspecies, and other ranks are often applied between and even within disciplines."[7] As an example, the NRC looked at the vertebrates classified as subspecies:

> Many of the subspecific and population-level taxa of [listed vertebrates classified as subspecies] were birds. In part, this is due to the ornithological tradition of recognizing certain kinds of variation at "subspecific" rather than "specific" level. A fish biologist looking at a similar kind of variation might well have used the species rank in describing what an ornithologist would consider a subspecies.[8]

An informal survey of ESA practitioners revealed that none were aware of listed subspecies that were not geographically distinct from other populations of the species to which they belonged. In other words, they could not point to examples of listed subspecies that could not also possibly qualify as distinct population segments. The Mount Graham red squirrel for example, is listed as an endangered subspecies. However, it is not known to be genetically different from the 29 other named subspecies of red squirrels that occur through the United States and Canada.

---

4. *See* 16 U.S.C. §§ 1532(8), (14).

5. 16 U.S.C. § 1532(16).

6. A taxon is simply a category or group of organisms.

7. National Research Council, Science and the Endangered Species Act 55 (1995).

8. *Id.*

What makes it unique is that it inhabits a very unusual and isolated geographic area. Why it was listed as a subspecies and not a distinct population segment is unclear. For practical purposes, it makes no difference, as both subspecies and distinct population segments listed under the ESA receive the same level of protection as listed species.

The two most important things to note about the "subspecies" category of listed species are (1) that it can contain plants and invertebrates, which the distinct population segment category cannot, and (2) that a subspecies will receive a lower priority for listing purposes than a species (*see* box on page 33). The Service will rightly consider the imminent extinction of a species more important than the imminent extinction of one subspecies belonging to that species. This is also true of distinct population segments.

B.3. Distinct Population Segments

The ESA also extends protection to "any distinct population segment of any species of vertebrate fish or wildlife which interbreeds when mature."[9] Although they constitute only a small fraction of vertebrate listings,[10] distinct population segments account for many of the listings of larger and more charismatic animals such as the bald eagle, gray wolf, and grizzly bear. The ESA does not protect distinct population segments of invertebrates or plants.

In 1996, the Fish and Wildlife Service published the Policy Regarding the Recognition of Distinct Vertebrate Population Segments Under the Endangered Species Act (the DPS Policy).[11] The goal of the DPS Policy was to create a more uniform method for identifying which distinct population segments should be treated as "species" for purposes of listing, delisting, or reclassification.[12] The DPS Policy enumerates three factors to be considered in deciding whether to treat a distinct population segment as a species:

- the discreteness of the population segment in relation to the remainder of the species to which it belongs;
- the significance of the population segment to the species to which it belongs; and

---

9. 16 U.S.C. § 1532(16).

10. *See* National Research Council *supra* note 7, at 55. *See, e.g.,* 61 Fed. Reg. 4722 (1996).

11. 61 Fed. Reg. 4722 (1996).

12. *See id.* at 4725.

- the population segment's conservation status in relation to the Act's standards for listing (i.e., is the population segment, when treated as if it were a species, endangered or threatened?).[13]

These factors are to be considered in order. The discreteness requirement is satisfied if either (1) the population is "markedly separated from other populations as a consequence of physical, physiological, ecological, or behavioral factors," or (2) the population is delimited by international government boundaries within which differences of exploitation and conservation are significant.[14]

To determine whether the discrete population segment meets the significance requirement, the DPS Policy suggests four classes of information which may be considered (but which are not meant to be exhaustive):

- persistence of the discrete population segment in an ecological setting unusual or unique for the taxon;
- evidence that loss of the discrete population segment would result in a significant gap in the range of taxon;
- evidence that the discrete population segment represents the only surviving natural occurrence of the taxon that may be more abundant elsewhere as an introduced species outside of its historic range; or
- evidence that the discrete population segment differs markedly from other populations of the species in its genetic characteristics.[15]

Considerations of discreteness and significance, like all other decisions made in the listing process, are to be based solely on the best scientific and commercial data available. However, FWS regards seriously Congress's expressed intent that the authority to list discrete population segments be used "sparingly and only when the biological evidence indicates that such action is warranted."[16]

The third factor described in the DPS Policy—the status of the distinct population segment as endangered or threatened—formalizes a policy that FWS has followed for the past decade in applying the ESA to distinct population segments. A consideration of the population's status

---

13. *Id.* at 4725.
14. *Id.*
15. *Id.*
16. S. Rep. No. 96-151, at 7 (1979).

recognizes that the FWS may list some populations of a species as endangered and others as threatened. For example, at one time, the American bald eagle was listed as endangered in some geographical locations, was considered threatened in others, and was not listed at all in still other areas.[17]

There is a discretionary component to the distinct population segment analysis that has created some friction between the Service and conservation groups. This component is related to geographic scale. In the case of the lynx, for example, conservation groups have pushed for the listing of five geographically distinct populations that occur in different parts of the United States. To date, the Fish and Wildlife Service's position is that there is only one population, the "North American population."

B.4. Between a Subspecies and a Distinct Population Segment: The Evolutionarily Significant Unit and Salmonids in the Pacific Northwest

On the ground, the future of the subspecies/distinct population segment issue appears to be in some hybrid of the two concepts. Perhaps contrary to the original intent of the law, it is becoming increasingly difficult to convince the Service to list groups of organisms unless it can be shown that they are both geographically distinct and genetically or evolutionarily different in a significant way.

In 1991, NMFS published a policy on evaluating Pacific salmon stocks for listing.[18] Under the policy, a stock of Pacific salmon will be considered to be a distinct population segment if it qualifies as an evolutionarily significant unit (ESU). The definition of an ESU is a stock that is

- substantially reproductively isolated from other nonspecific population units; and
- representative of an important component in the evolutionary legacy of the species.[19]

On the first criterion, "reproductive isolation," NMFS maintains that the level of isolation does not have to be absolute. Rather, after considering the available array of data, "it must be strong enough to

---

17. *See* 50 C.F.R. §§ 17.11 (amended 1995). In 1995, the FWS reclassified all previously endangered populations of the bald eagle within the lower 48 states to threatened status. 50 C.F.R § 17.11(h); 60 Fed. Reg. 36,000 (1995).

18. *See* 56 Fed. Reg. 58,612 (1991).

19. *Id.* at 58,618.

permit evolutionarily important differences to accrue in different population units." In further defining the second criterion, "representative of an important component in the evolutionary legacy," NMFS offers three questions it considers relevant to the determination:

- Is the population genetically distinct from other nonspecific populations?
- Does the population occupy unusual or distinctive habitat?
- Does the population show evidence of unusual or distinctive adaptation to its environment?[20]

The reference to genetics implies that NMFS' conceptualization of the ESU is somewhere between a subspecies and a distinct population segment. The process of defining an ESU, as defined by NMFS, indicates that the agency is attempting to step back from the specifics of the law and ask the general question: is it important to protect this particular group of organisms?

Indeed, before the ESU policy was published, some commentators expressed the concern that the concept of the ESU was too subjective and lacked specific guidelines for NMFS to follow in order to make a determination. NMFS replied, in the final publication of the policy, that the ESU policy did not contain a "simple rule" or "universal yardstick" whereby species determinations could be made. Rather, NMFS pointed out that, due to the varying amounts of data available and the differing opinions within the scientific community concerning Pacific salmon, a "species" determination under the ESU policy "will require some judgment."[21]

C. The Listing Process: How a Species Gets Listed

Species are considered for listing either at the initiative of the Service or as a result of a petition by any interested person or group.[22] The only procedural difference between the two cases is that in the case of a citizen petition, there is an initial 90-day period in which the Service must determine whether or not the petition presents evidence indicating that a listing may be warranted. This is essentially a screening process in which the Service decides whether or not there is enough information in the petition so that a full consideration of the species' status is possible.

---

20. *Id.*
21. *Id.* at 58,614.
22. *See* 16 U.S.C. § 1533(b)(3)(A).

Both the citizen petition that clears the 90-day process and the internally initiated petition receive similar processing within the Service. In both cases, the Service begins a 12-month process to decide if the species should be listed under the ESA. At the end of this period, the Service will conclude that listing is either "warranted" or "not warranted." A warranted determination is not the final hurdle for a species "seeking" ESA protection. Due to a lack of budget resources, the Service prioritizes among warranted species using a somewhat complex system. Priority species will be listed and receive full ESA protection. Less fortunate species will be classified as "warranted but precluded," and will face repeated journeys through the 12-month evaluation process.[23]

During the 12-month process, both the citizen petition and the internally initiated petition are evaluated in the same way. In other words, the substantive analysis of whether or not the species is in fact threatened or endangered is the same in either case.

C.1. The Substance of Listing: Listing Factors

The Service must determine whether or not a species is threatened or endangered "solely on the basis of the best scientific and commercial data available."[24] When considering a species for listing, the Service looks to five statutorily enumerated factors:

- the inadequacy of the present or threatened destruction, modification, or curtailment of its habitat or range;
- overutilization for commercial, recreational, scientific, or educational purposes;
- disease or predation;
- existing regulatory mechanisms;
- other natural or man-made factors affecting its continued existence.[25]

During the listing process, the Service is prohibited from considering the economic impacts of the listing.[26] In 1982, Congress inserted the word *solely* into the Section 4(b)(1)(A) phrase "solely on the best scientific and

---

23. U.S. Fish and Wildlife Service & National Marine Fisheries Service, Endangered Species Petition Management Guidance 13-14 (1996) (hereinafter FWS Petition Guidance).

24. 16 U.S.C. § 1533(b)(1)(A).

25. *See id.* §§ 1533(a)(1)(A)-(E). An example of the Service's application of each of these factors is in the accompanying summary in section C.2 of this chapter (The Alameda whipsnake).

26. *Id.* § 1533(b)(1)(A).

commercial data available." The legislative history sets forth the purpose
of this amendment:

> The addition of the word "solely" is intended to remove from the
> process of the listing or delisting of a species any factor not re-
> lated to the biological status of the species.[27]

In its comments to the amendments, the House Committee expressly
rejected President Reagan's Executive Order 12,291, which required economic analysis in all agency actions. The Committee's view was that
"economic considerations have no relevance to determinations regarding
the status of species."[28] The Committee explained the amendment in the
following manner:

> Applying economic criteria to the analysis of [the five listing
> factors] and to any phase of the species listing process is apply-
> ing economics to the determination made under Section 4 of the
> Act and is specifically rejected by the inclusion of the word
> "solely" in this legislation.[29]

C.2. An Example of the Application of the Five Listing Factors: The Alameda Whipsnake

The Alameda whipsnake is found in and around Oakland and Mt.
Diablo in the northern California counties of Alameda and Contra Costa.
The Fish and Wildlife Service published a final rule listing the Alameda
whipsnake as threatened on December 5, 1997. The following is a summary of the agency's conclusions under each of the five listing factors.[30]

(1) The Present or Threatened Destruction, Modification, or Curtailment of Habitat or Range: The Fish and Wildlife Service identified three
factors threatening the whipsnake's habitat: urban development and its
associated impacts; inappropriate grazing practices; and alteration of
suitable habitat by fire suppression. Highway and road construction
fragmented the whipsnake's habitat and restricted exchanges among the
five resulting populations. Agency biologists discovered that the habitat
for two of the isolated whipsnake populations had been reduced to a
narrow band of habitat (one mile wide in some areas) along a single
ridgetop. Isolated populations of an already depleted species could suffer from genetic problems, particularly the expression of deleterious

27. H.R. Rep. No. 97-567, 20, *reprinted in* 1982 U.S.C.C.A.N. 2,820.
28. *Id.*
29. *Id.*
30. *See* 62 Fed. Reg. 64,306 (1997).

genes and the loss of genetic variability, limiting the species' ability to adapt to environmental change. Residential and recreational development in each of the five habitat areas further threatened the viability of the already isolated whipsnake populations. For example, increased visitation to state parks and other protected areas where the whipsnake was known to exist heavily impacted the species' habitat. The Fish and Wildlife Service opined that open space plans and other proposed mitigation measures would further fragment whipsnake habitat with walking and bike paths.

(2) Overutilization for Commercial, Recreational, Scientific or Educational Purposes: In a brief discussion, the FWS expressed fear that though the whipsnake was not currently popular among reptile collectors, a federal listing might increase its value and lead to a rise in its popularity.

(3) Disease or Predation: While the impact of disease on the whipsnake was unknown, the final rule emphasized that the health of the species was being adversely affected by predators. These predators included native and non-native species. The predation threat from non-native species, including the red fox, rats, feral pigs, and feral and domestic cats and dogs, had been increased by urbanization and habitat fragmentation.

(4) The Inadequacy of Existing Regulatory Mechanisms: The Service determined that California's 1971 listing of the whipsnake as a threatened species under state law was not adequate to ensure the future well-being of the species. In addition, state agency discretion under the California Environmental Quality Act (CEQA) rendered that law ineffective in protecting the whipsnake or its habitat. "[O]nce significant impacts are identified [under CEQA]," wrote the Service, "the lead agency has the option to require mitigation . . . or to decide that overriding considerations make mitigation infeasible. In the latter case, projects may be approved that cause significant environmental damage, such as destruction of endangered species." The Service concluded that local political pressure for fire suppression and expansive developments, coupled with the inadequacy of state legislation, required federal intervention.

(5) Other Natural or Man-Made Factors Affecting Their Continued Existence: The Fish and Wildlife Service identified local fire suppression practices as both a direct and indirect threat to the whipsnake. Local fire suppression techniques exacerbated wildfires through the buildup of fuel, creating conditions for slow-moving, hot fires. The most intense fires are in the summer when the fuel is abundant and dry. Hatchling and adult whipsnakes move above ground in the summer and therefore face a greater risk of harm. The whipsnake is dependent on a mosaic of

open and closed canopy for both sun exposure to maintain body temperature and for protective cover from predators. FWS also found that vegetative changes due to fire suppression had led to alterations in the structure of whipsnake habitat: denser, closed tree canopies resulted in cooler surface conditions and less exposed ground area.

C.3. The Procedure of Listing: The Petition

The sections below explain the process for listing species in response to petitions from citizens. Much of this information is found in the FWS and NMFS policy and guidance document that outlines this process in much greater detail. The document, "Endangered Species Petition Management Guidance," July 1996, is available from either agency upon request.

C.3.a. Petition Requirements

The Service has developed guidelines to screen out inadvertent "petitions" that were not intended to trigger the ESA's petition review process. A petition should identify itself as a petition under the ESA, and clearly indicate the action requested by the petitioner.[31] The petition request should be dated, and contain the name, address, telephone number, institutional association, and signature of the petitioner. Generally, the Service resolves uncertainty about whether a request is a petition or not by requesting clarification from the author of the document.

C.3.b. Petition Management

The Service recognizes three general types of petitions:

- Type 1 petitions for actions under Section 4(b)(3) of the ESA;
- Type 2 petitions for actions encompassed by other provisions of the ESA; and,
- Type 3 petitions for action under the Administrative Procedure Act[32] (APA).[33]

---

31. See 50 C.F.R. § 424.14(a).

32. The ESA specifically provides that the rulemaking procedures of the Administrative Procedure Act shall apply to any regulation proposed by the Secretary in the course of implementing the ESA. This would include 90-day findings, 12-month findings, and proposed rules. 16 U.S.C. § 1533(b)(4).

33. See 5 U.S.C. §§ 551-559, 701-706.

Only Type 1 petitions are subject to the strict timetable provisions of the ESA. Type 1 petitions include requests to list, reclassify, or delist species and requests to revise critical habitat.

The FWS refers to Type 2 and Type 3 petitions as "near petitions." Type 2 petitions encompass requests for emergency action and designation of critical habitat in conjunction with the proposed listing of a species. "The Services always consider the need for an emergency rule or critical habitat designation when listing species, so petitions that specify such actions are considered in the context of the listing action. . . ."[34] Although such requests are common, neither request triggers the ESA's petition provisions. However, at a minimum, the Service must follow the requirements of the APA and acknowledge the receipt of the petition. While submission of a Type 2 petition may not obligate the Service to take action pursuant to the ESA, it is likely that the Service will treat such petitions as comments during the listing process and consider them accordingly.

Priority Rank of Listing Actions

The Service established the Type 1, Type 2, and Type 3 categories described above in order to identify *how* it should treat the various petitions it receives. In addition, the Service has set up a system to identify *in what order* it should treat new Section 4 activities. According to the rule for fiscal years 1998 and 1999, highest priority is to be given to consideration of emergency listings; next highest priority is reserved for resolving the status of outstanding proposed listings, processing new petitions, and carrying out delistings and reclassifications; lowest priority is given to processing critical habitat determinations.

See 63 Fed. Reg. 25,502 (1998); 63 Fed. Reg. 10,931, 10,931-35 (1998) (proposed guidance). *See also,* 61 Fed. Reg. 64,475, 64,480 (1996) (describing the supplemental priority system for fiscal year 1997).

The Service gives two examples of Type 3 petitions: designation of new critical habitat for an already listed species and petitions asking for issuance or revision of an existing rule.[35] Such petitions are reviewable only under the APA which states: "Each agency shall give an interested

---

34. FWS Petition Guidance 4-5, *supra* note 23.

35. *See id.* at 5.

person the right to petition for the issuance, amendment, or repeal of a rule."[36] The Service need only acknowledge the receipt of such a petition and "consider" the request. If action is taken, the Service must notify the petitioner, but Federal Register "notice and comment" are not required for Type 3 petitions.[37]

C.3.c. 90-Day Finding

In 1982, responding to the vast backlog of petitions, Congress fashioned a stricter statutory timetable for Service response and action. The 1982 amendments require the Service to determine, within 90 days of receipt of a petition, whether a petition presents "substantial scientific or commercial data that the petitioned action may be warranted."[38] The Service refers to this initial inquiry as the "90-day finding." The 90-day finding is a preliminary inquiry designed to manage the petition review process and ensure that there is enough information to conduct the more intensive rulemaking procedures.

In the course of a 90-day finding investigation, information contained in the petition is scrutinized not only for quantity and breadth but also for reliability. The Director of the FWS, in a clarification memorandum sent to all of the Regional Directors, announced: "The key consideration in evaluating a petition for substantiality involves demonstration of the adequacy and reliability of the information supporting the action advocated by the petition."[39] The Director outlined the necessary ingredients to make a "substantial" finding:

> A "substantial" finding should be made when the Service deems that adequate and reliable information has been presented or is available that would lead a reasonable person to believe that the petitioned action may be warranted.

> Among the most reliable and credible sources are papers published in the peer-reviewed scientific literature. Information provided by individuals with demonstrated expertise in the relevant subject area can also generally be considered reliable. Anecdotal information or information from sources without established records of subject-matter experience and expertise must be strongly corroborated to be considered substantial. Potentially, even a petition based on peer-reviewed publications may be

---

36. Administrative Procedures Act, 5 U.S.C. § 553(e).

37. FWS Petition Guidance 5, *supra* note 23.

38. 16 U.S.C. § 1533(b)(3)(A); 50 C.F.R. § 424.14(b).

39. Memorandum from the FWS Director to the FWS Regional Directors 2 (Nov. 30, 1995) (*contained in* FWS Petition Guidance, *supra* note 23, at app. A (1996)).

found not substantial if sufficient countervailing information is available.[40]

For purposes of the 90-day finding, "the responsible Service will use the information provided by the petitioner and information already available in the Service's files."[41] In light of the investigation carried out to reach a 90-day finding, a prospective petitioner would be well advised to thoroughly and completely prepare a petition and its supporting materials in accordance with the Service's policy guidelines. An absence of peer-reviewed literature or credentials for experts will potentially lead to a negative 90-day finding.

The Secretary must promptly publish the finding it makes at the end of the 90-day process in the Federal Register.[42]

C.3.d. 12-Month Findings

If, at the conclusion of the 90-day period, a petition is found to present substantial information indicating that the Service should consider a species for listing, the Service will begin investigating the status of the species and assembling evidence in support of a proposed rule. During a 12-month period, the Service collects and analyzes data in order to assess the species in terms of the five statutory listing factors.[43]

At the end of the 12-month period the Service determines whether the listing is "not warranted," "warranted" or "warranted but precluded."[44] The "Endangered Species Petition Management Guidance" document states that a species listing is not warranted when at the end of the 12-month review, "convincing data on biological vulnerability and threat are not available to support a proposal to list"[45]

If the Service finds "convincing information" that the listing is warranted, then it assigns the listing a priority number. Following a somewhat complex evaluation process (see box on page 47), the priority number is used to determine if the listing is warranted or warranted but precluded.[46] Only warranted species are proposed for listing.

---

40. *Id.*
41. FWS Petition Guidance, *supra* note 23, at 10.
42. *See* 16 U.S.C. § 1533(b)(3)(C)(ii).
43. For more on the five-factor listing inquiry see section C.1 of this Chapter (Section 4: Listing, Critical Habitat Designation, and Recovery Plans).
44. FWS Petition Guidance, *supra* note 23, at 13-14.
45. Id. at 13.
46. NMFS does not use listing priority to determine if a species is "warranted but precluded."

Endangered versus Threatened Designation

At the end of the 12-month period, a species can be proposed for listing as either an *endangered* or a *threatened* species.

The ESA defines an endangered species in the following language:

The term "endangered species" means any species which is in danger of extinction throughout all or a significant portion of its range other than a species of the Class Insecta determined by the Secretary to constitute a pest whose protection under the provisions of this Act would present an overwhelming and overriding risk to man.[47]

A threatened species is defined as "any species which is likely to become an endangered species within the foreseeable future throughout all or a significant portion of its range."[48]

By regulation, most threatened species are afforded similar, but not the same, protections against "takes" under Section 9 as endangered species.[49] With the exception of experimental populations that are "not essential to the continued existence of the species," the substantive provisions of Section 7 apply equally to endangered and threatened species.[50]

Upon a finding of warranted but precluded, the petition is automatically advanced into another 12-month review process. This process is repeated indefinitely until the listing is either found to be warranted or not warranted. For the purposes of reevaluation, such "recycled" petitions are treated as presenting "substantial scientific or commercial information that the petitioned action may be warranted," and thus escape repeating the 90-day finding process.[51]

C.3.e. Priority Ranking of Species

In 1978, recognizing that the backlog of warranted listing candidates coupled with the Service's limited budget made action on all qualified species impossible, Congress amended Section 4 to require the Ser-

---

47. 16 U.S.C. § 1532(6).

48. *Id.* § 1532(20).

49. See Chapter Four (discussing the different protections for threatened versus endangered species).

50. *See* 16 U.S.C. § 1539(j)(2)(C)(i).

51. *See id.* § 1533(b)(3)(C)(i).

vice to develop a system to identify species that should have priority for listing.[52] In 1983, the Fish and Wildlife Service adopted the current listing priority system (the 1983 Priority Guidelines).[53] The 1983 Priority Guidelines

Assigning Priority

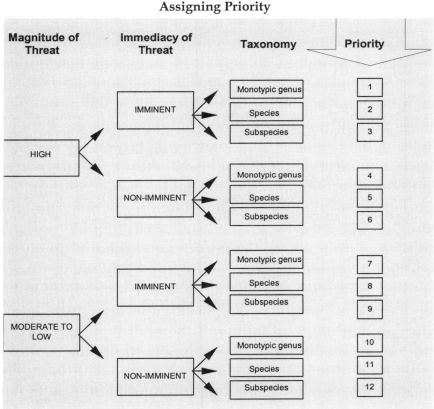

consider three factors in assigning a species a priority for listing: magnitude of threat; immediacy of threat; and species taxonomy. Using these three factors, the Service can assign a priority number between 1 and 12 to a candidate species. The lower the priority number, the higher the listing priority. If the resulting ranking priority given to a species exceeds the cutoff level set by the Secretary and the species otherwise qualifies for listing, the Service will classify the species as warranted but precluded.[54]

Decisions made at the beginning of the priority ranking process have enormous consequences for the resulting ranking, for example, if it is

---

52. *See id.* § 1533(h).

53. *See* 49 Fed. Reg. 43,098 (1983).

54. *See* 16 U.S.C. § 1533(b)(3)(B)(iii).

determined that the "magnitude of threat" facing an organism is "moderate to low," then that species cannot be given a priority number below a 6. The weightiness of the initial decisions implies a value choice made in the ranking process (from left to right in the box on page 47): magnitude of the threat is the most important consideration, with immediacy of the threat and the taxonomy of the organism having progressively less impact on the final priority ranking.

The "cutoff" point for reaching a warranted but precluded finding varies between FWS field offices, depending on that office's resources and caseloads. The relative ranking of species is not nationalized; rather, it is office specific. Individual field offices within a region may have different workloads and resource commitments and therefore have different bars for reaching a warranted but precluded finding. FWS field offices have no duty to publish their internal ranking guidelines and may change their cutoff points depending on other pending actions. Priority ranking levels are relative and not absolute, assigned by the field office only to help manage the listing process.[55] Therefore, a field office may reevaluate the ranking priority assigned to a species upon recycling a petition previously not acted upon due to a warranted but precluded finding.

For instance, upon consideration of a recycled petition urging the listing of the bull trout, the responsible field office in Region 1 revised the species' ranking from 9 to 3.[56] At the time the bull trout's priority status was revised, the FWS was under pressure from environmental groups that had filed suit over the original ranking, charging that the ranking of 9 was arbitrary and capricious. Six months after revising the priority ranking from 9 to 3, the field office reached a warranted but precluded finding by subsequently reversing its reclassification of the bull trout's priority ranking. In support of changing the priority ranking back from 3 to 9, the field office found that the Forest Service and the Bureau of Land Management, in the intervening six months before the revised classification, had initiated programs to reduce the threat to bull trout in the Columbia River Basin. Due to the new programs, the field office assigned a priority ranking of 9 for the second time to the bull trout on the grounds that the magnitude of threat was moderate and no longer as high as earlier determined.

On review of the priority ranking of the bull trout, the United States District Court of Oregon held the reclassification of priority ranking to be arbitrary and capricious, because the field office had relied on factors

---

55. *See* 48 Fed. Reg. 43,098-99 (1983).
56. *See* 60 Fed. Reg. 30,825 (1995).

that Congress had not intended be considered in the ranking decision and because the field office decision was inconsistent with its own biological findings.[57] On June 13, 1997, the Service published a proposed rule that, if adopted, would list the Klamath River population of bull trout as endangered and the Columbia River population of bull trout as threatened.[58] The case shows that there are limits to agency discretion in ranking species' priority.

C.3.f. Judicial Review of Findings

Affirmative 90-day or 12-month findings may not be challenged; only negative findings or "warranted but precluded" findings are subject to judicial review.[59] In *Building Industry Association of Southern California v. Babbitt*, [60] the plaintiffs challenged the listing of the fairy shrimp.[61] In addition to contesting the final rule listing the fairy shrimp, the plaintiffs also challenged the original petition to list the fairy shrimp, arguing that the petitions did not contain sufficient information to warrant an affirmative 90-day finding. Quoting the statute's language that only negative 90-day findings are subject to judicial review, the court concluded that the plaintiffs' challenge "must fail."[62]

C.4. From Proposed Rule to Final Rule

The Secretary is required to publish the 12-month finding and, in the case of a warranted species, the complete text of the proposed listing rule, in the Federal Register.[63] At the conclusion of the 12-month period, the Secretary must also:

- give notice of the proposed regulation to such professional scientific organizations as he deems appropriate;
- publish a summary of the proposed regulation in a newspaper of general circulation in each area of the United States in which the species is believed to occur; and

---

57. *See* Friends of the Wild Swan v. Service, 945 F. Supp. 1388, 1400 (D. Or. 1996).

58. *See* 62 Fed. Reg. 32,268 (1997).

59. *See* 16 U.S.C. § 1533(b)(3)(A).

60. 979 F. Supp. 893 (D.D.C. 1997).

61. Fairy shrimp is a collective term for several small shrimp species that inhabit vernal pools in California's Central Valley.

62. *See* 979 F. Supp. at 903-04.

63. *See* 16 U.S.C. § 1533(b)(5)(A)(i).

- promptly hold one public hearing on the proposed regulation if any person files a request for such a hearing within 45 days after the date of publication of general notice.[64]

The Secretary must also provide actual notice of the proposed regulation to appropriate state agencies and county jurisdictions in which the species occurs not less than 90 days before the effective date of the regulation.[65] With the cooperation and guidance of the Secretary of State, notice may also be given to foreign nations in which the species occurs.[66]

Once the proposed rule has been published, the Secretary has 12 months in which he or she must (1) publish a final listing rule; (2) withdraw the proposed listing; or (3) seek a 6-month extension.[67] The 6-month extension is available only when the Secretary can demonstrate that there is "substantial disagreement regarding the sufficiency or accuracy of the available data."[68] Otherwise, the proposed rule must be either finalized or withdrawn within a year. "The finding on which a withdrawal is based shall be subject to judicial review."[69] A withdrawn proposed rule cannot be re-proposed in the absence of "sufficient new information."[70]

C.4.a. Public Notice, Comment, and Hearing Requirements

A leading case on public comment and participation in the listing process is *Idaho Farm Bureau Federation v. Babbitt*.[71] At issue in the case was whether the Secretary committed procedural errors under the ESA and the APA in listing the Bruneau Hot Springs snail (the Springs snail). It was alleged that the FWS had violated these laws by (1) not allowing sufficient public comment and (2) not providing the public with a copy of a crucial United States Geological Survey (USGS) report. The Ninth Circuit held that the public comment period had been sufficient, but that the failure to produce the USGS report to the public was a significant procedural error.

Relying on its previous decisions, the court announced that "[t]he purpose of the notice and comment requirement is to provide for meaningful public participation in the rulemaking process."[72] According

---

64. *Id.* §§ 1533(b)(5)(C)-(E).
65. *See id.* § 1533(b)(5)(A)(ii).
66. *See id.* § 1533(b)(5)(A)(iii).
67. *See id.* § 1533(b)(6)(A).
68. *Id.* § 1533(b)(6)(B)(i).
69. *Id.* § 1533(b)(6)(B)(ii).
70. *See id.* § 1533(b)(6)(B)(ii).
71. 58 F.3d 1392 (9th Cir. 1995).
72. 58 F.3d at 1404.

to the facts of *Idaho Farm Bureau*, the FWS had originally scheduled a month-long public comment period on the proposed listing of the Springs snail. However, newspaper notice of the original comment period was not published until two days after the close of the comment period. FWS corrected its oversight by scheduling a second comment period to run for ten days. During that period, FWS received upwards of sixty comments on the proposed listing. The Court found the quantity and substance of the comments to demonstrate an understanding of the proposed listing and its relevant data; therefore, it found the public comment period adequate.

A separate issue in *Idaho Farm Bureau* was the question of whether FWS had violated the law by failing to disclose the USGS report to the public. The USGS report was one of the documents that the FWS had relied upon in deciding that the Springs snail warranted listing. The court found that the public should have been given a chance to examine the USGS report for two reasons: (1) the report provided unique information that was not duplicated in other reports, and (2) the FWS relied heavily upon the report in supporting its final rule. The court held that failure to produce the USGS report constituted significant procedural error.[73]

The court's holding in *Idaho Farm Bureau* contrasts with the recent holding in *Building Industry Association of Southern California*.[74] Faced with a similar situation, in which the FWS had not made a scientific study available to the public during the comment period, the court held that the failure to produce the study did not rise to the level of arbitrary and capricious.[75] The court based its holding on a finding that: (1) the final rule listing the fairy shrimp as endangered did not rest on the study in question but rather on a "broad constellation of data and factors"; (2) the fact that the fairy shrimp was rare had support elsewhere in the record; and (3) many experts had recommended listing the fairy shrimp without reference to the study in question.[76]

C.4.b. Remedy for Failure to Properly Include Public in Rule Making

The Ninth Circuit's remedy in *Idaho Farm Bureau* set an important precedent in regard to public participation in public review of

---

73. *See id.*

74. 979 F. Supp. 893 (D.C. 1997).

75. The standard for determining whether an agency action violates the Administrative Procedure Act is whether the agency action is "arbitrary and capricious." 5 U.S.C. § 706.

76. *See* 979 F. Supp. at 902-03.

proposed regulations under the ESA. Even though it found that the FWS had violated the ESA and the APA by failing to disclose the USGS report, the court refused to strike down the challenged regulation. Concerned about the future well-being of the Springs snail, the court gave the FWS a chance to correct its error, while leaving the listing decision (and its protections) in place:

> Ordinarily when a regulation is not promulgated in compliance with the APA, the regulation is invalid. However, when equity demands, the regulation can be left in place while the agency follows the necessary procedures. In the present case, concern exists regarding the potential extinction of an animal species. . . . The equitable concerns weigh toward leaving the listing rule in place while FWS remedies its procedural error and considers anew whether to list the Springs Snail.[77]

The extent to which courts will fashion similar remedies in future cases will depend on the facts of each case — as the Ninth Circuit made clear, its decision was based on the unique equities of the Springs snail case. The D.C. Circuit has supported this case-by-case approach to remedying procedural error made during the listing process.[78]

C.4.c. Peer Review

In 1994, the Service announced its endorsement of scientific peer review during the listing process and the formulation of draft recovery plans in *Endangered and Threatened Wildlife and Plants: Notice of Interagency Cooperative Policy for Peer Review in Endangered Species Act Violations* (the Peer Review Policy).[79] Peer review has long been the model that scientists have followed when judging the validity, importance, and acceptability of research findings and theoretical papers. Because the ESA mandates that listing decisions be made according to the "best biological and commercial information available," many commentators and regulators have argued that a peer review process is the only trustworthy and reliable yardstick for judging whether any given listing evidence is the "best."

---

77. 58 F.3d at 1405-06 (citations omitted).

78. *See generally* City of Las Vegas v. Lujan, 891 F.2d 927 (D.C. Cir. 1989).

79. *See* 59 Fed. Reg. 34,270 (1994). For a discussion of peer review in recovery plans see section F.2 of this Chapter (Section 4: Listing, Critical Habitat Designation, and Recovery Plans).

Peer Review in Practice

In the final rule to list the Alameda whipsnake as a threatened species, the FWS stated: "In accordance with the Service policy on peer review . . . the opinions of three independent scientists were also solicited. No responses were received from these specialists." Although FWS usually receives one or two comments back from its peer review requests, FWS has no authority to require responses from solicited experts.

For details see 62 Fed. Reg. 64,306, 64,309 (1997).

According to the Peer Review Policy, the Service should solicit "the opinions of three appropriate and independent specialists"[80] regarding the scientific and commercial evidence relevant to a listing decision. Although the Peer Review Policy does not set forth a specific timetable for the process, it is clear that it must take place — in order to be useful — within the statutory 12-month listing evaluation period.

Over the past several years, some in Congress have introduced legislation that would make peer review a mandatory part of the listing process. These proposals have aroused concern in the conservation community. The fear is that the benefits of peer review would be out-weighed by the harm to species resulting from further delay in the listing process. The Ad Hoc Committee on Endangered Species of the Ecological Society of America argued that:

> There is no scientific reason why listing, which is an administrative decision based on the available information, should require much time or agency resources. The uncertainty that may result from sparse information is part of the risk that is evaluated during the listing process. Adding independent peer review or other administrative processes to the listing process would unnecessarily lengthen the time to make a listing decision without providing any substantial benefits. The major problem with the listing process has been its slowness, not inadequacy of the quality of the listing decisions.[81]

---

80. *See id.*

81. Ecological Society of America Ad Hoc Committee on Endangered Species, *Strengthening the Use of Science in Achieving the Goals of the Endangered Species Act: An Assessment by the Ecological Society of America* 6(1) Ecological Applications 1, 4 (1996).

At this time, peer review is confined to a FWS policy statement and therefore cannot supersede the listing guidelines and timetables.

C.5. Judicial Review of Final Rules

As with most federal agency decisions, decisions made by the Service under the ESA can be challenged in court under the APA.[82] The APA's "arbitrary and capricious" standard is applied by courts to any challenged regulations, and to agency decisions such as the listing of a species or the issuance of incidental take permits.[83] The "arbitrary and capricious" standard makes it difficult, but not impossible, to challenge agency regulations and decisions: courts will uphold the Secretary's interpretation of the ESA so long as the interpretation is reasonable.[84] The reasonableness of an interpretation is evaluated by reference to the text, structure, and legislative history of the ESA.[85] Because the Service has expertise in the area of wildlife conservation and management, courts often begin with a presumption in favor of the Service when considering challenges to listing decisions.[86]

C.6. Emergency Listing

The Secretary may dispense with most procedural listing require-ments in the case of any emergency that poses "a significant risk to the well-being of any species of fish or wildlife or plants."[87] In such cases, the Secretary may make an emergency listing, which becomes effective im-mediately upon publication in the Federal Register. Emergency listings continue in force for 240 days and become permanent only if ordinary rulemaking procedures, such as providing an opportunity for notice and comment, are undertaken and completed within the 240-day period. Otherwise, the regulation ceases to have force. However, there is nothing in the law that would prevent the Service from re-issuing the emergency listing rule at the expiration of the 240 days.

The ESA requires that the Service monitor "warranted but pre-cluded" species and make prompt use of the emergency listing power to

---

82. See 5 U.S.C. § 706.

83. See e.g. Motor Vehicle Mfrs. Ass'n v. State Farm Mut. Auto. Ins. Co., 463 U.S. 29, 43 (1983); Wyoming Farm Bureau Fed'n v. Babbitt, 987 F. Supp 1349, 1364 (D. Wyo. 1997).

84. See Babbitt v. Sweet Home Chapter of Communities for a Great Oregon, 515 U.S. 687, 703 (1995) (citing Chevron U.S.A. v. Natural Resources Defense Council, 467 U.S. 837 (1984)).

85. See 515 U.S. at 695.

86. See Carlton v. Babbitt, 900 F. Supp. 526, 530 (D.D.C. 1995) (citing Marsh v. Oregon Natural Resources Council, 490 U.S. 360, 375-80 (1989)).

87. 16 U.S.C. § 1533(b)(7).

prevent "significant risk to the well being of any such species."[88] In *City of Las Vegas v. Lujan*,[89] a case involving the emergency listing of certain "warranted but precluded" populations of the desert tortoise, the D.C. Circuit characterized Congress's mandate to the Secretary to use his emergency listing powers as one of "shoot first and ask all of the questions later."[90] Previous to the decision to invoke his emergency listing powers, the Secretary had found that listing the desert tortoise was warranted but precluded on three separate occasions. In 1989, it was brought to the Secretary's attention that the Mojave population of the desert tortoise was threatened by a contagious, fatal, and incurable respiratory disease. Two months later, after some study, the Secretary published an emergency regulation listing the Mojave population of desert tortoises as endangered.

The City of Las Vegas challenged the emergency listing on numerous grounds. The most salient challenge was that the emergency listing was "arbitrary and capricious because it was based on inferior scientific evidence."[91] On summary judgment, the district court agreed with the plaintiffs that the decision was based on inferior scientific evidence. Nevertheless, the court ruled in favor of the Secretary, finding that it was within the Secretary's discretion to use his emergency listing powers as long as he provided, as required by the statute, the requisite notice to the states and detailed reasons for his decision.[92] The appellate court agreed with the result reached by the district court, but found stronger justification for reaching the same conclusion. As to the requirement that the Secretary withdraw an emergency regulation if "substantial evidence does not exist," the court reasoned that the Secretary need only rely on "the best appropriate data available to him."[93] "Congress contemplated," said the court, "that the Secretary would not inquire as thoroughly at the emergency listing stage."[94]

The test for determining whether the Secretary acted in an arbitrary or capricious manner in regard to the body and quality of scientific evidence relied on to reach an emergency listing decision turns on whether the Secretary "disregarded scientifically superior evidence that was

---

88. *See id.* § 1533(b)(3)(C)(iii).

89. 891 F.2d 927 (D.C. Cir. 1989

90. 891 F.2d at 932.

91. *Id.* at 931.

92. *See id.* (referencing City of Las Vegas v. Lujan, Memorandum Order, No. 89-2216 (D.D.C. Aug. 24, 1989)).

93. 16 U.S.C. § 1533(b)(7).

94. 891 F.2d at 932.

available to him at the time he published [the regulation]." The court explained that:

> At least for emergency listings (particularly of warranted but precluded species), however, [the emergency listing provision] merely prohibits the Secretary from disregarding available scientific evidence that is in some way better than the evidence he relies upon. Even if the available scientific and commercial data were quite inconclusive, he may—indeed must—still rely on it at that stage.[95]

In the case of the desert tortoise, the court found that there was ample evidence to support an emergency listing and no superior scientific evidence existed at the time of listing.

On April 2, 1990, the same day that the emergency listing expired, the Service published the final rule listing the Mojave population of the desert tortoise as endangered. At the same time, FWS listed parts of the Sonoran population as threatened, due to their similarity of appearance to members of the Mojave population. (*See* box below).[96]

Similarity of Appearance

Under very limited circumstances, Section 4(e) allows the Secretary to treat a species as threatened or endangered even though the species is not biologically threatened or endangered. If an unlisted species so closely resembles a listed species as to confuse identification of the listed species and therefore poses a threat to its protection, the Secretary may promulgate regulations protecting the look-alike species as if it were listed as threatened or endangered.[97] These species are listed because of their "similarity of appearance" to listed species; the regulations for these species are found in 50 C.F.R. §§ 17.50–17.52.

C.7. Delisting, Reclassification and Monitoring

In 1982, Congress addressed the concern that the endangered and threatened species lists "harbor a number of improperly listed species."[98]

---

95. *Id.* at 933 (emphasis added).
96. *See generally* 55 Fed. Reg. 12,178 (1990).
97. *See* 16 U.S.C. § 1533(e).
98. H.R. Rep. No. 97-567, 22, *reprinted in* 1982 U.S.C.C.A.N. 2822.

Lawmakers amended Section 4, requiring that the procedures and time frames used for the listing of species be followed in the delisting process.[99] Congress characterized its purpose in amending Section 4 as "to ensure that decisions in every phase of the process pertaining to the listing or delisting of species are based solely upon biological criteria and to prevent non-biological considerations from affecting such decisions."[100]

In 1984, the Service issued regulations implementing and further describing the delisting process mandated by the 1982 amendments.[101] The Service may delist a species only if one of the following criteria applies:

- the species has become extinct;
- the species has recovered; or,
- the original data upon which the species' listing was originally based was in error.[102]

The regulations stipulate that, for a species to be considered extinct, the Secretary must find that all previously identified individuals of the species have been extirpated from their range.[103] Additionally, "a sufficient period of time must be allowed before delisting to indicate clearly that the species is extinct."[104] A species may be delisted due to recovery "only if the best scientific and commercial data available indicate that it is no longer endangered or threatened."[105] For a species to be delisted due to erroneous data, a petitioner may either claim that: (1) the best commercial and scientific evidence available at the time of listing was in error, or (2) the interpretation of the best available evidence was in error.[106]

In addition to being delisted, a species can also be reclassified, from endangered to threatened or vice versa. A 1995 district court case helped interpret the reclassification procedure. In *Carlton v. Babbitt*,[107] plaintiffs appealed a denied petition to have two grizzly bear populations raised from "threatened" to "endangered" status.[108] The court found that the FWS, after determining that a petition is sufficient, must evaluate a

---

99. *See* 16 U.S.C. § 1533(b)(3).

100. H.R. Rep. No. 97-567, 22, *reprinted in* 1982 U.S.C.C.A.N. 2860.

101. *See* 49 Fed. Reg. 38,900 (1984).

102. 50 C.F.R. § 424.11(d).

103. *See* 50 C.F.R. § 424.11(d)(1).

104. *Id.*

105. 50 C.F.R. §§ 424.11(d)(2).

106. *See* 50 C.F.R. § 424.11(d)(3).

107. 900 F. Supp. 526 (D.D.C. 1995).

108. *See id.* at 528.

reclassification petition according to the five factors used in determining the species original listing status, that is, habitat destruction, overutilization, disease or predation, inadequate regulatory protections, and other natural or manmade factors.[109] The court instructed FWS to "consider each of the listing factors singularly and in combination with the other factors."[110] The court noted that usually courts defer to FWS's expertise in listing decisions.[111] However, in this case the court found that the Secretary's decision not to reclassify the Selkirk grizzly bear population as endangered was arbitrary, capricious, and unwarranted. The court found that "the defendants failed to sufficiently explain how they exercised their discretion with regard to the statutory listing factors and drew conclusions that cannot be supported by the evidence in the record."[112] The court further observed that the defendants had not adequately investigated or reviewed the evidence.[113]

In 1988, Congress once again demonstrated its concern over the fate of species languishing due to the large numbers of species awaiting listing. Noting that some of these species had undergone substantial declines in numbers, and several had become extinct before being protected, lawmakers enacted a series of monitoring requirements intended to prevent such occurrences.[114] Congress added a requirement that the Secretary take affirmative steps to monitor "warranted but precluded" species.[115]

The Secretary must also review the status of every listed species once every five years to determine whether any species should be reclassified or delisted.[116] Any change in the endangered and threatened lists as a result of this review must be made according to the regular Section 4 listing and delisting process. Two high-profile examples of reclassification and delisting were the 1995 reclassification of the remaining endangered populations of the bald eagle in the lower 48 states to threatened status[117] and the 1993 delisting of the eastern North Pacific stock of gray whales.[118]

---

109. *See id.* at 529. For more on the five factor listing inquiry see section C.1 of this chapter (Section 4: Listing, Critical Habitat Designation, and Recovery Plans).

110. 900 F. Supp. at 530.

111. *See id.*

112. *Id.* at 537.

113. *See id.*

114. *See* S. Rep. No. 100-240, at 8 (1987).

115. *See* 16 U.S.C. § 1533(b)(3)(C)(iii).

116. *Id.* § 1533(c)(2).

117. *See* 60 Fed. Reg. 36,000 (1995).

118. *See* 58 Fed. Reg. 3121 (1993).

D. Critical Habitat

A common misconception is that an area designated as "critical habitat" under Section 4 is magically transformed into something akin to a national park, where any modification of the landscape is illegal. This view is inaccurate for two reasons. First, critical habitat provisions apply only to federal or federally authorized activities. Critical habitat designation can affect private land, but only to the extent that a future activity on that land is subject to federal permitting, for instance, filling wetlands, or will be funded by the U.S. Treasury. Second, the law does not preclude all uses of designated critical habitat. Only those uses that destroy or adversely modify critical habitat violate Section 7(a)(2).[119] Despite these statutory limitations, many private landowners continue to fear that critical habitat designation will turn their backyard into "public land." This fear renders critical habitat designation controversial in many parts of the country.

Critical habitat designation is also a great time and resource drain on the FWS. In its proposed listing guidance for 1998 and 1999, the Service predicted that "[a] single critical habitat designation could consume up to twenty percent of the total listing appropriation [$1 million], thereby disrupting the Service's biologically based priorities."[120] For this reason, in its final listing guidance, the Service has made the designation of critical habitat its lowest priority among competing listing actions.[121]

D.1. Definition of Critical Habitat

The ESA defines critical habitat in the following manner:

i. the specific areas within the geographical area occupied by the species, at the time it is listed . . . on which are found those physical or biological features (I) essential to the conservation of the species and (II) which may require special management considerations or protection; and

ii. specific areas outside the geographical area occupied by the species at the time it is listed . . . upon a determination by the Secretary that such areas are essential for the conservation of the species.[122] The ESA specifies that critical habitat does not

---

119. *See* 16 U.S.C. § 1536(a)(2).
120. 63 Fed. Reg. 10,931, 10,933 (1998).
121. *See* 63 Fed. Reg. 25,502 (1998).
122. 16 U.S.C. § 1532(5)(A).

necessarily include all areas which the species could potentially occupy.[123] The Secretary retains discretion to determine what percentage of the species' entire range is essential to the conservation of the species.

The ESA requires that the area or features proposed for protection as critical habitat be those that are both "essential to the conservation of the species" and "which may require special management considerations or protections." The question of which physical features are essential to a species is closely related in application to interpretation and application of the "jeopardy standard" under Section 7 of the ESA. In other words, the Service only considers habitat essential if it is necessary to preserve

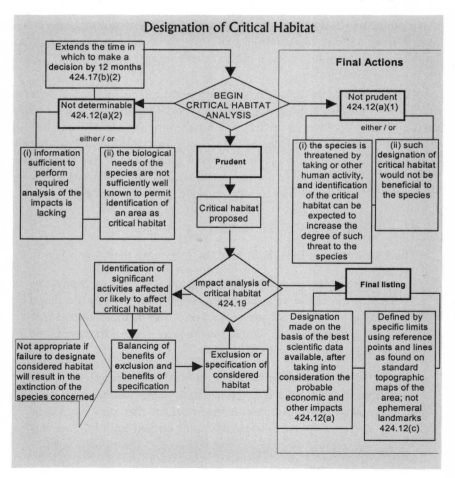

Designation of Critical Habitat

_____

123. *See id.* § 1532(5)(C).

the status quo of the population; it does not designate critical habitat with recovery in mind. Thus, although many commentators believe that the standard should be higher, essential habitat becomes in practice the minimum area that the species requires in order to survive.[124]

50 C.F.R. § 424.12(b) — Biological Criteria for the Designation of Critical Habitat

In determining what areas are critical habitat, the Secretary shall consider those physical and biological features that are essential to the conservation of a given species and that may require special management considerations or protection. These requirements include, but are not limited to the following:

(1) Space for individual and population growth, and for normal behavior;

(2) Food, water, air, light, minerals, or other nutritional or physiological requirements;

(3) Cover or shelter;

(4) Sites for breeding, reproduction, rearing of offspring, germination, or seed dispersal; and generally;

(5) Habitats that are protected from disturbance or are representative of the historic geographical and ecological distributions of a species.

When considering the designation of critical habitat, the Secretary shall focus on the principal biological or physical constituent elements within the defined area that are essential to the conservation of the species. Known primary constituent elements shall be listed with the critical habitat description. Primary constituent elements may include, but are not limited to, the following: roost sites, nesting grounds, spawning sites, feeding sites, seasonal wetland or dryland, water quality or quantity, host species or plant pollinator, geological formation, vegetation type, tide, and specific soil types.

The second requirement, that critical habitat contain features "which may require special management considerations or protection," has, in one instance, figured prominently in the Secretary's refusal to designate an area as critical habitat. In a case involving the proposed designation of

---

124. *See* Chapter 4, section D.2 (Section 7 and Critical Habitat).

critical habitat for the monk seal in the coastal waters of the northwest Hawaiian Islands, NMFS asserted that portions of a large area recommended by the monk seal recovery plan for critical habitat designation did not require special management considerations or protection.[125] NMFS made this finding despite having acknowledged that two types of human activity (deep-sea mining and commercial fishing operations) could affect monk seals and their habitat. In order to establish that the area was not in need of special management or special protection, NMFS found that a seabed mining industry was "likely years away," and also that existing fishery management plans already provided sufficient protection for the monk seal.[126]

D.2. The Critical Habitat Designation Process

The Secretary must designate critical habitat concurrently with listing a species unless the critical habitat is indeterminable or designation would be imprudent.[127] If there exists insufficient information on the species' habitat or the species' needs, then the Secretary may find the designation of critical habitat to be "not determinable."[128] The Secretary may reach a "not determinable" finding on two grounds: (1) a lack of information sufficient to perform the required analyses,[129] or (2) the biological needs of the species are not sufficiently known to identify its critical habitat.[130] If a "not determinable" finding is made, the time for designating critical habitat may be extended by up to 12 months.[131] If the designation of critical habitat would either further threaten or add no additional benefit to the species, then the Secretary may make a finding that the designation of critical habitat is "not prudent."[132] A not prudent finding, unlike a not determinable finding, is a final listing action. If the Secretary finds that the designation of critical habitat is both prudent and determinable, then, before designating any critical habitat, the Secretary must issue a proposed rule and hold a public comment period

---

125. *See generally* 51 Fed. Reg. 16,047-53 (1986).

126. *See id.* at 16,051.

127. *See* 16 U.S.C. § 1533(b)(2).

128. *See id.* § 1533(b)(6)(C)(ii).

129. *See id.* § 424.12(a)(2)(i).

130. *See id.* § 424.12(a)(2)(ii).

131. *See id.*

132. *See* 50 C.F.R. § 424.12(a)(1).

if any person files a request for one.[133] The Secretary must consider both scientific evidence and economic and other relevant factors.[134] Upon

A Critique of the Critical Habitat Regulations

The first reason the regulations are unlawful begins with an accepted principle of statutory construction, that a law will be interpreted to give effect to all of its portions so that no part will be "inoperative or superfluous, void or insignificant, and so that one section will not destroy another." Interior's interpretation of the law violates every clause just quoted by removing independent legal meaning for the term "critical habitat." . . . The only legal significance for critical habitat in the statute is its eligibility for protection, separate from the protections afforded to species from jeopardy in general. . . . Interior's regulations have eliminated the habitat inquiry, and thereby removed the more tangible and specific protection that critical habitat provides. . . . At this point the regulations are not simply interpretative; they repeal half of section 7(a)(2) — the half with the greater bite.

The second reason Interior's regulations are unlawful is that they restrict "critical habitat" to bare species survival, despite a legislative definition that requires considerably more. As noted above, the ESA defines critical habitat as that essential to the "conservation" of a species. The Act defines *conservation* as "the use of all methods and procedures which are necessary to bring any endangered species to the point at which the measures provided pursuant to [the Act] are no longer necessary." That is, to the point at which the species has recovered. To be sure, the Act further directs that "critical habitat shall not include the entire geographic area which can be occupied" by the species, but this restriction is qualified, again, by the requirement for designation of areas "essential for the conservation of a species."

For details see Oliver Houck, *The Endangered Species Act and Its Implementation by the U.S. Departments of Interior and Commerce*, 64 U. COLO. L. REV. 278, 300-01 (1993).

---

133. *See* 16 U.S.C. § 1533(b)(5).
134. *See id.* § 1533(b)(2).

considering economic and other relevant impacts, the Secretary may exclude certain areas from the final rule designated critical habitat.[135] After weighing all the relevant factors, the Secretary must publish the final designation in the Federal Register with a full description of the area and any necessary maps.[136]

D.2.a. The "Not Prudent" Standard

Implementing regulations describe when the designation of critical habitat would not be prudent:

- The species is threatened by taking or other human activity, and identification of critical habitat can be expected to increase the degree of such threat to the species, or
- Such designation of critical habitat would not be beneficial to the species.[137]

Although Section 4 is broadly phrased, the legislative history indicates that Congress intended the "prudency" exception to be narrowly construed. At the time of the 1978 amendments, when the critical habitat designation process was formally added to the Act, Congress noted that "[i]t is only in rare circumstances where the specification of critical habitat concurrently with the listing would not be beneficial to the species."[138] For instance, Congress noted that critical habitat designation would not be prudent if it would disclose the location of a listed species commonly sought by unscrupulous collectors.[139]

During the Reagan administration, however, the Service expanded the circumstances under which critical habitat designation would not be considered prudent. Section 4 regulations permit the Secretary to avoid designating critical habitat concurrently with listing whenever such designation "would not be beneficial to the species."[140] An official explanation of this provision indicates that the Secretary performs an informal balancing test on a case-by-case basis to determine whether critical habitat designation benefits a species:

[T]he Services will examine the balance between risk to a species that might be a consequence of designating its critical habitat

---

135. *See id.*
136. *See id.* § 1533(b)(6)(A)(ii).
137. 50 C.F.R. § 424.12(a)(1)(i)-(ii).
138. H.R. Rep. No. 95-1625, at 17, *reprinted in* 1978 U.S.C.C.A.N. 9453, 9484.
139. *See id.* at 16-17.
140. 50 C.F.R. § 424.12(a)(1)(ii).

and benefits that the species might derive from such designation
. . . In those cases in which the possible adverse consequences
would outweigh the benefits of designation of critical habitat, the
Services may forego such designation as matter of prudence.[141]

Critics state such a balancing test affords the Secretary broad discretion in an action that according to the Act should be mandatory.[142]

D.2.b. The Tide Turns: *NRDC v. DOI*

Although the balancing test employed by the Service is
discretionary, the Service's actual discretion over whether to designate
critical habitat at the time of listing is not unbounded. In 1997, the Ninth
Circuit scrutinized the FWS's decision not to designate critical habitat for
the threatened California gnatcatcher at the time the final listing was
made. In *Natural Resources Defense Council v. U.S. Dept. of Interior,* [143]
(*NRDC v. DOI*) the court narrowed the Secretary's discretion to decide
whether or not to designate critical habitat at the time of listing. Citing
the mandate of FWS regulations and excerpts from the 1978 Congressional Record, the Ninth Circuit concluded that "[t]he Service failed to
discharge its statutory obligation to designate critical habitat when it
listed the gnatcatcher as a threatened species, or to articulate a rational
basis for invoking the rare imprudence exception."[144]

According to FWS regulations, the designation of critical habitat is
not prudent when either of the two following conditions exist: (1)
identification of critical habitat would lead to an increased threat to the
species, or (2) designation of critical habitat would not be beneficial to
the species.[145] In *NRDC v. DOI*, the court asked "whether the agency
'considered the relevant factors and articulated a rational connection
between the facts found and the choice made.'"[146]

The court first considered whether FWS appropriately found that
designation of critical habitat would lead to an increased threat to the
gnatcatcher. In the final rule listing the gnatcatcher as threatened, the
Service claimed that publication of maps describing the critical habitat of

---

141. 49 Fed. Reg. 38,900, 38,903 (1984).
142. *See generally* Oliver Houck, *The Endangered Species Act and Its Implementation by the U.S. Departments of Interior and Commerce,* 64 U. Colo. L. Rev. 277, 300-01 (1993).
143. 113 F.3d 1121 (9th Cir. 1997).
144. 113 F.3d at 1127 (emphasis added) (citing 50 C.F.R. § 424.12(a)(1)(i)-(ii); H.R. Rep. No. 95-1625 (1978), *reprinted in* 1978 U.S.C.C.A.N. 9453).
145. *See supra* note 137 and accompanying text.
146. 113 F.3d at 1124 (quoting Resources Ltd., Inc. v. Robertson, 35 F.3d 1300, 1304 (9th Cir. 1993)).

the gnatcatcher would lead landowners to engage in prohibited takings activities.[147] The court rejected such an unsupported rationale:

> This "increased threat" rationale fails to balance the pros and cons of designation as Congress expressly required. . . . In this case, the Service never weighed the benefits of designation against the risks of designation. The final listing decision cited only eleven cases of habitat destruction, out of 400,000 acres of gnatcatcher habitat. The listing did not explain how such evidence shows that designation would cause more landowners to destroy, rather than protect, gnatcatcher sites.[148]

To support a not prudent decision on grounds that designation would lead to habitat destruction, the Service may not rely merely on an abstract principle or concern, but must base its decision on actual evidence of a real threat to the particular species.

Turning next to the question of whether FWS correctly found that designation of critical habitat would not be beneficial to the gnatcatcher, the court held that "[t]he Service's reliance on the 'no-benefit' exception to Section 4 designation was . . . improper."[149] The court's view was that the FWS had improperly expanded the narrow "no benefit" exception to Section 4 by changing the "beneficial to the species" test to a "beneficial to most of the species" test.[150] The court cited legislative history indicating that this exception was meant to prevent the imprudent designation of critical habitat areas only in the "rare circumstances where the specification of critical habitat concurrently with the listing would not be beneficial to the species."[151]

The court stated that "[b]y expanding the imprudence exception to encompass all cases in which designation would fail to control 'the majority of land-use activities occurring within critical habitat,' . . . the Service contravenes the clear congressional intent that the imprudence exception be a rare exception."[152]

The court next addressed the FWS's contention that because most of the potential critical habitat was privately owned, designation would provide "no benefit" to the species. The court cited the Service's own findings that over 80,000 of the 400,000 acres in question were publicly

147. *See* 58 Fed. Reg. 16,742, 16,756 (1993).
148. 113 F.3d at 1125.
149. *Id.* at 1126.
150. *Id.*
151. *Id.* (quoting H.R. Rep. No. 95-1625, at 17 (1978)).
152. *Id.* (citing 58 Fed. Reg. at 16,756).

owned and concluded that the species would indeed benefit.[153] Thus, the court found that the "no benefit" determination lacked a rational connection between the facts and the requirements of the law.

In the aftermath of the case, the Department of the Interior Solicitor's office provided guidance to the Service on the meaning of not prudent.[154] The Solicitor recommended that the Service take the following steps in explaining not prudent determinations:

- ensure that the facts discussed in the findings are internally consistent with the rest of the listing rule;
- include specific examples of specific risks which could lead to a "not prudent" finding;
- weigh specific risks against established benefits and show that the increased risk outweighs the benefit; and
- discuss the degree of overlap between Section 7's adverse modification standard and Section 7's jeopardy standard as applied to the habitat and species at issue . [155]

D.2.c. Consideration of Economic and Other Relevant Factors

The designation of critical habitat differs from most other ESA provisions because it can involve consideration of economic factors. A certain "core" area of critical habitat must be designated solely on biological factors: this is an amount that must be designated to prevent extinction of the species.[156] Any designation of critical habitat beyond the "core" area necessary for survival of the species, for example, a designation that would allow protection of an area into which an existing population could expand, depends on a balancing test. Under the law, the Secretary is to consider whether the economic benefits of not designating those areas exceed the biological benefits of designating them as critical habitat.[157]

This statutory balancing test did not exist before 1978, when the Secretary made critical habitat determinations solely on the basis of biological criteria. In 1978, however, Congress amended Section 4 to require the Secretary to designate critical habitat "after taking into

---

153. *See* 113 F.3d at 1126.
154. *See* Memorandum from Charles P. Raynor, Assistant Solicitor to the Director of United States Fish & Wildlife Service, *"Not Prudent" Findings Subject to Ninth Circuit Review* (Aug. 21, 1997).
155. *See id.* at 2-3.
156. 16 U.S.C. §§ 1533(b)(2), 1532(5)(A)(i).
157. *Id.* § 1533(b)(2).

consideration the economic impact, and any other relevant impact, of specifying any particular area as critical habitat."[158]

The "Additional Views" section of the 1978 House report on the ESA amendments succinctly describes the incongruities between the Section 4 critical habitat designation procedure and the rest of the ESA:

> In effect, then, the Secretary is given broad power to grant exemptions to the Endangered Species Act through a simple, unilateral administrative determination of his or her own. This is a process which stands in sharp contrast to the laboriously constructed exemption process, with its clear standards and procedural safeguards. . . .

***

> As currently written, the critical habitat provision is a startling section which is wholly inconsistent with the rest of the legislation. It constitutes a loophole which could readily be abused by any Secretary of the Interior who is vulnerable to political pressure, or who is not sympathetic to the basic purposes of the Endangered Species Act.[159]

The House report explaining the amendment noted that "[t]he consideration and weight given to any particular impact is completely within the Secretary's discretion."[160] The report went on to express lawmakers' expectations that the consideration of economic and other impacts would limit the designation of critical habitat. The House report emphasized, however, that even in areas where the Secretary expressly refuses to designate critical habitat, federal projects remain subject to the jeopardy standard of Section 7.[161]

The 1978 Amendments changed the designation process from a purely biological assessment to a social policy decision. Critics of the changes claim that the 1978 Amendments have significantly harmed the listing process.[162]

---

158. *Id.*

159. H.R. Rep. No. 95-1625, at 69 (1978), *reprinted in* 1978 U.S.C.C.A.N. 9543, 9484. This sentiment has been echoed by other commentators, *see, e.g.*, Michael Bean, The Evolution of National Wildlife Law 339 n.95 (1983).

160. H.R. Rep. No. 95-1625, at 17. Under the House version of the 1978 amendments, the Secretary could consider non-biological criteria only when designating critical habitat for invertebrate species. When the final version of the amended ESA emerged from committee, however, the limitation to invertebrate species had been dropped.

161. *Id.*

162. *See* James Salzman, *Evolution and Application of Critical Habitat Under the Endangered Species Act*, 14 Harv. Envtl. L. Rev. 311, 321-22 (1990). Some harsher effects of the changes

Along with the required analysis of economic impacts, critical habitat rulemakings are subject to a number of statutes and executive orders. Some of the statutes and executive orders that are applicable to critical habitat designations are the Regulatory Flexibility Act (5 U.S.C. § 601), the Paperwork Reduction Act (44 U.S.C. § 3501), Government Actions and Interference with Constitutionally Protected Property Rights (Executive Order 12,630), Regulatory Planning and Review (Executive Order 12,866), and Federalism (Executive Order 12,612).[163]

Currently, courts disagree as to whether the National Environmental Protection Act (NEPA) applies to the Service's designation of critical habitat.[164] That law requires government agencies to conduct environmental impact analyses of proposed major federal actions. In 1983, the Service published a determination that NEPA requirements did not apply to listings, delistings, the designation of critical habitat, reclassifications, or special rules issued with listings of threatened species.[165] Since that time, however, a split has developed among the federal circuit courts on the issue of whether critical habitat designation is subject to NEPA. The Sixth Circuit has long held that NEPA does not apply to listing decisions, but has remained silent on the question of whether NEPA applies to the designation of critical habitat.[166] The Ninth Circuit view is that NEPA does not apply to critical habitat designation.[167] The Tenth Circuit, on the other hand, has held that NEPA does apply, at least where the designation of critical habitat is equivalent to a "major federal action significantly affecting the quality of the human environment."[168] In light of this split between the circuits, it is likely that the Supreme Court would review the issue if given the opportunity.[169]

---

were removed by the 1982 Amendments. *Id.* at 323.

163. *See* U.S. Fish and Wildlife Service & National Marine Fisheries Service, Endangered Species Listing Guidance 89-90 (1996) (hereinafter FWS Listing Guidance).

164. For discussion of NEPA, *see* Chapter 6, section D.2.d (National Environmental Policy Act).

165. *See* 48 Fed. Reg. 49,244 (1983).

166. *See* Pacific Legal Foundation v. Andrus, 657 F.2d 829 (6th Cir. 1981).

167. *See* Douglas County v. Babbitt, 48 F.3d 1495 (9th Cir. 1995), *cert. denied*, 516 U.S. 1042 (1996).

168. Catron County Board of Commissioners v. United States Fish and Wildlife Service, 75 F.3d 1429, 1439 (10th Cir. 1996).

169. For a full discussion and background on *Catron*, *see* Richard W. Bertelson, III, Note, *Danger for the Endangered Species Act?: Catron County Board of Commissioners, New Mexico v. United States Fish and Wildlife Service*, 12 J. Nat. Resources & Envtl. L. 167 (1996-1997).

E.   The 1995-1996 Moratorium on Listing
and Designation of Critical Habitat

In April 1995, Congress rescinded from the FY1995 budget $1.5 million intended for ESA listing and critical habitat determinations.[170] This appropriations bill, Public Law 104-06, also placed a moratorium on using any remaining funds for listing determinations or designation of critical habitat (with a notable exception that the Service could use funds to determine that a species is no longer endangered but continues to be threatened). Congress went further, mandating that any court order requiring listing by a certain date would not be valid as long as funds were unavailable. The moratorium on listing and designation of critical habitat was continued by a number of congressional resolutions until it was lifted in April 1996.[171] The moratorium provides a dramatic example of Congress's power to influence action taken under the Endangered Species Act. For over a year, Congress prevented the Service from add-ing any new species to the endangered or threatened lists or designating any critical habitat for already listed species.

Congress enacted the moratorium not by changing the ESA, but by restricting funds available for its implementation. In *Environmental De-fense Center v. Babbitt*,[172] a case involving the listing of the California red-legged frog (the species made famous by Mark Twain in The Celebrated Jumping Frog of Calaveras County), the Ninth Circuit held Congress's methods valid and enforceable. It is well established that repeal of legis-lation by implication is disfavored.[173] However, through arguably circu-lar reasoning, the Court of Appeals found that Public Law 104-06 was not a repeal of the Secretary's duty to list species and designate critical habitat. The duty remained, said the court; Congress had simply and lawfully removed the Secretary's ability to carry out that duty. While recognizing the Secretary would have to use only limited funds to complete the listing of the frog, the court maintained that:

> taking final action on the California red-legged frog listing pro-posal would necessarily require the use of appropriated funds. The use of any government resources — whether salaries, employees, paper, or buildings — to accomplish a final listing would entail government expenditure. The government cannot make expenditures, and therefore cannot act, other than by

---

170. *See* Pub. L. No. 104-06 (April 10, 1995).

171. *See* Omnibus Consolidated Rescissions and Appropriations Act of 1996, Pub. L. No. 104-134 (April 25, 1996).

172. 73 F.3d 867 (9th Cir. 1995).

173. *See, e.g.,* TVA v. Hill, 437 U.S. 153, 190 (1978).

appropriation. Pursuant to Public Law 104-06, no appropriated funds are available to the Secretary to make a final listing that a species is disabled. Accordingly, the Secretary may not take final action on the California red-legged frog listing proposal at this time.[174]

The debate over the moratorium both inside and outside of Congress was bitter.

F. Recovery Plans

The goal of the ESA is to make itself unnecessary—to reach the point where listed species are no longer in danger of becoming extinct and where they have adequate habitat in which to thrive. In furtherance of that goal, Section 4(f) requires the Secretary to develop and implement recovery plans for all listed species.[175]

Recovery plans are largely misunderstood. It is often pointed out that the total price tag attached to implementing the specific line-items in recovery plans is well beyond the budget of FWS. For instance, the National Wilderness Institute estimated the total cost of implementing 1993 recovery plans would amount to nearly $1 billion, while FWS requested under 10 percent of that amount for implementing recovery plans in 1995.[176] Likewise, other critics noted that in 1992 "more than 80 percent [of recovery plans] had not achieved half the objectives listed in their plan."[177] Such criticism, while factually accurate, assumes all recovery plan objectives must be achieved for recovery to occur. On its web site, FWS addresses the question of costs:

> The recovery plan is best thought of as a menu. To have a healthy meal at a restaurant, one would not total an entire menu to arrive at the cost of one dinner. Not all the tasks in a recovery plan need be implemented to reach the recovery goal. For example, the recovery plan for the Ozark big-eared bat estimated spending for recovery at $2.6 million. This species is now consid-

---

174. 73 F.3d at 871-72.

175. *See* 16 U.S.C. § 1533(f).

176. National Wilderness Institute, Going Broke?: Costs of the Endangered Species Act as Revealed in Endangered Species Recovery Plans 1 (1994), *quoted in* J. B. Ruhl, *Section 7 (a)(1) of the "New" Endangered Species Act: Rediscovering and Redefining the Untapped Power of Federal Agencies' Duty to Conserve Species*, 25 Envtl. L. 1107, 1115 n.35 (1995).

177. Charles C. Mann & Mark L. Plummer, Noah's Choice: The Future of the Endangered Species Act 243 (1995).

ered stable; actual expenditures [including all federal and state spending] have totaled about $861,000.[178]

F.1. Content of Recovery Plans

Recovery plans generally include a discussion of species biology, past and present distribution, and the reasons for a species' listing as threatened or endangered. Plans also often include an estimate of target population, which is the point at which a species would be considered recovered. Recovery plans contain an outline or narrative that details actions or conditions necessary to promote species recovery. Plans may also identify federal agencies responsible for carrying out activities to implement species' recovery.

Recovery plans formulated prior to 1988, due to their unregulated content, rarely gave specific guidance on how best to recover listed species. For example, The Northern Rocky Mountain Wolf Recovery Plan directed federal agencies to "minimize direct, man-caused mortality."[179] To achieve this objective, the plan required agencies to "[m]ake provisions for minimizing or resolving conflicts between wolf recovery objectives and man."[180] Beyond the broad statement of purpose, the directive did not provide any field level guidance on how to minimize wolf-human conflicts. Without specifics, programs such as The Northern Rocky Mountain Wolf Recovery Plan were difficult to enforce or evaluate.

Recognizing these problems, Congress in 1988 added provisions to Section 4(f) that specified minimum contents of recovery plans.[181] Announcing that recovery plans should be "as explicit as possible," lawmakers noted that plans should contain "discrete measures to be taken for species, subspecies, populations, geographic subpopulations, or individuals."

Congress specifically called for three types of information to be included in the recovery plan. First, the plans must contain descriptions of "site-specific" management actions.[182] Congress noted that the charge to include "site specific" actions was designed to make recovery plans "as

---

178. United States Fish and Wildlife Service, *Endangered Species Recovery* (visited Aug. 19, 1999) <http://www.fws.gov/r9endspp/faqrecov.html>.
179. *See generally* U.S. Fish and Wildlife Service, Northern Rocky Mountain Wolf Recovery Plan (1985).
180. *Id.*
181. S. Rep. No. 100-240, at 9 (1987).
182. *See* 16 U.S.C. § 1533(f)(1)(B)(i).

explicit as possible."[183] Second, plans must contain "objective measurable criteria" to determine when a species has recovered and can be removed from the protected list.[184] Third, recovery plans must include estimates of the resources, time, and money necessary to achieve both the ultimate recovery of the species and the intermediate steps toward that goal.[185]

F.2. Preparation of Recovery Plans

Recovery plans are prepared in one of two ways: (1) FWS personnel supervise preparation of the plan, which is actually written by an outside group or individual under contract, or (2) FWS establishes its own "recovery team" to prepare the plan. Prior to 1994, recovery teams usually consisted of representatives from agencies charged with implementing the plan; scientists with expertise about the species involved; representatives from possibly affected industries; and FWS personnel. Under FWS's 1994 policy, Interagency Cooperative Policy on Recovery Plan Participation and Implementation Under the Endangered Species Act (1994 Recovery Plan Policy), the pool of possible participants in the recovery team was enlarged to include "other constituencies with an interest in the species and its recovery or the economic or social impacts of recovery." However, team members must be "recognized experts" who have knowledge of the species or skill in recovery plan implementation or design.[186]

Prior to 1988, the public was not given an opportunity to provide input into the plan formulation process or to comment on proposed recovery plans. In an attempt to increase public participation in the process, Congress amended Section 4(f) to require that the Secretary provide the public with notice and an opportunity to comment on recovery plans before approving new or revised plans.[187] Congress put very little bite into its requirement, requiring only that the Secretary "consider" all information presented during the comment period. It is unclear whether the Service must consider public comment concerning economic or other non-biological impacts of the recovery plan. The plain language of the amendment clearly states: "The Secretary shall consider all information presented during the public comment period."[188] It is possible that the term "information" denotes scientific or lay testimony that addresses

183. S. Rep. No. 100-240, at 9 (1987).
184. *See* 16 U.S.C. § 1533(f)(1)(B)(ii).
185. *See id.* § 1533(f)(1)(B)(iii).
186. 59 Fed. Reg. 34,272, 34,273 (1994).
187. *See* 16 U.S.C. § 1533(f)(4).
188. *Id.* (emphasis added).

biological considerations. However, it is equally likely that the term "all" was meant to encompass every comment made during the public comment period. Considering FWS's inclusion of constituencies interested in the economic or social impacts of species recovery on recovery teams, it seems likely that FWS would consider non-scientific information during the public comment period.

The ESA places no time constraints on the completion of recovery plans; however, in the 1994 Recovery Plan Policy, the FWS required recovery plans to be completed within 2½ years after final listing.[189] In *Oregon Natural Resource Council v. Turner*, the court affirmed the Secretary's broad discretion in regard to the timing of developing recovery plans.[190] The duty to prepare a recovery plan will be violated only if the Secretary "affirmatively determines not to develop a recovery plan, or possibly that the time lapse after listing and before development and publication of a recovery plan was so great and so unreasonable as to amount to a complete failure to fulfill a duty."[191]

F.3. Peer Review of Recovery Plans

Peer review in conjunction with the development of draft recovery plans is less formal and prescriptive than peer review in listing decisions: for draft recovery plans, the Service will only use scientific peer review "where appropriate." However, in regard to the formulation of draft recovery plans, the Peer Review Policy encourages the use of expertise and opinions from appropriate local, state, and federal agencies; tribal governments; academic scientific groups and individuals; and any party that may possess pertinent information in regard to the plan.[192] The difference in the approach to peer review between listing decisions and the formulation of draft recovery plans is attributable to the very different purposes and impacts of the two actions. Listing decisions are weighty and have legal force to back them up, while, on the other hand, recovery plans are simply advisory documents with little or no legal significance. Also, the broader range of expertise allowed at the draft recovery plan stage underscores the fact that many interests and stakeholders must be allowed to participate in the formation of a robust and effective plan.

189. 59 Fed. Reg. 34,272-73 (1994).

190. *See* 863 F. Supp. 1277, 1282-83 (D. Or. 1997).

191. *Id.* at 1282.

192. *See* 59 Fed. Reg. 34,270 (1994).

Priority of Actions in a Recovery Plan

The recovery priority guidelines set forth a system to prioritize activities identified in individual recovery plans as necessary for species recovery. This priority system divides recovery activities into three categories. Priority 1 actions include measures necessary to prevent extinction or irreversible decline of a species. Priority 2 actions include measures necessary to prevent significant population decline or habitat degradation. Lastly, Priority 3 actions include everything necessary for full recovery of a given species. Arguably, federal agencies are obligated to carry out any recovery action classified as Priority 1. Because these tasks are by definition necessary to prevent the extinction of a listed species, failure to implement them would jeopardize the continued existence of listed species in violation of Section 7(a)(2).

For details see 48 Fed. Reg. 43,098.

F.4. Priority Guidelines: Ranking System and Parity Among Species

Like the system for ranking candidate species for listing, a priority system guides recovery plan development. Section 4(f) directs the Secretary to give priority to species most likely to benefit from recovery plans, particularly species facing pressure from construction or other developmental or economic activities.[193] The FWS published recovery priority guidelines in 1983.[194] The guidelines set recovery plan development and implementation priorities by combining the immediacy of threats to a species' survival with the species' recovery potential. The term "recovery potential" represents an estimate of a species' chances for recovery based on how well the threats to its existence are understood and how much management is necessary to remedy those threats. The recovery priority guidelines also consider genetic distinctiveness of listed species, with monotypic genera taking precedence over subspecies and population segments. Finally, among species with equal recovery priorities, those facing conflict from economic activities, such as construction, are considered first.

---

193. *See* 16 U.S.C. § 1533(f).
194. *See* 48 Fed. Reg. 43,098.

In 1988, Congress expressed concern that the Secretary was disproportionately allocating recovery funds among species. A Senate report accompanying the 1988 ESA amendments noted that during a five-year period ending in 1986, approximately half of the funds available for development and implementation of recovery plans were spent on only five percent of listed U.S. species. The report also noted that the Secretary set aside scant money for recovery of listed insects, mollusks, crustaceans, and plants. In an effort to force the Secretary to allocate recovery resources more evenly among listed species, Congress inserted into Section 4(f) a requirement that recovery plans be developed and implemented "without regard to taxonomic classification." From 1989 to 1991, the Service did little to live up to Congress's exhortation, spending most of its budget of $171 million on only 10 species.[195]

F.5. Legal Weight of Recovery Plans

The legal weight and enforceability of recovery plans are not well defined. FWS takes the position that recovery plans are "guidance documents" that do not bind the government.[196] Environmental groups have tried to use recovery plans to force government action, but it is still unclear if this tactic will succeed. A claim could be made that the failure to implement a recovery plan leaves a species on the brink of extinction indefinitely, and that indefinite status is equivalent to jeopardizing the species in violation of Section 7. In an unpublished case, *In Defense of Endangered Species v. Ridenour*,[197] the court faced the claim that the wolf recovery plan limited the government's consideration of alternatives. The court refused to resolve the claim, holding the issue was not ripe in that case, but noted the resolution would involve "complicated analysis of federal law. . . ."[198]

Even if recovery plans are unenforceable against the government, they can still have legal weight in supporting the government's conser-

---

195. *See* Robert J. Barro, *Federal Protection: Only Cute Critters Need Apply*, Wall St. J., Aug. 4, 1994, at A12.

196. *See, e.g.*, U.S. Dept. of Justice, Memorandum in Support of Federal Defendants' Motion to Dismiss, submitted in Hawaii Audubon Society v. Lujan, No. 91-00191 (D. Hawaii) (filed Apr. 4, 1991), *quoted in* Robert Meltz, *Where the Wild Things Are: the Endangered Species Act and Private Property*, 24 Envtl. L. 369, 376 (1994); *see also* Endangered and Threatened Species Listing and Recovery Priority Guidelines, Fed. Reg. 43,098, 43,103 (1983).

197. 19 F.3d 27 (9th Cir. 1994).

198. *See id.*

vation measures. For example, in *Carson-Truckee Water Conservation District v. Watt*, the Ninth Circuit held that the Secretary, in accordance with the recommendations of a recovery plan, could devote unappropriated water in a federally administered reservoir to the preservation of a listed species, refusing to sell water to future applicants.[199]

---

199. *See* 741 F.2d 257 (9th Cir. 1984).

CHAPTER THREE

Section 7: Requirements for Federal Agencies

A. Introduction

The ESA protects listed species in several ways. Section 7, which requires federal agencies to both act and refrain from acting for the benefit of listed species, is perhaps the most important protection accorded to species by the law. Unlike Section 9, which is concerned with protecting individual members of listed species from harm, Section 7 is conceptually oriented toward the continued survival of entire species.

Section 7 has three major components: (1) it requires all federal agencies to *pro-actively work toward the conservation* of listed species;[1] (2) it requires all federal agencies considering a project or action to *consult with the Service* to insure that the proposed activity is "not likely to jeopardize the continued existence" of any listed species or will not "result in the destruction or adverse modification" of its critical habitat;[2] and (3) with a very limited exception, it *prohibits federal agencies from either jeopardizing listed species or degrading their habitat.*[3]

Section 7 is important for a variety of reasons. First, the federal government manages about a third of the nation's land, more than 700 million acres. These lands provide habitat for a large number of endangered species. Although many endangered species occur only on private land, especially in areas east of the Rocky Mountains, federal lands have been and will continue to be an important component of any long-range plan to protect biodiversity in the United States. Section 7 ensures that activities on these lands are consistent with the survival of endangered species there.

In addition, Section 7 protects species from activities authorized, funded, or carried out by federal agencies, regardless of whether those activities are conducted on federal land. Federal actions such as dam construction tend to be large in scale, so that even one federal project is capable of significantly reducing a species' long-term chance of survival.

---

1. *See* 16 U.S.C. § 1536(a)(1) ("Section 7 (a)(1)").

2 *See id.* § 1536(a)(2) ("Section 7 (a)(2)").

3. *See id.*

Section 7 allows the public to participate in the final approval of most Habitat Conservation Plans (HCPs).[4] Although the public cannot participate throughout much of the HCP process, when plans are being negotiated between the Service and private landowners, Section 7 indirectly creates the opportunity for public comment on the HCP.

The Section 7 consultation process, whereby federal agencies are required to work with the Service to assess the impacts of proposed activities on listed species, has proven to be useful in generating important and previously nonexistent biological data on species and systems.

Finally, Section 7 is important because it creates the potential for leadership by federal agencies with respect to endangered species. Long-term conservation of endangered species will be a challenging and expensive task; federal leadership on this issue will be critical in ensuring that private efforts are forthcoming and meaningful.

B. What Duties Does Section 7(a)(1) Impose on Federal Agencies?

Section 7(a)(1) provides that all federal agencies shall "in consultation with and with the assistance of the Secretary, utilize their authorities in furtherance of the purposes of this chapter by carrying out programs for the conservation of endangered species and threatened species listed pursuant to [the ESA]."[5] Exactly what this provision requires the various federal agencies to do remains unclear, although a recent Fifth Circuit case has interpreted it as requiring some positive action on the part of an agency.[6] Other courts have yielded to agency discretion, refusing to order agencies to create conservation programs. A strong, mandatory Section 7(a)(1) has the potential to greatly improve implementation of the ESA. It remains to be seen whether the Fifth Circuit view will be adopted more broadly, or whether courts will continue to leave the matter wholly to federal agency discretion.

At the very least, Section 7(a)(1) allows a federal agency the discretion to give the conservation of endangered species priority over its more central and traditional missions. Thus, in cases where interested parties challenge agency actions intended to conserve species, the agency will be on solid ground in defending its actions based on its obligations under Section 7(a)(1).

---

4. For more on HCPs, see Chapter Five, Incidental Takes and Habitate Conservation Plans.

5. 16 U.S.C. § 1536(a)(1).

6. Sierra Club v. Glickman, 156 F.3d 606 (5th Cir. 1998).

B.1. The Baseline: Section 7(a)(1) Allows Federal Agencies to Prioritize Conservation of Listed Species

In *Carson-Truckee Water Conservation District*,[7] the plaintiff argued that the Bureau of Reclamation was obligated to release from the Stampede Reservoir only the bare minimum amount of water necessary to ensure the survival of two endangered fish species living downstream, leaving additional water available for sale to the plaintiffs. The district court rejected this position and asserted that the ESA required the agency to give endangered species priority over all other water uses until fish recovery was achieved.[8]

On appeal, the Ninth Circuit upheld the district court, reasoning that the Bureau of Reclamation was merely complying with the law in following the ESA mandate to "use programs under [its] control for conservation purposes where threatened or endangered species are involved."[9]

Carson-Truckee thus stands for the proposition that federal agencies may use Section 7(a)(1) as a "shield against judicial attack on [agency] decisions that further" the goal of species conservation.[10]

B.2. Agency Conservation Programs: More to Come?

During the first 20 years of the ESA, federal agencies for the most part ignored the Section 7(a)(1) requirement that, in consultation with the Service, they "utilize their authorities in furtherance of the purposes of [the ESA] by carrying out programs for the conservation of" listed species. Due to the vast amount of land under federal control, and the wide scope of federal activities, a fully implemented Section 7(a)(1) would almost certainly enhance the nation's efforts to conserve listed species. Yet to date, the section remains "the sleeping giant of the ESA programs."[11]

Two recent events, however, provide hope that the sleeping giant will be awakened—either by the courts or by the Service. First, in September of 1994, the Service brought twelve federal agencies together to sign a Memorandum of Understanding, which recognized the agencies' "common goal of conserving [listed species] by protecting and managing

---

7. 549 F. Supp. 704 (E.D. Cal. 1983), *aff'd*, 741 F.2d 257 (9th Cir. 1984).

8. *See id.* at 712 (holding that Washoe Project Act obligations were superseded by the ESA and Indian fishery rights).

9. 741 F.2d at 262.

10. J. B. Ruhl, *Section 7 (a)(1) of the "New" Endangered Species Act: Rediscovering and Redefining the Untapped Power of Federal Agencies' Duty to Conserve Species*, 25 Envtl. L. 1107, 1130 (1995).

11. *Id.* at 1108.

their populations and the ecosystems upon which those populations depend."[12] Each signatory promised to:

1. Use its authorities to further the purposes of the ESA by carrying out programs for the conservation of federally listed species, including implementing appropriate recovery actions that are identified in recovery plans.
2. Identify opportunities to conserve federally listed species and the ecosystems upon which those species depend within its existing programs or authorities.
3. Determine whether its respective planning processes effectively help conserve threatened and endangered species and the ecosystems upon which those species depend.
4. Use existing programs, or establish a program if one does not currently exist, to evaluate, recognize, and reward the performance and achievements of personnel who are responsible for planning or implementing programs to conserve or recover listed species or the ecosystems upon which they depend.[13]

Although probably not enforceable in court against the signing agencies, the Memorandum signals at the very least an intent by the Service to prod other agencies into complying with the law and sharing the burden of ESA implementation.

Perhaps more important to the future of Section 7(a)(1) is the Fifth Circuit case of *Sierra Club v. Glickman*, decided in late 1998.[14] In that case, the Sierra Club sued the U.S. Department of Agriculture, claiming that the agency violated Section 7(a)(1) "by failing to consult with FWS and failing to utilize its authorities to carry out programs" for endangered species dependent on water flow out of the Edwards Aquifer in Texas.[15] After reviewing the legislative history of the ESA and Section 7(a)(1), the court concluded that "Congress intended to impose an affirmative duty on each federal agency to conserve each [listed] species. In order to

---

12. Memorandum of Understanding Between Federal Agencies on Implementation of the Endangered Species Act Signed September 28, 1994, [July-Dec.] Daily Env't. Rep. (BNA) No. 188, at E-1 (September 30, 1994). The agencies that signed the agreement were FWS, NMFS, the U.S. Forest Service, the U.S. Department of Defense, the U.S. Army Corps of Engineers, the Bureau of Land Management, the Bureau of Mines, the Bureau of Reclamation, the Minerals Management Service, the National Park Service, the U.S. Coast Guard, the Federal Aviation Administration, the Federal Highway Administration, and the Environmental Protection Agency. All told, the signees are responsible for the management of more than 600 million acres of land.

13. *Id.* at E-5. For a more detailed analysis of the Memorandum of Understanding, *see* Ruhl, *supra* note 10, at 1144-53.

14. 156 F.3d 606 (5th Cir. 1998).

15. *Id.* at 610.

achieve this objective, the agencies must consult with FWS as to each of the listed species, not just undertake a general consultation."[16]

The Department of Agriculture argued that its duties under Section 7(a)(1) were not judicially reviewable "because there is 'no law to apply'" and "because it has a substantial amount of discretion in developing programs for the benefit of Edwards-dependent species."[17] Unlike most other courts that have weighed these arguments,[18] the Fifth Circuit was not persuaded. "[G]iven the specific requirements of Section 7(a)(1)," said the court, "in any given case there is more than enough law against which a court can measure agency compliance."[19] The court rejected the agency's "discretion" argument, which it paraphrased as "because [we, the USDA, enjoy] a substantial amount of discretion as to ultimate

---

A Reagan-Watt Era Argument for Limiting Agency Duties Under Section 7(a)(1)

One argument for limiting the duty of other agencies under Section 7 is that if Congress had intended such a result—one that would require all agencies to affirmatively protect all species under any actions taken—it would not have included Section 7(a)(2) and the elaborate Section 7 exemption process within the statute. Arguably, if both mandates apply to all agency actions, the directives to conserve listed species would subsume the Section 7(a)(2) jeopardy provisions. The contemporary wisdom of this argument is best captured in the Solicitor General's denunciation of the result in *Carson-Truckee Water Conservation District v. Watt*. The Solicitor General argued that Section 7(a)(1) acts as an enabling clause which grants agencies the authority to take actions to promote species recovery, *but that Section 7(a)(2) does not obligate the agencies to take any action at all.*

For details see Memorandum to the Director, U.S. Fish and Wildlife Service, from the Associate Solicitor, Conservation and Wildlife, U.S. Department of the Interior (Sept. 7, 1983).

---

16. *Id.* at 616.

17. *Id.* at 617.

18. *See, e.g.,* Coalition for Sustainable Resources, Inc. v. United States Forest Service, 48 F. Sup.2d 1303 (D. Wyo. 1999), and the cases cited therein at 35. *See also* Seattle Audubon Society v. Lyons, 871 F. Supp. 1291 (W.D. Wash. 1994).

19. 156 F.3d at 618.

program decisions, [we have] unreviewable discretion to ignore Section 7(a)(1) altogether."[20]

The Fifth Circuit ordered the Department of Agriculture to comply with the district court's order "to develop, in consultation with FWS, an organized program for utilizing USDA's authorities for the conservation of the Edwards-dependent endangered and threatened species as contemplated by the ESA."[21]

Of course, even if all circuits adopt the Fifth Circuit's approach in *Sierra Club*, there will be limitations on what agencies will be required to do. As the Fifth Circuit noted, the "duty to consult and the duty to conserve are tempered by the actual authorities of each agency."[22]

C. Section 7(a)(2): What Federal Agencies Must and Cannot Do

The difference between the respective goals of Sections 7(a)(1) and 7(a)(2) is stark. Section 7(a)(1) speaks in terms of "carrying out programs for the conservation of" listed species, with "conservation" being defined in the ESA as those measures necessary to bring the species off the ESA list.[23] In other words, the theme is *recovery*. The purpose of Section 7(a)(2), on the other hand, is merely to insure that federal actions do not harm a species' chances for survival. The provision bars only those agency actions that would take the species' overall health below its *status quo*. The theme is not one of recovery but of "*no jeopardy.*"

The stated goal of Section 7(a)(2) is to "insure that any action authorized, funded, or carried out by [a federal agency] is not likely to jeopardize the continued existence of any [listed species] or result in the destruction or adverse modification of [a listed species' critical habitat]." This is the "prohibitive" or "substantive" portion of Section 7(a)(2). The agency carrying out the action, and not the Service, has ultimate responsibility for insuring that the agency action does not jeopardize a species or destroy or adversely modify (illegally degrade) its habitat.

The ESA and federal regulations do however require that the Service be involved in the process by which an agency determines whether its proposed action will jeopardize a listed species or illegally degrade its habitat. Section 7(a)(1) imposes on federal agencies a "duty to consult" with the Service whenever a listed species can be found within the area

---

20. *Id.*

21. *Id.*

22. *Id.* at 616, citing Platte River Whooping Crane Trust v. Federal Energy Regulating Comm'n, 962 F.2d 27, 34 (D.C. Cir. 1992) for the proposition that Section 7(a)(1) does not expand an agency's existing authorities to conserve endangered species. *See also* Sierra Club v. Babbitt, 65 F.3d 1502, 1510 (9th Cir. 1995).

23. 16 U.S.C. §§ 1536(a)(1), 1532(3).

that will be affected by the agency action.[24] This is the "affirmative" or "procedural" facet of Section 7(a)(2).

All federal agencies must comply with both the substantive and procedural requirements of the law.

C.1. Procedural Compliance: An Overview

Before commencing an agency action, the agency proposing the action (the action agency) must determine whether the proposed action will "likely affect" a listed species or one that is proposed for listing (proposed species). The first step in this process is for the agency to request information from the Service as to whether or not any such species are located in the area of a proposed agency action (the action area). If so, the action agency must conduct a "biological assessment" to determine whether its project (if carried out) would likely affect the listed or proposed species.[25] If the agency concludes, after completing the biological assessment, that a protected species is likely to be adversely affected, the action agency must initiate a "formal consultation" with the appropriate "expert agency."[26] The expert agency will be either the Fish and Wildlife Service or NMFS, depending on the species involved.

After formal consultation, the expert agency must issue a written statement setting forth its "biological opinion" and a summary of the information on which that opinion is based.[27] If the expert agency finds that the proposed project will not jeopardize the species or illegally degrade its habitat, the action agency may proceed with its proposed activity. However, if the expert agency determines that the project is likely to do either of these things, the action agency will have to decide how to proceed. In a biological opinion finding likely jeopardy, the expert agency must—to the extent possible—suggest "reasonable and prudent alternatives" to the agency's proposal that would avoid such a result.[28] The action agency may choose among the alternatives and proceed accordingly. In the case where no alternatives exist, the action agency may apply to the Endangered Species Committee for an exemption from the law.[29]

---

24. The Section 7(a)(2) "duty to consult" with the Service regarding proposed federal actions is separate and distinct from the Section 7(a)(1) "duty to consult" with the Service in developing and carrying out programs for conserving listed species.

25. 16 U.S.C. § 1536(c)(1).

26. *See id.*

27. *Id.* § 1536(b)(3)(A).

28. *Id.*

29. *See id.* §§ 1536(e), 1536(h).

Ecosystem Protection Through Section 7

Consultation requirements under Section 7 may provide a tool for ecosystem protection. Although as written the ESA is largely a means of protecting individual species, its preamble states "the purposes of this act are to provide a means whereby ecosystems upon which endangered species or threatened species depend may be conserved." In 1994 FWS and NMFS made it their official policy to consider impacts on ecosystems when taking action under the ESA. In their policy statement, the agencies pointed out that "species will be conserved best not by a species by species approach but by an ecosystem conservation strategy that transcends individual species."

Jason Patlis argues that if the Service decided to pursue ecosystem protection, Section 7 provides both the opportunity and the tools necessary to do so. While not particularly suited to providing ecosystem protection during site-specific consultations, the requirements of Section 7 can guard ecosystems during "programmatic actions" and "coordinated actions." Programmatic actions are those that may not have any planned site disturbances or incidental takes, but are nonetheless long-term and have some degree of uncertainty concerning their outcome or impacts. Patlis points out that programmatic actions lend themselves to the application of the incremental consultations provided for in 50 C.F.R. § 402.14(k) and that such ongoing consultation over a long time frame can more easily incorporate measures to protect ecosystems.

Coordinated actions are those actions in which many agencies act together on a common issue. An example of coordinated consultations is PACFISH, a salmon-recovery strategy developed by the Bureau of Land Management and NMFS. Patlis argues that coordinated activities provide an excellent opportunity to take a broader view of species protection and incorporate ecosystem protections into the consultation procedure. Further, coordinated activities enable agencies to overcome political boundaries and increase the cost-effectiveness by working to protect newly listed species from the outset, as well as improving the science used by coordinated consultations to do the mapping and other analyses needed for ecosystem protection.

For details see Jason Patlis, *Biodiversity, Ecosystems, and Endangered Species, in* Biodiversity and the Law 43 (William J. Snape III ed., 1996); Notice of Interagency Cooperative Policy for Ecosystem Approach to the Endangered Species Act, 59 Fed. Reg. 34,273.

C.2. Preliminary Determinations
C.2.a. Applicable Agency Actions

An agency proposing an agency action must determine whether any listed or proposed species is present in the action area.[30] "Action" is defined in the ESA regulations as "all activities or programs of any kind authorized, funded, or carried out, in whole or in part, by federal agencies."[31] Besides the umbrella category of action, Section 7 applies to "major construction activities," by federal agencies for which regulations are given greater detail.[32]

C.2.b. Requests for Information

If the action agency is aware that listed or proposed species occur in the action area, the agency must provide the expert agency with written notification of the species and critical habitat that are being included in the biological assessment. If the action agency is unsure as to whether listed or proposed species occur in the action area, the agency must submit to the expert agency a written request for a list of any listed or proposed species or designated or proposed critical habitat that may be present in the action area.[33]

Within 30 days of a notification, the expert agency shall either concur with or revise the action agency's list. In the case of a request, the expert agency shall within 30 days advise the action agency in writing whether, based on the best scientific and commercial data available, any species or critical habitat may be present in the action area, including listed, proposed, and candidate species.[34]

If the expert agency advises that no listed or proposed species is present in the area of the proposed action, no further consultation or biological assessment is required, and the proposed action may commence. If the expert agency determines that a *proposed* species is present in the action area, the action agency must confer with the expert agency pursuant to Section 7(a)(4). However, the action agency need not prepare a biological assessment unless the proposed listing becomes final.[35] If the expert agency determines that *listed* species are present in the area of the proposed action, the action agency must conduct a biological assessment to determine whether the action is likely to affect those species. In this

---

30. *See* 50 C.F.R. § 402.12(b).

31. *See id.* § 402.02.

32. *See id.* §§ 402.02, 402.12.

33. 50 C.F.R. § 402.12(c).

34. *See id.* § 402.12(d).

35. *See id.* § 402.12(d)(1).

case, the expert agency must provide the action agency with all available information regarding the species and their critical habitat and may recommend discretionary studies or surveys that may provide better information for assessment.[36]

C.2.c. Informal Consultation

Informal consultation is an optional process that includes all discussions and correspondence between the expert and action agencies designed to assist the action agency in determining whether formal consultation or a conference is required.[37] The informal consultation may preclude or provide the basis for initiating formal consultation.

If the action agency preliminarily determines that an action "may affect" a protected species but is "not likely to adversely affect" the species, it may attempt an "informal consultation" with the expert agency An action agency's "not likely to adversely effect" determination becomes final for consultation purposes only when the expert agency concurs in writing.[38] If the expert agency does not concur, the agency must proceed to formal consultation. Even under informal consultation, the action agency must wait for expert agency concurrence before proceeding with the project. Informal consultation is not bound by any timetable; it may continue as long as adverse impacts can be completely avoided.

C.2.d. Biological Assessments

Biological assessments are designed to help the action agency determine whether it must formally consult with an expert agency or enter into mandatory conferences concerning the proposed action. Although the contents of a biological assessment are discretionary, they generally include the following:

- the results of on-site inspections to determine the presence of a listed or proposed species;
- the views of recognized experts on the species at issue;
- a review of the literature and other information;
- an analysis of the effects of the action on the species and habitat, including a description of any known unrelated nonfederal activities in the action area that are likely to impact the species; and

---

36. *See id.* § 402.12(d)(2).
37. *See id.* § 402.13(a).
38. *See id.* § 402.14(b)(1).

- an analysis of alternative actions considered by the action agency for the proposed action.[39]

The contents of an Environmental Impact Statement (EIS), prepared as part of the action agency's compliance with NEPA, may be sufficient to constitute a biological assessment. In *Mobil Oil Corp. v. ICC*,[40] the court refused to halt an agency action for an alleged failure to prepare an assessment because it found that statements within an EIS prepared for the action were sufficient to constitute a biological assessment. Given that Section 7(c) explicitly links preparation of a biological assessment with NEPA procedures, this approach appears valid. An agency's failure to conduct a biological assessment, with the knowledge that an endangered species is in the action area, constitutes a violation of the ESA.[41]

The biological assessment must be completed within 180 days after the date on which it is initiated—that is, 180 days from the date the action agency determines that a biological assessment is necessary.[42] The action agency must submit the completed biological assessment to the expert agency for review. The expert agency must respond in writing within 30 days as to whether it concurs with the findings of the biological assessment.[43]

If the biological assessment indicates that the proposed action is not likely to adversely affect a protected species, the project can be initiated if the expert agency writes an opinion concurring with the biological assessment.[44] However, if the biological assessment indicates that the proposed action is likely to adversely affect a listed species, the action agency must enter into formal consultation proceedings with the expert agency.

C.3. Conferences Regarding Proposed Species

Conferences between representatives of the action agency and the expert agency are required for all federal actions that are likely to (1) adversely affect the continued existence of a species *proposed* to be listed, or (2) result in the destruction or adverse modification of the species' proposed critical habitat.[45] The conference is designed to assist the action

---

[39]. *See id.* § 402.12(f).

40. 685 F.2d 624 (D.C. Cir. 1982).

41. Thomas v. Peterson, 589 F. Supp. 1139 (D. Idaho 1984), *aff'd in part, rev'd in part,* 753 F.2d 754 (9th Cir. 1985).

42. *See* 50 C.F.R. § 402.12(i).

43. *See id.* § 402.12(j).

44. *See id.* §§ 402.12(j), 402.12(k), 402.14(b)(1).

45. *See* 16 U.S.C. § 1536(a)(4).

agency in identifying and resolving potential conflicts at an early stage in the planning process. Generally, the action agency initiates the conference with the expert agency. However, the expert agency may request a conference if, after a review of the available information, it determines that a conference is required for a particular action.

The conference consists of informal discussions concerning the proposed action.[46] During the conference, the expert agency will make advisory recommendations regarding ways to minimize or avoid adverse effects. If the proposed species is subsequently listed or the proposed critical habitat is designated prior to completion of the action, the action agency must review the action to determine whether formal consultation is required. If requested by the action agency and deemed appropriate by the expert agency, an opinion issued at the conclusion of the conference may be adopted as the biological opinion when the species is listed or its critical habitat is designated. The conference opinion may only be adopted as the biological opinion if no new significant information is developed and no significant changes to the action alter the content of the opinion.[47]

The conclusion reached, and any recommendations developed, during the conference must be documented by the expert agency and provided to the action agency. However, the style and magnitude of the document will vary with the complexity of the conference. And if formal consultation is also required for a particular action, the expert agency must provide the results of the conference with the biological opinion.[48]

C.4. Formal Consultation

Formal consultations are required for *all* federal actions that are likely to adversely affect a *listed* species or result in the destruction or adverse modification of its critical habitat. Formal consultations determine whether a project is likely to jeopardize the continued existence of a listed species or to destroy or adversely modify critical habitat. The conclusion is developed fully in the expert agency's written biological opinion.

C.4.a. Initiation

Formal consultation is initiated by a written request from an action agency to an expert agency upon the determination that a proposed agency action is likely to adversely affect a listed species. The request

---

46. *See* 50 C.F.R. § 402.10.

47. *See id.*

48. *See id.* § 402.10(e).

must include (1) a description of the action being considered, the specific area that may be affected, any listed species or critical habitat that may be affected, and the manner in which the action may affect any listed species or critical habitat; (2) relevant reports, including any EIS, environmental assessments, or biological assessment prepared on the proposal pursuant to Section 7(c); and (3) any other relevant information available on the proposed actions, the affected listed species, or its critical habitat.[49]

The action agency must also provide the expert agency with the best scientific and commercial data available for an adequate determination of the effects that the action may have on listed species or critical habitat. This may include the results of studies or surveys conducted by the action agency.[50] Within 30 working days after receiving an initiation package, the expert agency should acknowledge in writing its receipt of the consultation request, advise the action agency if there are any data deficiencies, and request either the missing data or a statement in writing that the data are not available.[51] The responsibility for conducting and funding any studies belongs to the action agency.[52]

C.4.b. Time Frames for Consultation

Formal consultations should be concluded within 90 days of initiation, and the expert agency's biological opinion should be delivered to the action agency within 45 days thereafter.[53] Formal consultation is initiated on the date the request is first received by the expert agency, if the action agency has provided all relevant data; if not, the formal consultation is considered initiated on the date the expert agency receives all relevant data in the initiation package.[54]

The regional director of the expert agency is responsible for ensuring that the consultation is completed and the biological opinion is prepared and delivered within 135 days of initiation. The consultation cannot be "suspended." However, when the expert agency determines that additional data would provide a better information base to formulate a biological opinion, the agency may request an extension of formal consultation and request that the action agency obtain additional information regarding the extent to which the action may affect listed species or criti-

---

49. *See id.* § 402.14(c).

50. *See id.* § 402.14(d).

51. *See* U. S. Fish and Wildlife Service and National Marine Fisheries Service, Endangered Species Consultation Handbook 4-6 (1998) (hereinafter CONSULTATION HANDBOOK).

52. *See* 50 C.F.R. § 402.14(f).

53. *See id.* § 402.14(e).

54. *See* Consultation Handbook, *supra* note 51, at 4-5 to 4-7.

cal habitat. Likewise, if more time is needed by the expert agency to analyze the data or prepare the final opinion (or by the action agency to provide data or review a draft opinion), an extension can be requested by either party.[55]

When the action agency asks to review the draft biological opinion, these time frames continue to apply. However, no final opinion will be issued before the 135th day while the action agency is reviewing the draft. Once comments to the draft are received by the expert agency, the biological opinion is finalized and delivered to the action agency. If comments on the draft opinion result in major changes or clarification, a time extension can be sought by the expert agency or the action agency. If the expert agency has not received those comments by the 125th day, the expert agency checks with the action agency to negotiate an extension. If the expert agency receives the action agency's comments less than 10 days before the end of the established deadline, the expert agency is automatically entitled to a 10-day extension to deliver the opinion.[56]

C.4.c. Biological Opinion

If the biological opinion indicates that the proposed action is *not likely to jeopardize* a protected species, the project can be completed. However, if the biological opinion indicates that the proposed action is likely to jeopardize a protected species, the action agency must implement reasonable and prudent alternatives to avoid the likelihood of jeopardy, alternatives outlined in the biological assessment. If no reasonable and prudent alternatives exist, the action agency has three alternatives: (1) seek an exemption; (2) cancel the project; or (3) continue with the project and risk violating the ESA.[57]

Required Content of a Biological Opinion. According to FWS regulations, the formal biological opinion includes the following:

- address, salutation, introduction, and consultation history;
- a description of the proposed action;
- the status of the species;
- the environmental baseline in the action area;
- the effects of the action;

---

55. *See* 50 C.F.R. § 402.14(f).

56. *See id.* § 402.14(g)(5).

57. The Service or a private party can request, pursuant to the ESA or the APA, that a court stop an agency project if the project does not comply with Section 7, 16 U.S.C. § 1540; 5 U.S.C. § 706. In addition, pursuant to Section 9 of the ESA, the action agency and its officers may be liable for civil and criminal penalties to the extent they unlawfully take listed species, 16 U.S.C. § 1538.

- the cumulative effects of reasonably foreseeable future non-federal actions;
- the jeopardy/no jeopardy conclusion;
- reasonable and prudent alternatives;
- an incidental take statement;
- conservation recommendations;
- a reinitiation notice; and
- a list of the literature cited.[58]

Consultation history: This section of the biological opinion outlines the history of the consultation request and includes information regarding the following:

- any informal or prior formal consultations on the action;
- documentation of the date consultation was initiated and a chronology of subsequent requests for additional data, meetings, and extensions; and
- other applicable past or current actions.[59]

Description of the proposed action: This section of the biological opinion includes the following:

- a description of the proposed action;
- a description of the action area; and
- a description of conservation activities, if any, proposed as part of the action.

This section summarizes in the biological opinion the expert agency's understanding of the proposal. Proposed conservation activities represent actions to be implemented by the action agency or the applicant that will contribute to the recovery of the species under review. Conservation activities proposed or mandated by the expert agency are described elsewhere.[60]

Status of the species: This section of the biological opinion describes the current status of the species over its entire range and its critical habitat at the time of consultation. Its purpose is to present the biological or ecological information on the species needed to formulate the biological opinion. This analysis documents the effects of all past human and natural activities or events that have led to the current status of the species and the ecosystems on which the species depends.[61]

---

58. *See* Consultation Handbook, *supra* note 51, at 4-13 to 4-14; *see also* 50 C.F.R. §§ 402.14(h)-(j).

59. *See* Consultation Handbook, *supra* note 51, at 4-12.

60. *See id.* at 4-14 to 4-18.

61. *See id.* at 4-19 to 4-22.

Environmental baseline: This is an analysis of the collective effects of past and ongoing human and natural factors that have led to the current status of the species or its critical habitat within the proposed area. This baseline is then projected into the future to establish the "current" survival of the species. During a jeopardy consultation, the proposed action will be factored into the analysis so that a comparison may be drawn between the "present" future baseline and the "projected" future baseline.[62]

Effects of the action: This section is part of the environmental baseline and describes all direct and indirect effects on the species or its critical habitat arising from the proposed action. Direct effects encompass the direct or immediate impact of the project on the species or its habitat. Indirect effects include the future impacts anticipated from the action.[63]

Cumulative effects: This section includes the effects of future state, local, or private actions that do not involve any federal action and are reasonably certain to occur within the action area being considered in the biological opinion. This analysis is the last factor to be considered in formulating the biological opinion. Cumulative effects may be the deciding factor in determining the likelihood of jeopardy or adverse modification.[64] However, the cumulative effects section is frequently the least documented part of the biological opinion, primarily due to the lack of definitive information on future state, local, or private actions.

Biological opinion: This section states the expert agency's conclusion as to the severity of the adverse effects on the species or its critical habitat.[65]

Reasonable and prudent alternatives: This section lays out reasonable and prudent alternative actions the expert agency believes must be taken by the action agency to avoid the likelihood of jeopardy to the species or the destruction or adverse modification of critical habitat. Obviously in many cases, the proposed action does not jeopardize species and no alternative is necessary. If needed, however, the alternatives must represent options that are lawfully available to the action agency. Reasonable and prudent alternatives are limited to those alternatives that

- the expert agency believes will avoid the likelihood of jeopardy or adverse modification of critical habitat;

---

62. *See generally* Deborah L. Freeman & Carmen M. Sower, *Against the Flow: Emerging Conflicts Between Endangered Species Protection and Water Use*, 40 Rocky Mtn. Min. L. Inst. 23-1, 23-11 (1994); *see also* Consultation Handbook, *supra* note 51, at 4-22 to 4-23.

63. *See* Consultation Handbook, *supra* note 51, at 4-23 to 4-30.

64. *See id.* at 4-29 to 4-30.

65. *See id.* at 4-31 to 4-39.

- can be implemented in a manner consistent with the intended purpose of the action;
- can be implemented consistent with the scope of the action agency's legal authority and jurisdiction; and
- are economically and technologically feasible.[66]

Incidental take statement: An agency action may result in taking some individuals of listed species incidental to the action. Such an incidental take cannot, however, jeopardize the continued existence of the species.[67] Every biological opinion must contain an incidental take statement, even if the known incidental take is zero. If the possibility of an incidental take exists, the incidental take statement must contain:

- a description of the incidental take;
- the amount or extent of incidental taking of the species;
- reasonable and prudent measures to minimize incidental take;
- terms and conditions for the implementation of such reasonable and prudent measures, including monitoring and reporting requirements;
- instructions for handling and disposition of dead, injured, or sick listed species; and
- a statement requiring reinitiation of consultation if the incidental take limits are exceeded.[68]

Incidental take statements establish the limits on the amount or extent of incidental takes in various ways, including the extent of habitat, the amount of kill, or the type or degree of harassment. Reasonable and prudent measures to minimize the amount or extent of the anticipated incidental take cannot alter the basic design, location, scope, duration, or timing of the action and may only involve minor changes.[69] The action agency must comply with the terms and conditions in order to implement the specified reasonable and prudent measures. These terms and conditions include, but are not limited to, monitoring and reporting requirements tailored to the nature of the action and the particular needs of the species involved.[70]

Conservation recommendations: Although conservation recommendations are not required under the ESA, those recommendations may be included as a separate item in the consultation package when the action

66. *See id.* at 4-40 to 4-41.

67. *See* 16 U.S.C. § 1536(b)(4).

68. *See also* 50 C.F.R. §§ 402.14(i)(1), (4).

69. *See also* 50 C.F.R. § 402.14(i)(2).

70. *See generally* Consultation Handbook, *supra* note 51, at 4-43 to 4-53.

agency identifies the discretionary actions it may implement. Conservation recommendations have the following purposes:

- suggesting how an action agency can assist species' conservation under 16 U.S.C. § 1536(a)(1);
- minimizing or avoiding the adverse effects of a proposed action on listed species or critical habitat after the terms of the incidental take permit are implemented; or
- recommending studies to improve understanding of a species' biology or ecology.

Wherever possible, these actions should be tied to tasks identified in recovery plans.[71]

Conservation measures may be provided separately or at the end of the consultation package, but they should not be incorporated anywhere in the biological opinion where they can be confused with the opinion itself. Conservation recommendations are advisory and not intended to carry any binding legal force.[72] Compliance with these recommendations is not a precondition for a subsequent finding of "no jeopardy" or "no anticipated incidental take."[73]

Reinitiation notice: The four conditions that alert the action agency of the need for reinitiating formal consultation are as follows:

- new information reveals that the action may affect listed species or critical habitat to an extent or in a manner that was not previously considered;
- the action is modified in a manner that causes adverse effects to the listed species or its critical habitat that were not previously considered;
- a new species is listed, or critical habitat is designated that the action may affect; or
- the extent or amount of incidental take is exceeded.[74]

Literature cited: The ESA requires that biological opinions are based on the best scientific data available. This section should identify the scientific and commercial data used in developing the biological opinion.[75]

C.5. Early Consultation for Federal Permittees

If a prospective applicant for a federal permit or license "has reason

---

71. For further discussion, see Chapter Two, section F (Recovery Plans.

72. 50 C.F.R. § 402.14(j).

73. *See id.; see also* Consultation Handbook, *supra* note 51, at 4-59 to 4-60.

74. *See* 50 C.F.R § 402.16; *see also* Consultation Handbook, *supra* note 51, at 4-60.

75. *See* Consultation Handbook, *supra* note 51, at 4-56.

to believe that an endangered species or a threatened species may be present in the area affected by his project and that implementation of such action will likely affect such species," the applicant may request that the agency from which it seeks the permit or license (the licensing agency) enter into early consultation with the respective expert agency.[76]

Early consultation is an optional process that occurs before an applicant files an application for a federal permit or license. Although early consultation is conducted between the licensing and expert agencies, the prospective applicant should be involved throughout the consultation process.[77]

To qualify for an early consultation, a definite proposal must outline the action and its effects, and the applicant must certify that he intends to implement the proposal if it is authorized.[78] The licensing agency conducting the early consultation has the same responsibilities and must follow the same procedures as action agencies in formal consultations.[79] Likewise, the "preliminary" biological opinion must contain the same information as a biological opinion issued after formal consultation, although "the incidental take statement provided with a preliminary biological opinion does not constitute authority to take listed species."[80]

C.6. Emergency Consultation

The emergency consultation procedures allow action agencies to incorporate endangered species concerns during an emergency. For the purposes of the ESA, an emergency situation involves (1) an act of God, (2) a disaster, (3) a casualty, or (4) a national defense or security emergency.[81]

Initiation of formal consultation does not begin until the emergency is under control. However, the action agency is required to notify the expert agency as soon as possible after a "may affect" determination has been reached and must commence informal consultation where adverse impacts are reasonably foreseeable. Although the formal consultation occurs after the response to the emergency, it is treated like any other formal consultation.

An action agency must provide the following additional information to initiate a formal consultation after an emergency: (1) a description of

---

76. 16 U.S.C. § 1536(a)(3); *see also* 50 C.F.R. § 402.11(b).
77. *See* 50 C.F.R. § 402.11(a).
78. *See id.* § 402.11(b).
79. *See id.* § 402.11(d).
80. 50 C.F.R. § 403.11(e); *see also* Consultation Handbook, *supra* note 51, at 7-1 to 7-4.
81. *See* 50 C.F.R. § 402.05(a).

the nature of the emergency; (2) a justification for the expedited consultation; and (3) an evaluation of the emergency or the response to the emergency on affected species and their habitats.[82]

C.7. Irreversible and Irretrievable Commitments

Action agencies are prohibited from making an "irreversible or irretrievable commitment of resources" to a proposed action at any point prior to a final determination that the action will not illegally harm a species or its habitat. Thus, it cannot commit resources during the initial evaluation of whether species are present in the action area, during the biological assessment process,[83] throughout the consultation process,[84] or while the biological opinion is being written.

The "commitment of resources" includes far more than actually starting work on the project or proposal. It includes any act by the agency that obligates it in any way to perform all or part of the project.[85] The rationales for this rule are simple. First, committing resources to a project that is later cancelled would be an unwise use of resources. More important, a premature commitment of resources has the potential to create an awkward political situation, where an agency (or an affected private party) can attempt to leverage its early investment of resources into a waiver of Section 7. This was the case in *TVA v. Hill*,[86] where TVA tried to avoid Section 7 by pointing to the fact that it had already put significant federal funds into the project. Although this argument did not persuade the Supreme Court, it did eventually persuade Congress to exempt the project from Section 7.

As to whether or not a commitment of resources is irreversible or irretrievable, at least one court has developed a test.[87] A commitment of resources will be deemed irreversible or irretrievable when

- at the time an agency commits resources to a project, there is a reasonable likelihood that the project, at any stage of development, will violate Section 7(a)(2), and
- the resource expenditure is not salvageable; in other words, it is not useful for another approach to the project or for an entirely different project.

---

82. See *id.* § 402.05(b); *see also* Consultation Handbook, *supra* note 51, at 8-1 to 8-5.

83. See 16 U.S.C. § 1536(c)(1); 50 C.F.R. § 402.12(b)(2); No Oilport! v. Carter, 520 F. Supp. 334 (W.D. Wash. 1981).

84. See 16 U.S.C. § 1536(d); *see* Conner v. Burford, 848 F.2d 1441, 1455 n.34 (9th Cir. 1988).

85. No Oilport! v. Carter, 520 F. Supp. 334, (W.D. Wash. 1981).

86. See 437 U.S. 153 (1978).

87. North Slope Borough v. Andrus, 486 F. Supp. 332 (D.D.C. 1980), *aff'd*, 642 F.2d 589 (D.C. Cir. 1980).

D. Substantive Protections

Section 7(a)(2) requires that each federal agency "insure that any action authorized, funded, or carried out by such agency . . . is not likely to jeopardize the continued existence of any endangered species or threatened species or result in the destruction or adverse modification of habitat" critical to such species.[88] Applying these black and white legal terms to the gray world of ecosystems and organisms is not an easy task. Scientists will in most cases not be able to provide a "yes" or "no" answer to the question of whether a proposed action is "likely to jeopardize the continued existence" of a listed species. A scientific response to such a question will be couched in terms of probabilities. The ESA does not provide guidance on how the specific analysis of the "jeopardy" or "adverse modification" questions should be answered. While the Service has made an attempt to clarify these processes in its regulations and policy statements, final decisions will always involve a substantial amount of Service discretion.

D.1. The Jeopardy Standard

Current federal regulations provide that to "jeopardize the continued existence of" means to "engage in an action that reasonably would be expected, directly or indirectly, to reduce appreciably the likelihood of both the survival and recovery of a listed species in the wild by reducing the reproduction, numbers, or distribution of that species."[89]

The Service's view is thus that an agency action must imperil both the survival *and* the recovery of a species in order to constitute jeopardy.[90] Under this interpretation of the law, a project that does not appreciably reduce the likelihood of a species' survival may proceed, regardless of its potential impact on recovery. The only projects that may not proceed are those that would imperil both survival and recovery. Agency critics note that the use of the word "recovery" in the regulations is therefore meaningless. Any action that appreciably reduces the likelihood that a species will survive will obviously reduce that species' chances of recovery as well.[91]

---

88. 16 U.S.C. § 1536(a)(2).

89. 50 C.F.R. § 402.02.

90. *See* Oliver A. Houck, *The Endangered Species Acts and Its Implementation by the U.S. Departments of Interior and Commerce*, 64 U. Colo. L. Rev. 278, 322 (1993).

91. *See id.* at 317-29.

D.2. Section 7 and Critical Habitat

As interpreted by the Service, the statutory language in Section 7(a)(2) prohibiting destruction or adverse modification of critical habitat gives species no additional protection beyond the jeopardy standard. In current regulations, the phrase "destruction or adverse modification" is defined as "a direct or indirect alteration that appreciably diminishes the value of critical habitat for both the survival and recovery of a listed species."[92] By tying this language into the "jeopardy" regulation language cited above, the Service has folded the critical habitat question into the "jeopardy" question. The result is that the *only* question the Service will ask in assessing whether a proposed action will violate Section 7 is: "Will the action likely jeopardize the continued existence of the species?" If a proposed action will modify a species' critical habitat to the extent that chances of recovery will be diminished, but continued existence will not be threatened, then the regulations will allow that action to proceed.

Critics argue that this interpretation is flawed in that it renders the statutory protection of critical habitat meaningless. Under legal principles, regulations that render statutes "inoperative or superfluous, void or insignificant" exceed agency authority and are not permitted.[93]

Despite the fact that the regulations seem to void the critical habitat protections intended by Congress in Section 7(a)(2), courts have occasionally enjoined agency actions where it can be shown that those actions will result in harm to critical habitat.[94] And several cases show a correlation between the failure to designate critical habitat and subsequent failure by courts to enjoin federal actions adversely affecting habitat important to listed species.[95]

---

92. 50 C.F.R. § 402.02.

93. C.F. Communications Corp. v. Federal Communications Comm'n, 128 F.2d 735, 739 (D.C. Cir. 1997).

94. *See* Idaho Rivers United v. National Marine Fisheries Services, 1995 WL 877502 (W.D. Wash. Nov. 9, 1995) (enjoining location of a mine in the Salmon National Forest, critical habitat of the Snake River spring and summer Chinook salmon); Seattle Audubon Soc'y v. Evans, 771 F. Supp. 1081 (W.D. Wash), *aff'd*, 952 F.2d 297 (1991) (enjoining timber sales in the areas of national forests of Washington, Oregon, and northern California, critical habitat of the Northern spotted owl).

95. *See, e.g.*, Sierra Club v. Froehlke, 534 F.2d 1289 (8th Cir. 1976); Enos v. Marsh, 769 F.2d 1363 (9th Cir. 1985); Missouri Coalition for the Environment v. Corps of Engineers, 678 F. Supp. 790 (E.D. Mo. 1988), *aff'd*, 866 F.2d 1025 (8th Cir. 1989), *cert. denied*, 493 U.S. 820 (1989); Pyramid Lake Paiute Tribe v. U.S. Department of Navy, 898 F.2d 1410 (9th Cir. 1990); Stop H-3 Ass'n v. Dole, 740 F.2d 1442 (9th Cir. 1984), *cert. denied*, 471 U.S. 1108 (1985).

D.3. Application of Section 7 to Powers Delegated to States

Some federal laws, such as the Clean Water Act (CWA), are administered either by the federal government or by state government.[96] When administered by the federal government, Section 7 clearly applies, but the outcome is less clear if the federal law is administered by a state. The CWA states that the Environmental Protection Agency must approve state programs that meet enumerated criteria. The list of criteria does not include ESA compliance.[97] The question is whether the EPA must require state programs to meet Section 7 protections, whether the EPA has the option to require Section 7 protections, or whether the EPA cannot require Section 7 protections. In *American Forest & Paper Ass'n v. U.S. E.P.A.*, the Fifth Circuit held that the EPA cannot require Section 7 protections in a state-managed CWA program.[98] No other circuit has decided this question, which could become increasingly important as states take over administration of certain federal laws.

D.4. Exemptions

If a proposed action fails to meet the requirements of Section 7(a)(2), the action agency may seek an exemption from the Endangered Species Committee.[99]

D.4.a. Exemption Process

A federal agency, the governor of the state in which an agency action would occur, or a permit or license applicant (the exemption applicant) may apply for an exemption if, after consultation under Section 7(a)(2), the expert agency's biological opinion indicates that the agency action would violate Section 7(a)(2).[100] An exemption applicant must submit a written application to the Secretary of the Interior no later than 90 days after the completion of the consultation process.[101]

The Secretary must determine, within 20 days after the receipt of the application, whether the action agency

- carried out the consultation responsibilities in good faith and made a reasonable and responsible effort to develop and fairly

96. *See* Clean Water Act, 33 U.S.C. §§ 1251(b), 1251(d).
97. *See id.* § 1342(b).
98. *See* American Forest and Paper Ass'n v. U.S. E.P.A., 137 F.3d 291, 294 (5th Cir. 1998).
99. *See* 16 U.S.C. § 1536(e).
100. *See id.* § 1536(g)(1).
101. *See id.* § 1536(g)(2)(A).

consider modifications or reasonable and prudent alternatives to the proposed action;
- conducted a biological assessment; and
- refrained from making any irreversible or irretrievable commitment of resources.

If the action agency has met these requirements, the Secretary will accept the application.[102]

Within 140 days after an application's acceptance, the Secretary must submit a comprehensive report to the Committee.[103] Within 30 days after receiving the Secretary's report, the Committee must make a final determination as to whether to grant an exemption. The Committee may grant an exemption if, by a vote of not less than five of its members, it takes the following actions:

- determine that there are no reasonable and prudent alternatives to the agency action, the benefits of such action clearly outweigh the benefits of alternative course of action and that such action is in the public interest, the action is of regional or national significance, and the action agency did not make any irreversible and irretrievable commitment of resources; and
- establish reasonable mitigation and enhancement measures so as to minimize the adverse effects of the action on the protected species or its critical habitat.[104]

Any action for which an exemption is granted shall not be considered to be a taking of any protected species with respect to any activity that is necessary to carry out such action.[105]

D.4.b. Exemptions in Practice

The cumbersome exemption mechanism is little-used.[106] The Committee rejected an exemption for the Tellico Dam, but that decision was later overturned by an act of Congress. Second, the Committee granted an exemption for the Gray Rocks Dam, basing its decision on the adoption and implementation of habitat mitigation measures developed during project settlement negotiations. Thirteen Oregon timber sales were granted exemptions from the ESA's protection of the Northern

---

102. *See id.* § 1536(g)(3).

103. *See id.* § 1536(g)(5)

104. *See id.* § 1536(h)(1).

105. *See id.* § 1536(o)(1).

106. *See generally,* Houck, *supra* note 90, at 297. For further discussion of the exemption process in practice, *see* Jared des Rosiers, *The Exemption Process under the Endangered Species Act: How the "God Squad" Works and Why,* 66 Notre Dame L. Rev. 825 (1991).

spotted owl; however, that decision was later overturned by the Ninth Circuit due to the fact that three of the seven cabinet members had illegal *ex parte* contact with then-President Bush.[107]

Endangered Species Committee: Makeup and Organization

The Committee is a cabinet-level body composed of seven members: the Secretary of Agriculture; the Secretary of the Army; the Chairman of the Council of Economics Advisors; the Administrator of the Environmental Protection Agency; the Secretary of the Interior; the Administrator of the National Oceanic and Atmospheric Administration; and an individual, appointed by the President, from each of the affected states.

The Secretary of the Interior (Secretary) serves as the Chair of the Committee. The Committee meets at the call of the Chair or five of its members, and all meetings and records of the Committee are open to the public. The presence of five members of the Committee, or their representatives, constitutes a quorum for the transaction of any function of the Committee.

E. Judicial Review of Agency Decision-Making under Section 7

Citizens have legal standing to challenge the procedural and substantive integrity of agency decision-making under Section 7. Action agencies' procedural and substantive noncompliance with Section 7 can be challenged under Section 11(g) of the ESA. Likewise, the Service can be forced to comply with nondiscretionary procedural requirements of Section 7 under Section 11. In a recent case, the Supreme Court held that substantive opinions of the Service were reviewable under the Administrative Procedure Act.[108]

As discussed above, Section 7 obliges the Secretary and other federal agencies to carry out several nondiscretionary procedural duties. Such duties include preparing biological assessments and using the best scientific and commercial data available.

Courts make their own independent determinations of whether the Secretary and federal agencies have complied with Section 7's procedural requirements. Plaintiffs bear the burden of establishing a procedural violation by showing that the circumstances trigger a procedural

---

107. *See* Portland Audubon Soc'y v. Endangered Species Committee, 984 F.2d 1534 (9th Cir. 1993).

108. Bennett v. Spear, 520 U.S. 154 (1997).

requirement and the required procedures have not been followed.[109] The way an agency action actually affects listed species is irrelevant to a procedural Section 7 claim.

One of the most common Section 7 procedural claims is that the Secretary or a federal agency did not use the best scientific and commercial data available when deciding whether an agency met the requirements of Section 7(a)(2). These challenges succeed only if plaintiffs can point out relevant data that was not considered by the Secretary or agency. If a court determines that the agency followed the statutory procedures in good faith, it will not disturb the final agency conclusion. On the other hand, if a reviewing court finds procedural flaws, it will find a violation of Section 7(a)(2) and most likely enjoin the project.[110]

It is also possible for citizens to challenge the expert agency's biological opinion and/or the action agency's "no jeopardy" conclusion on substantive grounds. A citizen can argue that these agency decisions were wrong—the proposed project would jeopardize the continued existence of the species. In the case of such a challenge, a court will give deference to the agency, and will overturn the agency decision only if it finds that it was arbitrary and capricious. This is a difficult standard for a potential plaintiff to overcome and thus, substantive challenges to Section 7 decision-making are rarely successful.[111]

---

109. Thomas v. Peterson, 753 F.2d at 765.

110. *See* Conservation Law Found. v. Watt, 560 F. Supp. 561, 573 (D. Mass. 1983); Thomas v. Peterson, 753 F.2d at 764.

111. *See* Mausolf v. Babbitt, 125 F.3d 661 (8th Cir. 1997). Southwest Center for Biological Diversity v. United States Bureau of Reclamation, 6 F. Supp.2d 1119 (D. Ariz. 1997); Strahan v. Linnon, 967 F. Supp. 581 (d. Mass. 1997); Center for Marine Conservation v. Brown, 917 F. Supp. 1128 (S.D. Tex. 1996). *But see* Greenpeace v. National Marine Fisheries Service, 80 F. Supp.2d, 1137 (W.D. Wash. 2000).

CHAPTER FOUR

Section 9: Protecting Members
of Listed Species

A. Introduction

Section 9 of the ESA is meant to protect the individual members of listed species. Unlike Section 7, where an activity is evaluated in terms of its effect on the overall wellbeing of a listed species, activities under Section 9 are viewed through the lens of individual harm. Generally speaking, Section 9 prohibits persons from doing harm to members of listed species. This includes direct forms of harm such as killing an individual organism, and indirect forms of harm such as the destruction of habitat where individuals reside or breed. Section 9 also prohibits activities connected with or flowing out of harm to organisms, such as the transportation, possession or sale of individuals.[1]

There are two other notable features of Section 9 that distinguish it from Section 7. First, while Section 7's provisions apply only to federal agencies and permittees, Section 9 applies to all "persons," including private individuals, corporations, and federal and non-federal government officials and entities.[2] Second, Section 9 gives greater protection to fish and wildlife than plants and can give greater protection to endangered species than threatened species. In contrast, Section 7 does not make such distinctions.

There are several exceptions to the general Section 9 prohibition on "taking" individual members of listed species. As set forth in Section 10 of the ESA, the Service may issue "take permits" for various reasons, including scientific research, subsistence use by Alaska natives, experimental populations, and undue economic hardship. The most frequently issued and controversial take permits are issued pursuant to Section 10(a)(1)(B) (so-called "incidental take permits"), which can only be issued in conjunction with the approval of a Habitat Conservation Plan (HCP). Beginning in the early 1990s, the Service increased the use of incidental take permits and HCPs as a tool for resolving the conflict between alteration and use of private land and the ESA. Most endangered

---

1. *See* 16 U.S.C. § 1538(a).
2. *See* 16 U.S.C. §§ 1538(a), 1532(13).

species have at least some part of their habitat on privately owned land.[3] Chapter Five of this Handbook is devoted to an in-depth discussion of HCPs.

B. To Whom Do Section 9's Prohibitions Apply?

The prohibitions of Section 9 apply to "any person."[4] "Person" is defined broadly in the ESA, and includes government entities as well as individuals and business entities.[5] Not only is it unlawful for any person who is subject to the jurisdiction of the United States to commit the acts prohibited in Section 9, but Section 9(g) makes it also unlawful to attempt to commit, solicit another to commit, or cause to be committed any such act.[6]

The section's specific prohibitions, such as the Section 9(a)(1) ban on takes, are read in conjunction with Section 9(g); hence, the ESA not only prohibits acts that constitute takes, but also prohibits acts that cause the actions that constitute takes.[7] Thus, as explained by the court in *Strahan v. Coxe*, if a person takes an endangered species pursuant to the authority of some governmental entity, that governmental entity "may be deemed to have violated the provisions of the ESA."[8] In supporting its holding, the *Strahan* court noted other similar decisions:

- *Sierra Club v. Yeutter*, 626 F.2d 429, 438-39 (5th Cir. 1991), which found that the Forest Service's management of timber stands was a take of the red-cockaded woodpecker in violation of the ESA;
- *Defenders of Wildlife v. Administrator, Enviornmental Protection Agency*, 882 F.2d 1294, 1301 (8th Cir. 1989), which held that the EPA's registration of pesticides containing strychnine violated the ESA, both because endangered species had died from ingesting strychnine bait and because that strychnine could only be distributed pursuant to the EPA's registration scheme; and

---

3. In 1993, close to 80 percent of ESA-protected species had some or all of their habitat on private land; more than a third of the species inhabit no federal land at all. *See* U.S. General Accounting Office, Endangered Species: Information on Species Protection on Nonfederal Lands 4-6 (1994).

4. *See* 16 U.S.C. § 1538.

5. *See id.* § 1532(13).

6. *See id.* § 1538(g).

7. *See, e.g.,* Strahan v. Coxe, 127 F.3d 155, 163 (1st Cir. 1997), *cert. denied,* 525 U.S. 830 (1998).

8. 127 F.3d at 163 (rejecting a legal challenge to the trial court's finding that the state of Massachusetts violated the ESA through its scheme for regulating commercial fishing).

- *Loggerhead Turtle v. County Council of Volusia County*, 896 F. Supp. 1170, 1180-81 (M.D. Fla. 1995), which held that the county's authorization of vehicular beach access during turtle mating season constituted a take of the turtles in violation of the ESA.

Following *Strahan*, an appeal of *Volusia County* labeled as an "accepted notion" that governmental authorization of third party actions could itself constitute a take.[9]

Plaintiffs or prosecutors bear the burden of establishing a violation of Section 9.[10] Specific intent is not required for violations of Section 9. In other words, a court will not inquire as to whether an alleged violator intended to, for example, kill a listed bird by cutting down the tree in which it was roosting. Rather, a court will focus on the general intent of the alleged violator—did he or she knowingly cut down the tree? Knowledge of the law is not an essential element in civil or criminal violations of the ESA.[11] However, punishment can vary depending on the violator's mental state, with more willful violators receiving stiffer penalties.[12]

C.1. Endangered Fish and Wildlife: The Prohibition Against Takes

Section 9's most significant prohibition pertaining to endangered fish and wildlife is the prohibition against taking members of listed species.[13] The prohibition applies on the high seas as well as within the United States and its territorial waters. To "take" is defined as "to harass, harm, pursue, hunt, shoot, wound, kill, trap, capture, or collect, or to attempt to engage in any such conduct."[14]

C.1.a. The Definition of "Harm"

Of the various terms included within the definition of take, by far the most controversial and difficult to define has been "harm." FWS regulations provide that within the definition of take, to harm means "[to perform] an act which actually kills or injures wildlife. Such act may include significant habitat modification or degradation where it actually

---

9. Loggerhead Turtle v. City Council of Volusia City, 148 F.3d 1231, 1327 (11th Cir. 1998).

10. *See, e.g.*, Sierra Club v. Block, 614 F. Supp. 488, 492 (D.D.C. 1985).

11. *See* United States v. Ivey, 949 F.2d 759, 766 (5th Cir. 1991) (citing the statute and legislative history).

12. See Chapter Seven (Bringing Suit Under the ESA).

13. 16 U.S.C. §§ 1538(a)(1)(B)-(C).

14. *Id.* § 1532(19).

kills or injures wildlife by significantly impairing essential behavioral patterns, including breeding, feeding or sheltering."[15]

There have been three significant court cases related to this regulation. The first two, involving the endangered palila bird, primarily addressed factual issues tying habitat destruction with taking.[16] Although the regulatory definition of harm requires a finding of actual death or injury to individuals, the reality is that destroying habitat — while clearly harming individuals — rarely produces "corpses." The palila cases stand for, among other things, the proposition that taking-level harm to members of listed species from habitat destruction can be proven without actual corpses, for example, by showing that the habitat destruction reduced the population of the species in that area.

The third important case in this area was the Supreme Court's 1995 decision in *Babbitt v. Sweet Home*.[17] In that case, the plaintiffs took a different tack in trying to weaken Section 9's protection of listed species' habitat. They argued that the regulation was invalid, claiming that the regulatory definition of harm effectively expanded the scope of protections provided by the law itself.

C.1.b. Background: The Palila Decisions

The *Palila* cases set the parameters for controversies over the meaning of "harm." In the *Palila* cases, the plaintiffs argued that the state of Hawaii's activities in maintaining populations of feral goats and sheep for hunting constituted an illegal take of palilas because the goats and sheep destroyed palila habitat. The state did not contest the fact that the goats and sheep destroyed palila habitat, but argued instead that the destruction of habitat caused by the goats and sheep was not a take under the ESA. In both *Palila I* and *Palila II*, the Ninth Circuit upheld district court findings that the state's goat and sheep management activities did indeed qualify as illegal takes of the palila.

When *Palila I* was brought in 1979, the regulatory definition of harm was as follows:

---

15. 50 C.F.R. § 17.3.

16. *See* Palila v. Hawaii Dept. of Land & Natural Resources, 471 F. Supp. 985 (D. Haw. 1979) (*Palila I*), aff'd, 639 F.2d 495 (1981) (*Palila I Appeal*); and Palila v. Hawaii Dept. of Land & Natural Resources, 649 F. Supp. 1070 (D. Haw. 1986) (*Palila II*), aff'd, 852 F.2d 1106 (9th Cir. 1988) (*Palila II Appeal*).

17. 515 U.S. 687 (1995).

"Harm" in the definition of "take" in the Act means an act or
omission which actually injures or kills wildlife including acts
which annoy it to such an extent as to significantly disrupt essential behavioral patterns, which include, but are not limited to,
breeding, feeding or sheltering: significant environmental modification or degradation which has such effects is included within
the meaning of "harm."[18]

The state of Hawaii appealed the district court's ruling in *Palila I* that
maintaining the feral animals was a take of the palila. After the district
court was upheld on appeal, an Interior Department Solicitor's Opinion
concluded that the Ninth Circuit's decision "demonstrates fundamental
confusion over the distinction between habitat modifications and takings,"[19] and argued that habitat modification alone did not legally constitute a taking. In that opinion, the Solicitor interpreted Section 9 as
prohibiting habitat modification only when it could be shown that modification actually resulted in the death of or injury to individual members
of a listed species.[20] Following this line of thinking, the Fish and Wildlife
Service subsequently adopted the above-quoted definition of harm that
remains in effect to this day.[21]

This new definition of harm was at issue in the second palila case.
Palila II was factually similar to *Palila I*, except that it involved a different
species of feral sheep, the mouflon. In *Palila II*, the state argued that the
new definition of harm, with its greater emphasis on actual death or injury to members of listed species, precluded the *Palila I* result. The state
contended that because no evidence of actual death or injury to birds had
been presented, the court could not find that a taking had occurred.

After a trial, the district court in *Palila II* rejected the state's arguments and held that the new definition of harm was not substantially
different from the previous definition upon which it had relied in deciding *Palila I*.[22] The *Palila II* court also rejected the state's argument that
evidence of death or injury to specific individual members of a listed
species was necessary for it to find that a take had occurred. The court
found that the presence of feral sheep was in fact harming the palila
population as a whole and that the maintenance of the sheep population

18. 50 C.F.R. § 17.3 (repealed 1981).

19. 46 Fed. Reg. 29,492 (1981).

20. *See id.* at 29,491.

21. *See id.* at 54,748.

22. *See* Palila v. Hawaii Dept. of Land & Natural Resources, 631 F. Supp. 787, 789 (D. Haw.
1985).

thus constituted an illegal take of the palila. [23] On appeal, the Ninth Circuit affirmed this holding.[24]

C.1.c. The Supreme Court's Decision in *Sweet Home*

In *Sweet Home*, the Supreme Court rejected the plaintiffs' claim that the regulatory definition of harm was invalid under the ESA.[25] The Court considered the text and structure of the Act, its legislative history, and the 1982 amendment that provided for incidental take permits,[26] and determined that it is reasonable, under the *Chevron* standard, for the regulatory definition of harm to include "significant modification or degradation where it actually kills or injures wildlife."[27]

Specifically, the Court found it reasonable for harm to refer to indirect as well as direct harm to species, and observed that the statutory term *harm* would be surplusage if it did not encompass indirect injuries.[28] The Court noted the government's arguments that activities that cause only minimal or unforeseeable harm would not violate the Act as it is construed in the harm regulation,[29] and rejected the dissent's claims that the regulation "dispenses with the foreseeability of harm" or "fail[s] to require injury to particular animals."[30] The Court indicated that the harm regulation, which simply implements the ESA, is subject to the "knowingly violates" language that appears in Section 11 of the Act,[31] and to ordinary requirements of proximate causation and foreseeability.[32] The elements of an ESA harm case therefore are that the defendants caused, in a proximate and foreseeable manner, actual death or injury to identifiable members of the listed species. The remaining questions are how strictly these elements will be applied.

---

23. *See* 649 F. Supp. at 1077.

24. *See* 852 F.2d at 1110.

25. 515 U.S. 687 (1995).

26. For discussion of incidental take permits, see Chapter Five (Incidental Takes and Habitat Conservation Plans).

27. 515 U.S. at 697 (referring to Chevron U.S.A. Inc. v. Natural Resources Defense Council, Inc., 467 U.S. 837 (1984)).

28. *See* 515 U.S. at 697-98.

29. *See id.* at 699.

30. *See id.* at 700 n.13.

31. 16 U.S.C. §§ 1540(a)(1), 1540 (b)(1).

32. 515 U.S. at 700 n.13.

C.1.d. Prospects after *Sweet Home*

Although the regulatory definition of "harm" has withstood a facial challenge, questions remain as to the scope of its application. *Sweet Home* was a 6-3 decision, but at least four justices (O'Connor, who concurred in *Sweet Home*, and Scalia, Rehnquist, and Thomas, who dissented) believe that the *Palila II* appeal, which set the standard for applicability, was wrongly decided. Most likely, then, the definition of harm has not yet been entirely settled.[33]

Scalia, Rehnquist, and Thomas would reject the regulatory definition of harm that applied in *Palila II*. Although accepting the validity of the regulation itself, O'Connor argued that the Ninth Circuit misapplied it in the *Palila II* appeal; it is not clear how the other five justices who upheld the "harm" regulation would view its application to the facts of *Palila II*. According to O'Connor, the Ninth Circuit in the *Palila II* appeal should not have held

> that a state agency committed a "taking" by permitting feral sheep to eat mamane-naio seedlings that, when full-grown, might have fed and sheltered endangered palila. . . . Destruction of the seedlings did not proximately cause actual death or injury to identifiable birds; it merely prevented the regeneration of forest land not currently inhabited by actual birds.[34]

In addition to arguing that the Ninth Circuit misapplied the "harm" regulation in *Palila II*, Justice O'Connor invited Congress to revisit the question of FWS authority, and invited FWS to narrow the scope of the regulatory definition of "harm."[35]

Even in the wake of *Sweet Home*, the Ninth Circuit still interprets "harm" rather broadly. For example, in *Marbled Murrelet v. Babbitt*,[36] the court made it clear that Ninth Circuit case law was not changed by *Sweet Home*, and held that "a habitat modification which significantly impairs the breeding and sheltering of a protected species amounts to 'harm' under the ESA."[37]

---

33. *See* 515 U.S. at 714 (Justice O'Connor, concurring, notes that under her interpretation of 50 C.F.R. § 17.3, the *Palila II Appeal* was wrongly decided), 715 (Justice Scalia, dissenting, and joined by Chief Justice Rehnquist and Justice Thomas, would strike down the regulation, even under the Chevron standard).

34. *Id.* at 713-14 (Justice O'Connor, concurring).

35. *See id.* at 714.

36. 83 F.3d 1060 (9th Cir. 1996).

37. *Id.* at 1067.

C.2. The Definition of "Harass"

The regulations define "harass" as follows:

"Harass" in the definition of "take" in the Act means an intentional or negligent act or omission which creates the likelihood of injury to wildlife by annoying it to such an extent as to significantly disrupt normal behavioral patterns which include, but are not limited to, breeding, feeding or sheltering.[38]

No cases have relied on this definition alone to find a take of an endangered species, but a decision involving harassment under the Marine Mammal Protection Act (MMPA) suggests how such cases might be analyzed. In dictum, a Ninth Circuit panel suggested that the definition of harass in the ESA requires "direct and severe" disruptions of an animal's natural behavior.[39] The court observed that the definition in 50 C.F.R. § 17.3 "requires significant disruption of 'normal' behavioral patterns," and noted that the "[d]eterrence of abnormal . . . activity is not proscribed."[40] The court held that the defendant's actions—firing a rifle into the water behind some porpoises in an attempt to deter them from eating bait off a fishing line—did not constitute unlawful harassment of the porpoises under the Marine Mammal Protection Act or its regulations.[41]

C.3. "Reasonably Certain Threat of Imminent Harm"

To prove a take, it will not suffice to show that a take may have occurred, or might occur in the future. Rather, a take must have occurred already or must be reasonably certain to occur.[42] To prove a take, it suffices to show that a reasonably certain take is imminent.[43] Whether a showing of imminence is necessary in such a case is not always clear in the case law.

---

38. 50 C.F.R. § 17.3.
39. United States v. Hayashi, 22 F.3d 859, 864 (9th Cir. 1993) (as amended, 1994) (discussing the ESA's regulatory definition of "harass" from 50 C.F.R. § 17.3 in connection with the interpretation of "harass" for purposes of the MMPA, 16 U.S.C. § 1362(13)).
40. Id.
41. See id. at 866. See also Tepley v. National Oceanic & Atmospheric Admin., 908 F. Supp. 708 (N.D. Cal. 1995) (holding that insufficient evidence had been presented to support a finding that an underwater photographer harassed whales within the meaning of the MMPA).
42. See Marbled Murrelet v. Babbitt, 83 F.3d 1060, 1068 (9th Cir. 1996); Forest Conservation Council v. Rosboro Lumber Co., 50 F.3d 781, 783 (9th Cir. 1995). But see American Bald Eagle v. Bhatti, 9 F.3d 163 (1st Cir. 1993) (upholding a finding that deer hunting on a state reservation did not cause takes of bald eagles absent a showing that the hunt caused any actual harm to bald eagles).
43. Marbled Murrelet, 83 F.3d at 1066.

In *Marbled Murrelet*, the Ninth Circuit described its holding in *Rosboro* as follows: "a reasonably certain threat of future harm is sufficient to support a permanent injunction under the ESA."[44] The court emphasized that the holding remains good law, and that the trial court had found that there was a reasonable certainty of imminent harm.[45] While this is settled law in the Ninth Circuit, not all circuits have reached the issue of when injunctive relief is available.

How strictly courts will apply the "imminence" requirement is unclear. An argument can even be made that a reasonably certain threat is sufficient to obtain an injunction, that imminence is unnecessary, and that the requirements of certainty, proximate causation, and standing are sufficient to prevent unjust application of Section 9. A district court expressly declined to read an immediacy requirement into Section 9's ban on takes in *Palila II*. In that case, the defendants admitted that an activity then underway could harm a protected species in the future, but argued that the activity did not constitute a take because it was not presently harming the species.[46] Calling this view "shortsighted," the court enjoined the challenged activity as a take.[47] This example shows that imminence may lose much of its meaning, but other courts or circuits may be more strict.

C.4. Endangered Fish and Wildlife: Other Prohibitions

Section 9 prohibits the violation of any regulation that pertains to an endangered species of fish or wildlife.[48] In addition, Section 9 explicitly forbids the following actions:

- the possession, sale, and transport of illegally taken endangered species;[49]
- the shipment of endangered species in interstate or foreign commerce for commercial purposes;[50]
- the sale of endangered species in interstate or foreign commerce;[51]

---

44. *See id.* at 1068.
45. *Id.*
46. *See Palila II*, 649 F. Supp. at 1075.
47. *See id.*
48. *See* 16 U.S.C. § 1538(a)(1)(G); *see also* 50 C.F.R. § 17.31 (prohibitions regarding endangered wildlife).
49. *See* 61 U.S.C. § 1538(a)(1)(D).
50. *See id.* § 1538(a)(1)(E).
51. *See id.* § 1538(a)(1)(F).

- the importation of endangered species into the United States and the export of such species from the United States.[52]

Just as with the take prohibition, courts have interpreted other Section 9 prohibitions broadly. Thus, for example, in *Delbay Pharmaceuticals v. Department of Commerce*,[53] the court upheld the seizure of sperm whale products held in the course of a commercial activity as a violation of Section 9, even though the products were legally imported under a hardship exemption[54] to the Endangered Species Conservation Act of 1969. The court also held that Congress desired the broadest possible applications of Section 9's prohibitions.[55] In *Cayman Turtle Farm v. Andrus*,[56] the court found that Section 9's ban on importing protected species applied to commercially farmed specimens of protected species. And in *United States v. 3,210 Crusted Sides of Caiman Crocodilus Yacare*,[57] the court held that hides shipped from Bolivia to Paris on a flight that made an unscheduled landing in the United States were imported into the United States within the ESA's definition of "import."

C.5. Federal Preemption of State Endangered Species Laws

Congress intended the ESA to preempt state wildlife conservation laws to a very limited extent. Accordingly, the ESA preempts only those state laws relating to interstate or foreign trade in, or import or export of, an endangered species. States are free to restrict sales of endangered species so long as they do not interfere with federally permitted commerce. State laws are preempted only to the extent that they

- permit what is prohibited by the Act or its implementing regulations, or
- prohibit what is allowed by exemption or permit under Section 10(d).

For example, in *Man Hing Ivory and Imports, Inc. v. Deukmejian*,[58] the Ninth Circuit held that the ESA preempted a state law that banned the import of elephant products for commercial purposes. The state law was preempted because federal implementing regulations specifically

---

52. *See id.* § 1538(a)(1)(A).
53. 409 F. Supp. 637 (D.D.C. 1976).
54. For details on the hardship exemption, *see* section E.2.a of this chapter (Hardship and Subsistence).
55. 409 F. Supp. at 642.
56. 478 F. Supp. 125 (D.D.C. 1979).
57. 636 F. Supp. 1281 (S.D. Fla. 1986).
58. 702 F.2d 760 (9th Cir. 1983).

allowed limited trade in elephant products under special purpose permits, which were granted under Section 10(d) authority.

On the other hand, in *Cresenzi Bird Importers, Inc. v. New York*,[59] the court held that federally issued permits "to engage in business as an importer or exporter of wildlife" did not preempt New York state law banning the sale of wild birds. The court explained that only Section 10(d) permits have a preemptive effect. The permits in *Cresenzi*, aimed at controlling inhuman and unhealthful conditions in the transportation of wild birds and animals, were authorized under a different section of the act (Section 9(d)).

C.6. Endangered Plants

Section 9 imposes different prohibitions on acts involving endangered plants from those involving endangered fish and wildlife. A member of a listed plant species occurring on private land generally will not be protected by Section 9 unless it is protected under an applicable state law.[60] Section 9 does extend some protection to plants found on federal land.

C.6.a. Prohibitions Against Removal

Section 9(a)(2)(B) makes it illegal for any person to "remove and reduce to possession," or to "maliciously damage or destroy" any endangered plant on federal land.[61] On non-federal land, it is against the law to "remove, cut, dig up, or damage or destroy any [endangered plant] . . . in knowing violation of any law or regulation of any state or in the course of any violation of a state criminal trespass law."[62]

FWS interprets the prohibition on removing plants from federal land and reducing them to possession as applying only to "a person who removes an endangered plant from its location . . . and holds it as his/her own."[63] Thus, persons collecting plants for possession or sale (including seeds and cuttings) would violate Section 9, but not so those who merely displace or destroy endangered plants in the course of activities such as logging or mining. Legislative history indicates that this interpretation is consistent with congressional intent.[64]

---

59. 658 F. Supp. 1441 (S.D.N.Y.), *aff'd*, 831 F.2d 410 (2d Cir. 1987).
60. Plants on private land will be protected by Section 7 if a private landowner applies for an HCP, or if an activity on private land is subject to federal permitting.
61. 16 U.S.C. § 1538(a)(2)(B).
62. *Id.*
63. 50 Fed. Reg. 39,681, 39,686 (1985).
64. H.R. Rep. No. 467, at 15 (1988).

Legislative history also sheds light on how Section 9 should be applied with respect to endangered plants on non-federal land. The protections were not meant to interfere with the traditional rights of landowners; they were intended only to increase the deterrent effect of state laws protecting plants.[65]

C.6.b. Other Prohibitions

Section 9 prohibits the violation of any regulation that pertains to an endangered species of plant.[66] Section 9 similarly prohibits the import or export of endangered plants into or out of the United States,[67] and bans interstate and foreign commerce in such species.[68] The restrictions applicable to plants differ, however, from those applicable to fish and wildlife in that Section 9 does not make unlawful the mere possession of illegally obtained plants.[69] Therefore, a person within the United States who possesses a plant specimen that someone else has illegally taken will not violate the law unless the specimen was acquired in an interstate transaction. However, this same person would potentially be subject to federal prosecution under the Lacey Act, which makes it unlawful for any person to "import, export, transport, sell, receive, acquire, or purchase any fish or wildlife or plant taken or possessed in violation of any law, treaty, or regulation of the United States."[70]

D. Protection of Threatened Species

Section 9 prohibits the violation of any regulation that pertains to species of fish, wildlife, or plants that are listed as threatened pursuant to Section 4.[71] Section 4(d) requires the Service to issue regulations that it deems "necessary and advisable to provide for the conservation of [threatened] species."[72] This regulatory power allows the Service to accord threatened species the same protection that Section 9 provides for endangered species.[73]

---

65. See S. Rep. No. 240, at 12 (1987).
66. See 16 U.S.C. § 1538(a)(2)(E); see also 50 C.F.R. § 17.61 (prohibitions regarding endangered plants).
67. See 16 U.S.C. § 1538(a)(2)(A).
68. See id. §§ 1538(a)(2)(C)–(D).
69. Compare id. § 1538(a)(1)(D) (fish and wildlife) with id. § 1538(a)(2)(C) (plants).
70. 16 U.S.C. § 3372(a)(1). See 50 Fed. Reg. 39,681, 39,686 (1985).
71. See 16 U.S.C. §§ 1538(a)(1)(G) (fish or wildlife), 1538(a)(2)(E) (plants).
72. Id. § 1533(d).
73. See id.

Federal regulations pertaining to threatened fish and wildlife may not apply in those states that have entered into cooperative agreements with the federal government regarding conservation of resident threatened species of fish or wildlife.[74]

D.1. Regulations Pertaining to Threatened Species

Current FWS regulations extend most aspects of Section 9 protection to threatened species. The regulations provide that specific threatened species may be excepted from such favored treatment by rule.[75] The "special rules" are usually justified on the grounds that they further the conservation of the species.[76] By contrast, NMFS regulations protecting threatened species from take are issued on a species by species basis.[77] NMFS has in the past occasionally listed species as threatened without providing any Section 9 protections, at least on a temporary basis.[78]

D.1.a. The Secretary's Discretion in Promulgating Regulations That Affect Threatened Species

As noted above, Section 4(d) requires the Service to write regulations when it deems such regulations "necessary and advisable" for the conservation of threatened species. While the legal requirement to write these regulations is stated in mandatory "shall" terms, the "necessary and advisable" language creates room for agency discretion. There is no case law on the issue of whether the Service must write regulations to protect threatened species. Although FWS has written general regulations protecting threatened species, NMFS has to date only done so for selected species. It is unclear whether the agency can be compelled to write regulations for all species under its jurisdiction. There is, however, case law that requires 4(d) regulations, once written, to serve valid conservation purposes.[79]

---

74. *See id.*

75. *See* 50 C.F.R. §§ 17.31 (wildlife and fish), 17.71 (plants).

76. *See* part D.1.a of this chapter (The Secretary's Discretion in Promulgating Regulations that Affect Threatened Species).

77. *See* 50 C.F.R. § 227.

78. *See, e.g.,* Endangered and Threatened Species: Listing of Several Evolutionary Significant Units (ESUs) of West Coast Steelhead, 62 Fed. Reg. 43,937-44,001 (1997) (codified at 50 C.F.R. §§ 223.102, 224.101).

79. Sierra Club v. Clark, 577 F. Supp. 783 (D. Minn. 1984), *aff'd & rev'd,* 755 F.2d 608 (8th Cir. 1985) (regulations allowing sport trapping of threatened wolf species invalid). For an in-depth discussion of that case, see Keith J. Halleland, *Sierra Club v. Clark: The Government Cries Wolf,* 11 Wm. Mitchell L. Rev. 969 (1985). *See also* State of Louisiana ex rel. Guste v.

E. Exceptions to the Prohibitions

Circumscribed exceptions from the prohibitions of Section 9 are found in sections 9 and 10 of the ESA,[80] and in the federal regulations. In addition, Section 10 and Section 7 create broad statutory exceptions to the prohibitions, allowing takes under certain conditions when the "taking is incidental to, and not the purpose of, the carrying out of an otherwise lawful activity."[81] The incidental take provisions were established by Congress in amendments to the ESA in 1982. Before those amendments took effect, the interplay of sections 7 and 9 led to the possibility that a proposed federal action could satisfy the no-jeopardy standard of Section 7(a)(2) (which operates on the aggregate species level) but still violate the Section 9 ban on takings (which operates on the individual animal level).[82] The 1982 amendments authorized incidental takes in connection with projects that met the Section 7 no-jeopardy standard.[83] Also in 1982, Congress loosened the restrictions on private and state land-use decisions that resulted from Section 9's absolute ban on taking endangered species by creating a permit process whereby non-federal entities can apply for permission to incidentally take listed species in the course of an

Alaska Natives and Native Hawaiians

Native Alaskans, but not native Hawaiians, have special hunting privileges under Section 10 of the ESA. This distinction between groups was upheld against a constitutional challenge in *United States v. Nuesca*, 945 F.2d 254, 257-58 (9th Cir. 1991). The *Nuesca* court denied the Hawaiian defendants' claim that the ESA violates the Equal Protection Clause by treating one aboriginal group differently from another. The court held that Congress had a rational basis for distinguishing between the groups, noting that as a group, Alaska Natives maintain a traditional culture that depends for subsistence on the taking of certain endangered species and that it had not been established that subsistence hunting was of similar importance to a significant number of native Hawaiians.

Verity, 853 F.2d 322 (5th Cir. 1988) (regulations prohibiting take of threatened species upheld).
80. 16 U.S.C. §§ 1538, 1539.
81. *Id.* § 1539(a)(1)(B).
82. *See* H.R. Rep. No. 567, 97th Cong., 2d Sess. 26 (1982), *reprinted in* U.S.C.C.A.N. 2826.
83. 16 U.S.C. §§ 1536(b)(4), 1536(o).

otherwise lawful activity.[84] These broad incidental take exceptions are discussed in detail in Chapter Five.

A person alleged to have violated a Section 9 prohibition and who claims the benefit of a permit or a statutory exemption bears the burden of proving that the permit or exemption is applicable.[85]

E.1. Exceptions in Section 9

Provisions in Section 9 allow authorized state officials to take members of listed species when acting pursuant to a state-federal cooperative agreement.[86] Other provisions govern members of listed species that are held in captivity or controlled environments."[87]

E.2. Narrow Exceptions in Section 10

Various provisions in Section 10 allow actions that would otherwise violate the ESA.

E.2.a. Hardship and Subsistence

Hardship exemptions are available in certain cases where a person has entered into a contract involving a species before notice has been published that the species is considered for listing, if the subsequent listing of the species would cause undue economic hardship.[88] Undue economic hardship includes, but is not limited to, "substantial economic loss" or the "curtailment of subsistence."[89]

With some exceptions, Section 10 exempts Native Alaskans who reside in Alaska, and non-native permanent residents of Alaskan native villages from violations of Section 9 when they take or import threatened or endangered species for subsistence purposes. Further, they may sell non-edible byproducts of those species that are made into native handicrafts or clothing.[90]

---

84. *Id.* § 1539(a)(1)(B).

85. *Id.* § 1539(g).

86. *Id.* §§ 1538(a)(2), 1535(g)(2). *See also id.* § 1535(c) (outlining cooperative agreements); 50 C.F.R. §§ 17.21(c)(5), 17.31(b).

87. *See* 16 U.S.C. § 1538(b).

88. *See id.* § 1539(b)(1).

89. *See id.* § 1539(b)(2).

90. *See id.* § 1539(e).

E.2.b. Reintroductions to Enhance the Survival of a Species

Section 10 authorizes the Secretary to permit acts otherwise prohibited under Section 9 if those acts serve scientific purposes or enhance the propagation or survival of the affected species.[91] These permits can apply to acts that are necessary to establish and maintain experimental populations, defined in 16 U.S.C. § 1539(j)(1), which are subject to special provisions. In general, each member of an experimental population is treated as a threatened species,[92] which means that the protections accorded to the experimental population are those set forth in the regulations.[93]

The attempt to establish experimental populations can have unexpected results, as illustrated by the status of wolves in Yellowstone National Park and central Idaho. The gray wolf is listed as an endangered species in the lower forty-eight states (except for Minnesota, where it is listed as threatened). In accordance with a recovery plan for the species, Canadian gray wolves were released in Yellowstone and central Idaho. These wolves were labeled an "experimental" population, and regulations allowed ranchers to kill wolves that attacked livestock.[94] Some ranchers and environmentalists opposed elements of the reintroduction program in *Wyoming Farm Bureau Federation v. Babbitt*.[95] Ranchers, hoping to block the reintroduction of wolves, claimed that wolves already inhabited the area; environmentalists, hoping to require full protection for all wolves, made similar claims. Because experimental populations must, by definition, be geographically separate from non-experimental populations, the designation of the population as experimental would be inappropriate if a wolf population were already present. Nevertheless, the Fish and Wildlife Service argued for the "experimental" designation as necessary and supported its action by defining the word "population" to exclude isolated individuals.[96] The district court held that such a designation was unlawful under the Endangered Species Act because it had the effect of reducing the protection afforded to non-introduced wolves, and therefore the entire release program was unlawful. The court ordered that the released wolves be removed, but stayed the order pending appeal.[97] This holding was criticized in the neighboring 9th Circuit.[98]

---

91. *See id.* § 1539(a)(1)(A).

92. *See id.* § 1539(j)(2)(C).

93. *See id.* §§ 1538(a)(1)(G), 1538(a)(2)(E).

94. *See* 50 C.F.R. § 17.84(i).

95. 987 F. Supp. 1349 (D. Wyo. 1997).

96. *See id.* at 1370.

97. *See id.* at 1375.

98. *See* United States v. McKittrick, 142 F.3d 1170, 1175 (9th Cir. 1998).

E.2.c. Other Exceptions

Special exemptions apply to certain items (sperm whale oil, sperm whale oil derivatives, finished scrimshaw, and the raw material for scrimshaw) that were lawfully held in the United States prior to the passage of the ESA.[99] Other exceptions apply to antiques,[100] and to certain transshipments through the United States and certain mistaken shipments into the United States.[101]

E.3. Exceptions in the Federal Regulations

Federal regulations allow any person to take an endangered or threatened species in defense of his or her own life or the life of another.[102] In addition, certain federal or state employees may take individual members of protected species upon finding that those individuals represent "a demonstrable but nonimmediate threat to human safety."[103] The animal can be killed, however, only when it is not "reasonably possible" to eliminate the threat to human safety by capturing and relocating it.[104] It is unlawful, though, to take an endangered or threatened species in defense of property, including livestock: in *Christy v. Hodel*,[105] the Ninth Circuit upheld the validity of regulations preventing the killing of grizzly bears that preyed upon domestic sheep.

F. The Legality of Section 9 Prohibitions

As discussed in detail below, arguments that Section 9's prohibitions are unconstitutional or conflict with other rights have generally proven unsuccessful.

F.1. Takes and Due Process Rights

As the use of sections 9 and 10 of the Endangered Species Act has grown in the last decade, an active public and scholarly debate has emerged about whether the Act can stand up to Constitutional "takings"

---

99. 16 U.S.C. § 1539(f).

100. *See id.* § 1539(h).

101. *See id.* § 1539(i); *see also* Carpenter v. Andrus, 485 F. Supp. 637 (D.D.C. 1976) (holding that endangered species en route to a foreign country and mistakenly shipped to the U.S. are not subject to seizure; codified in an amendment to 16 U.S.C. § 1539(i)).

102. *See* 50 C.F.R. § 17.21(c)(2) (endangered species); *id.* § 17.31(a) (threatened species).

103. *See id.* §§ 17.21(c)(3)(iv), 17.31(a).

104. *Id.*

105. 857 F.2d 1324 (9th Cir. 1988).

challenges under the 5th and 14th Amendments.[106] Under the takings clause, "private property [shall not] be taken for public use, without just compensation."[107]

> ## "Takes" and "Takings"
>
> For those unfamiliar with legal jargon, Constitutional "takings" might be confused with the Endangered Species Act's prohibition against "takes." The ESA's prohibition against takes refers to actions that harm endangered or threatened species. On the other hand, the Constitutional prohibition applies to uncompensated governmental takings of private property.

Until the late 1980s and early 1990s, takings violations were rarely found,[108] and the test for finding a takings violation was vague.[109] In recent years, however, the United States Supreme Court has revived takings protections in cases such as *Lucas v. South Carolina Coastal Council*,[110] *Dolan v. City of Tigard*,[111] and *Nollan v. California Coastal Commission*.[112] In these cases, discussed briefly on page 123, the Court has established a set of tests that help to facilitate takings analyses.

As of 1998, no takings cases have been decided on the issue of ESA-related private land regulation.[113] However, several congressional bills and numerous statements from property rights advocates suggest that property owners should be compensated, in whole or in part, for ESA regulation of their property under Section 9.[114] Some proponents of

---

106. *See, e.g.*, Bruce Babbitt, *ESA & Private Property: The Endangered Species and "Takings:" A Call for Innovation Within the Terms of the Act*, 24 Envtl. L. 355 (1994); Susan Shaheen, *The Endangered Species Act: Inadequate Species Protection in the Wake of the Destruction of Private Property Rights*, 55 Ohio St. L.J. 453 (1994); Barton H. Thompson, Jr., *The Endangered Species Act: A Case Study in Takings and Incentives*. 49 Stan. L. Rev. 305, 324-43 (1997); Written Statement of Ike C. Sugg, Fellow in Wildlife and Land-Use Policy, Competitive Enterprise Institute, before the Endangered Species Task Force of the House Committee on Resources, May 18, 1995.

107. U.S. Const. amend. V.

108. *See* Thompson, *supra* note 106, at 324.

109. *See* Paula C. Murray, *Private Takings of Endangered Species as Public Nuisance: Lucas v. South Carolina Coastal Council and the Endangered Species Act*, 12 UCLA J. Envtl. L. & Pol'y 119, 121 (1993).

110. 505 U.S. 1003 (1992).

111. 512 U.S. 374 (1994).

112. 483 U.S. 825 (1987).

113. *See* note 106, at 456; Thompson, *supra* note 106, at 325.

114. *See* Endangered Species Conservation Act of 1995, S. 1364, 104th Cong., 1st Sess. (1995); Private Property Protection Act of 1995, H.R. 925, 104th Cong. 1st Sess. (1995);

strengthened takings protections suggest that, for example, property owners should be compensated for "any diminution in value" caused by regulatory action taken under the Act.[115]

Occasionally, federal statutes that prohibit the taking of certain wildlife have come under indirect attack by allegations that damage to private property caused by the protected wildlife is an unconstitutional taking of property without just compensation. Courts generally reject such arguments. In *Christy v. Hodel*,[116] the Ninth Circuit held that the ESA and regulations pertaining to grizzly bears, as applied to prevent the killing of bears in defense of property, did not deprive plaintiffs of property without due process of law. In *Mountain States Legal Foundation v. Hodel*,[117] the Tenth Circuit concluded that damage to grazing land by animals protected by the Wild Free-Roaming Horses and Burros Act did not constitute a taking of property because landowners are not deprived of the economically viable use of the lands. The Sixth Circuit agreed in *United States v. Kepler*,[118] in a case upholding a defendant's conviction for illegally transporting species in interstate commerce against a Fifth Amendment challenge.

F.2. Takings Challenges to State Regulatory Action

Courts have generally rejected arguments that state law regulation of habitat requires compensation under the Fifth and Fourteenth Amendments. In *Southview Associates, LTD. v. Bongartz*,[119] vacation home developer Southview sued members of the Vermont Environmental Board after the Board denied its application for a development permit. The development permit (sought pursuant to a Vermont land use statute) was denied on the grounds that the development would significantly impair a deeryard. The Court of Appeals for the Second Circuit held that Southview did not suffer a physical taking, as Southview retained the right to possess and sell the land, and many uses remained available to Southview or another owner. The Court also determined that Southview's regulatory taking and substantive due process claims were not ripe for review because Southview could not show that the decision made by the Board was final and because Southview had never sought compensation in the Vermont Courts.

Thompson, *supra* note 106, at 306.

115. *See* Babbitt, *supra* note 106, at 357 (summarizing views of ESA critics).

116. 857 F.2d at 1331.

117. 799 F.2d 1423 (10th Cir. 1986).

118. 531 F.2d 796 (6th Cir. 1976).

119. 980 F.2d 84 (2d Cir. 1992).

Takings and the ESA

Constitutional takings protections were at their nadir when Congress passed the ESA in 1973. Since the Supreme Court's 1978 decision in *Penn Central Transportation Co. v. New York City*, takings law has changed significantly.

Many commentators assumed that the new era of takings law would enable property owners to judicially challenge land use regulation under the ESA. Attention has focused on *Lucas v. South Carolina Coastal Council*, both because of its rejection of the benefit-harm distinction previously used to insulate many environmental regulations from takings restraints, and because of its holding that regulations depriving property owners of all economically viable uses of their property constitute takings. Decisions of the Court of Federal Claims have further heightened interest in *Lucas* by holding that regulations that deprive property owners of *almost all* economically viable uses of their property, or all economically viable uses of *part* of their property, can be unconstitutional takings in some situations.

Property rights advocates also have identified opportunities for challenging ESA actions under other recent Supreme Court decisions. Relying on *Loretto v. Teleprompter Manhattan CATV Corp.* and *Nollan v. California Coastal Commission*, property advocates have urged that Section 9 of the ESA requires compensation because it authorizes the "physical occupation" of property by endangered species. Less attention has been focused on *Dolan v. City of Tigard* and the aspects of *Nollan* that require any conditions that the government imposes on the development of property both to have a nexus and to be "roughly proportional" to the harms from development that the government seeks to avoid. . . . However, *Dolan* and *Nollan* could limit the FWS's ability to demand habitat set asides and other mitigation measures as a condition for a Section 10 ITP.

For details see Thompson, The Endangered Species Act: A Case Study in Takings & Incentives, 49 Stan. L. Rev. 305, 324-25, footnotes omitted.

In *Florida Game and Fresh Water Fish Commission v. Flotilla, Inc.*,[120] residential developer Flotilla brought a takings claim against the Commission arising from the Commission's restrictions on subdivision development activity near bald eagle nesting sites. The Court held that the restriction to protect the nesting sites affecting the development of 48 acres of a 173-acre parcel did not deprive the developer of most or all of its interests in the property. In evaluating and rejecting the developer's regulatory takings claim, the Court weighed six factors:

- whether there is a physical invasion of property;
- whether the regulation precludes all economically reasonable use of the property;
- whether the regulation confers public benefit or prevents public harm;
- whether the regulation promotes health, safety, welfare or morals of the public;
- whether the regulation is arbitrarily or capriciously applied; and
- the extent to which the regulation curtails investment-backed expectations.

F.3. Takes and the Commerce Clause

A federal court upheld the Section 9 take prohibition against a Commerce Clause challenge in a 2-1 decision in *National Ass'n of Home Builders v. Babbitt*.[121] The court held that the Commerce Clause gives Congress the authority to regulate wildlife and to regulate the use of non-federal lands, even when the protected species in question exists only within the borders of a single state. In this case, the takes in question would have resulted from the expansion of a road intersection, which was intended to improve access to a hospital for emergency vehicles. The species at issue was the Delhi Sands flower-loving fly, an endangered species found only in California.

The two justices who upheld the take prohibition differed on the rationales for the holding. Applying the analytical approach set forth by the Supreme Court *United States v. Lopez*,[122] Judge Wald argued that in prohibiting takes of endangered species, the law regulates the use of the channels of interstate commerce by enabling the government to control the transport of species in interstate commerce and by ensuring that the channels of interstate commerce are not used for immoral or injurious

---

120. 636 So. 2d 761 (Fla. 1994).
121. 130 F.3d 1041 (D.C. Cir. 1997) *cert. denied*, 524 U.S. 937 (1998).
122. 514 U.S. 549 (1995).

purposes.[123] The possibility that the extinction of an individual endangered species might be of a de minimis nature does not affect the analysis, which must consider the aggregate effect of the extinction of all similarly situated species.

In addition, Judge Wald argued that the law regulates activities that have a substantial relation to interstate commerce, finding that Congress could rationally conclude (1) that the intrastate activity that was regulated by Section 9 prevents the destruction of biodiversity and therefore protects interstate commerce, which relies upon biodiversity, and (2) that Section 9 prevents the adverse effects of interstate competition.[124] That a regulated activity might be local or might be non-commercial does not affect the analysis, so long as the activity has a substantial effect on interstate commerce.

Judge Henderson, concurring, rejected the channels-of-commerce argument. She argued that the law regulates activities that have a substantial relation to interstate commerce, but distinguished her reasons from those espoused by Judge Wald.[125] The distinctions are subtle; indeed, Judge Wald found Judge Henderson's reasoning to be "substantially similar" to her own.[126]

In a comprehensive dissent, Judge Sentelle argued that the federal government used the Interstate Commerce Clause to regulate activity that is neither interstate nor commerce.

F.4. Takes and the Rights of Native Americans

One important, highly charged, and still unanswered question about the ESA is exactly how it applies to Native Americans, whose hunting and fishing rights may conflict with the ESA's take prohibition. Native American groups generally say the ESA does not apply to them, arguing that their rights can only be terminated by clear intent in acts of Congress. The federal government generally argues that the ESA does apply. In holding that the Act prohibits Native Americans on the Seminole reservation from the non-commercial hunting of endangered Florida panthers, a district court noted in *United States v. Billie* that "on-reservation hunting rights are not absolute when a species . . . is in danger of extinction."[127]

---

123. *See* 130 F.3d at 1046.

124. *See id.* at 1052.

125. *See id.* at 1057-58 (Henderson, concurring).

126. *See id.* at 1046.

127. 667 F. Supp. 1485, 1492 (S.D. Fla. 1987).

In *United States v. Dion*, the Supreme Court did not reach the question whether the ESA abrogated Native American rights; but the Court held unanimously that the Bald Eagle Protection Act did abrogate treaty rights to hunt eagles. [128] That abrogation eliminated the possibility of using the treaty as a defense to ESA prosecution arising from the same conduct. The Court also noted that the Bald Eagle Protection Act and the ESA "prohibit exactly the same conduct" with respect to eagles for the same reasons.[129] In determining whether an act of Congress has abrogated treaty rights, "[w]hat is essential is clear evidence that Congress actually considered the conflict between its intended action on the one hand and Native American treaty rights on the other, and chose to resolve that conflict by abrogating the treaty."[130] So, for example, a court has held that members of the Chippewa tribe have a treaty right to sell certain migratory bird feathers, a right that Congress chose not to abrogate in enacting the Migratory Bird Treaty Act.[131]

---

128. *See* 476 U.S. 734, 745 (1986).

129. *Id.* at 746.

130. *Id.* at 739–40.

131. *See* United States v. Bresette, 761 F. Supp. 658, 660 (D. Minn. 1991).

CHAPTER FIVE

Section 10: Incidental Takes and Habitat Conservation Plans

A. Introduction

The majority of present and potential habitat for listed species in the United States exists on non-federal property owned by private citizens, states, municipalities, Native American tribal governments, and other non-federal entities.[1] Conservation efforts on non-federal property are thus critical to the survival and recovery of many endangered and threatened species. Although Section 7 can occasionally restrict activities on non-federal land, Section 9 is the primary ESA tool by which activities that affect listed species on non-federal land are regulated.

While Section 9 does not require landowners to take affirmative action to help species, it does restrict land uses by prohibiting the take of species through habitat modification.[2] This restriction has created some opposition to the ESA within the development community.[3] Section 9 has occasionally proven to be a real or perceived thorn in the side of developers and resource extractors, as evidenced by recent controversies surrounding such species as the northern spotted owl in the Pacific Northwest timber country, the Stephen's kangaroo rat (K-rat) in heavily populated Riverside County in Southern California, and the Mojave Desert tortoise in Nevada's growing Clark County.

Under the ESA's statutory structure, non-federal entities that cause a take through habitat modification (or otherwise) are subject to liability under Section 9. The only way to avoid such liability is to come within an exemption established by Section 10(a). Prior to 1982, Section 10(a) only allowed incidental takes for research and scientific purposes, or in cases of emergency or hardship. Members of the development community criticized the Section 9 prohibition against takes as overly restrictive and

---

1. *See* U.S. General Accounting Office, Endangered Species: Information on Species Protection on Non-Federal Lands 4-6 (1994).

2. *See* Chapter Four (Section 9: Protecting Members of Listed Species).

3. *See, e.g.,* Todd Woody, *Taking on Endangered Species: The Rat, the Farmer, and the Feds,* Legal Times, July 24, 1995, at 8; Craig Manson, *Species and Habitat Conservation: Natural Communities Conservation Planning: California's New Ecosystem Approach to Biodiversity,* 24 Envtl. L. 603, 606 (1994).

inflexible.[4] In the 1982 amendments to the ESA, Congress tried to address these concerns by expanding Section 10(a) to include the possibility of incidental takes for non-federal entities. For the most part, the amended Section 10(a) lay dormant until the mid-1990s, when the application rate for incidental take permits (ITPs) rose dramatically. Presently, incidental take permits and habitat conservation plans (HCPs) are a staple of endangered species law in the United States.[5]

This chapter focuses not on case law, but on the administrative process of developing, approving, and monitoring HCPs written in connection with applications for Section 10 ITPs. As of the summer of 2000, only two courts had found an HCP to be legally inadequate.[6] This relative absence of case law suggests that HCP challenges are difficult to win. With the proliferation of HCPs around the country, however, many additional HCP suits are pending or anticipated in the near future.

B. Incidental Take Statements and Incidental Take Permits

In 1982, Congress amended the ESA to allow the take of listed species under certain conditions when the "taking is incidental to, and not the purpose of, the carrying out of an otherwise lawful activity."[7] Although Section 10 incidental take permits apply to private and other non-federal lands, they are best understood in the context of Section 7 incidental take statements, which apply to federal actions.

B.1. Incidental Take Statements for Federal Actions

Under Section 7 of the ESA, federal agencies and federal permittees (for example, holders of a Section 404 Clean Water Act permit) can circumvent the strict Section 9 prohibition against takes by entering into Section 7 consultations with the Service. If, during the consultation process, a federal agency or permittee can prove that its take is not purposeful and "does not jeopardize the continued existence of the species," that agency or permittee can obtain an "incidental take statement" from the Service and be exempted conditionally from Section 9's prohibitions.[8] Once a federal agency or federal permittee begins formal consultation, the Service must conduct a scientific analysis and publish a Biological

---

4. *See* Timothy Beatley, Habitat Conservation Planning: Endangered Species and Urban Growth, 19 (1994).

5. See U.S. Fish & Wildlife, Habitat Conservation Plans and the Incidental Take Permitting (visited October 24, 2000) <http://endangered.fws.gov/hcp/hcpplan.html>.

6. *See* part D.4.c. of this chapter (Legal Options for Outside Parties).

7. 16 U.S.C. § 1539(a)(1)(B).

8. *Id.* §§ 1536(b)(4), 1536(o).

Opinion.[9] If the Service finds that "no jeopardy" to the species exists, the Service describes measures to minimize takes, if any are needed, and the proposed action by the federal agency or permittee can go forward.[10]

Incidental Take Statements in Practice: A Critique

The operation of the Bureau of Reclamation's Central Valley Project (a California irrigation water supply project) has had a devastating effect on the winter-run Chinook salmon. The U.S. Fish and Wildlife Service's incidental take statement, constrained by the Project's water supply contracts and the realities of severe drought conditions, requires only monitoring and plans to reduce fish mortality. "These measures hardly 'insure' prospects for the winter-run Chinook in any ordinary sense of the word, and mortality will remain 'significant.' Consultation under the ESA has not saved the winter-run Chinook. It has purchased them a seat at the argument."

For details see Oliver A. Houck, *The Endangered Species Act and Its Implementation by the U.S. Departments of Interior and Commerce*, 64 U. COLO. L. REV. 278, 328-329 (1993) (quoting NATIONAL MARINE FISHERIES SERVICE, SOUTHWEST REGION, BIOLOGICAL OPINION ON THE EFFECT OF THE CENTRAL VALLEY PROJECT ON SACRAMENTO RIVER WINTER-RUN CHINOOK SALMON 44-48 (1992).

A Section 7 incidental take statement must spell out how the incidental takes that result from the proposed activity will affect the species.[11] When possible, the Secretary must estimate the number of individuals likely to be taken,[12] but an incidental take statement that fails to cite a numerical impact on the species is not necessarily invalid. Congress anticipated that impacts would be difficult to estimate on some occasions.[13] An incidental take statement must also identify "reasonable and prudent measures that the Secretary considers necessary or appropriate to minimize [the] impact" of incidental takes on the species[14] and it

---

9. *See id.* § 1536(b)(3)(A).

10. *See id.* §§ 1536(a)(2), (b)(4).

11. *See id.* § 1536(b)(4)(i).

12. *See* H.R. Rep. No. 97-567 at 27 (1982), *reprinted in* 1982 U.S.C.C.A.N. 2827.

13. *See* Pacific Northwest Generating Coop. v. Brown, 822 F. Supp. 1479, 1510 (D. Or. 1993), *aff'd*, 38 F.3d 1058 (9th Cir. 1994).

14. 16 U.S.C. § 1536(b)(4)(ii).

must establish "terms and conditions" to implement those measures.[15] The regulations, however, require that such measures "cannot alter the basic design, location, scope, duration, or timing of the action and may involve only minor changes."[16] If at any time during the agency project the actual take exceeds the level specified in the incidental take statement, the agency must immediately reinitiate Section 7 consultation with the Service.[17]

Once an incidental take statement is issued, it is irrelevant whether a particular incidental take results from suboptimal or even incompetent implementation of mitigation measures, so long as the terms and conditions of the statement are met and the maximum level of incidental take is not exceeded. For instance, in *Mt. Graham Red Squirrel v. Espy*, the Ninth Circuit held that even if two endangered squirrels that had died during tagging had been mishandled, their deaths would fall within the incidental take allowance that had been established. Therefore, unintended deaths during the implementation of mitigation measures can still fall within an incidental take limit.[18]

In at least some circumstances, the issuance of a Section 7 incidental take statement allows parties who are not federal agencies to engage in incidental takes without applying for Section 10 incidental take permits. The Ninth Circuit, in *Ramsey v. Kantor*, held that a party that is neither a federal agency nor a Section 7 applicant can lawfully take individuals of a listed species without obtaining a Section 10 permit, provided the party's actions are contemplated by a Section 7 incidental take statement and are conducted in compliance with the requirements of the statement.[19]

B.2. Section 10(a)(1)(B): Incidental Take Permits for Non-Federal Entities

In 1982, Congress created a permit scheme analogous but not identical to the Section 7 incidental take statement described above, under which non-federal entities can apply for permission to incidentally take listed species in the course of otherwise legal activities.[20] Section 10 ITPs are available to state, municipal or tribal governments, corporations or businesses, associations, and private individuals. Section 10 ITPs can also

---

15. *Id.* § 1536(b)(4)(iv).
16. 50 C.F.R. § 402.14(i)(2).
17. *See id.* § 402.14(i)(4).
18. *See* 986 F.2d 1568, 1580 (9th Cir. 1993).
19. *See* 96 F.3d 434, 441-42 (9th Cir. 1996).
20. *See* 16 U.S.C. § 1539(a)(1)(B).

be obtained by combinations of these parties, such as watershed councils and joint power authorities.[21]

In order to secure a Section 10 ITP, the applicant must submit an HCP to the Service.[22] The Service will evaluate the proposed HCP to determine whether the plan meets legal requirements. The HCP must also be made available for public comment before the Section 10 ITP can be granted.[23] One feature that distinguishes a Section 10 ITP from a Section 7 incidental take statement is that the applicant must engage in mitigation measures to offset the impacts that the proposed development will have on the species.[24] This requirement is not mirrored

Habitat Conservation Plan Requirements:

In applying for an incidental take permit, the applicant must submit a habitat conservation plan that specifies the following:

(1) how the proposed activity will affect listed species;

(2) what steps the applicant will take to monitor, minimize, and mitigate such impacts, what funding will be available to carry out these steps, and how the applicant will deal with unforeseen circumstances;

(3) what alternatives that would not result in takes were considered by the applicant and why those alternatives were rejected, and;

(4) other measures that the Secretary specifies as necessary or appropriate for the purpose of the plan.

For details see 16 U.S.C. § 1539(a)(2)(A).

in the Section 7 incidental take process.[25] Incidental take statements must minimize their impact but are not expressly required to mitigate it.[26]

---

21. *See generally* U.S. Fish and Wildlife Service & National Marine Fisheries Service, Habitat Conservation Planning and Incidental Take Permit Processing Handbook (Nov. 1996) (hereinafter HCP Handbook) (visited Oct. 24, 2000) <http://endangered.fws.gov/hcp/hcpbook.html>.

22. For details of the HCP approval process, *see* Albert C. Lin, *Participants' Experiences with Habitat Conservation Plans and Suggestions for Streamlining the Process*, 23 Ecology L.Q. 369 (1996).

23. *See* 16 U.S.C. § 1539(c).

24. *See id.* § 1539(a)(2)(B).

25. *See* Melinda E. Taylor, *Promoting Recovery or Hedging a Bet Against Extinction: Austin, Texas's Risky Approach to Ensuring Endangered Species' Survival in the Texas Hill Country*, 24 Envtl. L. 581, 594 (1994).

The ESA requires that HCPs only cover listed species, but legislative history indicates some congressional desire for conservation plans to address unlisted species as well.[27] If a plan considers unlisted as well as listed species, subsequent listing of species in the area would require minimal (if any) changes to the plan, and the permitted activity could continue uninterrupted. Nevertheless, the Service views the inclusion of unlisted species in HCPs as optional.[28]

Incidental Take Permits Issuance

Section 10 provides that after an opportunity for public comment on conservation plans, the Secretary is required to issue an incidental take permit if the following conditions are met:

(a) the Secretary has received such "assurances as he may require that the plan will be implemented," and

(b) the Secretary finds that

(a) the take will be incidental (as opposed to intentional, which would be the case for hunting);

(b) the applicant will minimize and mitigate the impacts of any such take, to the greatest extent practicable;

(c) the applicant will ensure that the plan is adequately funded;

(d) the take will not appreciably reduce the likelihood that the species will survive and recover in the wild; and

(e) any measures specified by the Secretary as necessary or appropriate will be met.

A permit will contain those terms and conditions that the Secretary deems necessary or appropriate, including any reporting requirements that are deemed necessary for determining whether the permittee is complying with those terms and conditions. The Secretary must revoke a permit if he or she finds that the permittee is not complying with the applicable terms and conditions.

For details see 16 U.S.C. § 1539(a)(2)(A)-(C).

---

26. See 16 U.S.C. § 1537(b)(4).
27. See H.R. CONF. REP. NO. 97-835 at 30 (1982), reprinted in 1982 U.S.C.C.A.N. 2860, 2871.
28. See 50 C.F.R. § 17.32; 50 Fed. Reg. 39,681-83 (1995).

The Secretary's grant of an ITP is a federal action subject to the consultation requirements and substantive mandates of Section 7.[29] Thus, the Secretary is required to find that the take will not appreciably reduce the likelihood of the survival and recovery of the species in the wild.[30]

B.3. Background on Habitat Conservation Plans

Before 1994, habitat conservation planning under Section 10 was relatively rare. In the first ten years after the enactment of Section 10(a)(1)(B), only 11 HCPs had been approved. The apparent lack of enthusiasm for HCPs might have been caused by a lack of familiarity with the process, by the unsettled issue of whether habitat destruction violated Section 9, by the possibility in some cases of obtaining a Section 7 permit instead, or by the belief by some landowners that the Section 10 ITPs did not guarantee freedom from additional restrictions. Gradually, more HCPs were approved as non-federal entities and the Fish and Wildlife Service became more knowledgeable about the HCP process (the National Marine Fisheries Service has been much less involved in HCPs). The pace of HCP approval dramatically increased in the mid-1990s with administrative changes designed to speed HCP processing and guarantee no additional restrictions on property use. The number of approved HCPs rose to over 300 by August, 2000.[31] The Clinton Administration and Interior Secretary Bruce Babbitt have championed HCPs, stating that such plans are the key to preventing "environmental train wrecks."[32]

HCPs can allow incidental takes for any number of years.[33] The first HCP in the nation, prepared for San Bruno Mountain in 1983, expires after 30 years but can be revoked if the plan is not successfully implemented.[34] More recent plans are often valid for 50 to 100 years. For example, one 11.36-acre HCP, issued to a construction company in Florida to protect the bald eagle, eastern indigo snake, and two state-listed species, lasts for just under 100 years—and it is renewable.[35] Other

29. See H.R. Conf. Rep. No. 97-835, at. 29-30 (1982), reprinted in 1982 U.S.C.C.A.N. 2860.

30. See 16 U.S.C. § 1539(a)(2)(B)(iv).

31. See U.S. Fish and Wildlife Service, Endangered Species Habitat Conservation Planning (visited Oct. 24, 2000) <http://endangered.fws.gov/ hcp/index.html>.

32. Id.

33. See 65 Fed. Reg. 35242, 35255-56 (2000) (hereinafter HCP Handbook Addendum); U.S. Fish and Wildlife Service, Addendum to the Habitat Conservation Planning Handbook (visited Oct. 24, 2000) <http://endangered.fws.gov/hcp/addendum.html>.

34. See Beatley, supra note 4, at 32.

35. See National Wildlife Federation (hereinafter NWF), Regional Habitat Conservation Plan Summaries (visited Oct. 24, 2000) <http://www.nwf.org/nwf/endangered/hcp/plnsum.html>.

HCPs are for a much shorter duration. The one issued to Wal-Mart Stores, Inc. in Florida to protect the Florida scrub jay, eastern indigo snake, blue-tailed mole skink, and sand skink, lasted for one year without the possibility of renewal.[36] While permission to take listed species operates only for the time specified in the ITP, many land dedications or use restrictions are permanent.

The lack of HCP case law and the exploding number of HCPs is no indication of a consensus as to their usefulness in protecting the environment. If property-rights advocates express concerns over the operation of ESA Section 9, environmentalists often express concern over the substance of, and approval procedures for, HCPs. Among the charges leveled against the current HCP process are the lack of meaningful public participation; the lack of independent scientific involvement and assessment; inadequate mitigation measures; net loss of habitat; failure of plans to provide for species recovery; and inadequate funding for mitigation. These concerns are heightened when HCPs cover larger areas, multiple species, and unlisted species (for which data is generally less reliable), and when the HCP as written and as subject to the No Surprises rule leaves little room for flexibility.[37] Some of the criticisms are legal in nature and may result in court challenges and possible legislative changes. Others are purely policy arguments over whether HCPs truly conserve either habitats or species. In this chapter, we present primarily a guide to HCP law and regulations as they are currently applied, rather than an assessment of how well the system works.

C. Types of Habitat Conservation Plans

An HCP will usually fall within one of the following broad categories: individual single species, individual multi-species, regional single species, and regional multi-species. Small landowners, or others whose activities have a "negligible" impact on target species, have the opportunity to apply for a relatively new type of individual HCP, called a low-effect HCP.

C.1. Individual Habitat Conservation Plans

Individual HCPs are those developed by a single landowner. For example, the Simpson Timber Company has an HCP which was issued in 1992 and covers 380,000 acres of land in Northern California. Other ex-

---

36. See id.
37. See Tara Mueller, Guide to the Federal and California Endangered Species Laws 58 (1994). For further discussion of the No Surprises policy, see part E.3.d. of this chapter.

amples of individual HCPs include an HCP covering 0.5 acres, issued in 1994 to an individual landowner in Brevard County, Florida; an HCP covering 62 acres, issued in 1992 to the Lake Line Mall in Williamson County, Texas; and an HCP covering 30,000 acres, issued to the International Paper Company in Southern Alabama.[38]

Individual HCPs can encompass either single or multiple species. For example, the Simpson Timber Company HCP focuses on only one listed species, the northern spotted owl, while the Millacoma Tree Farm HCP covers not only the northern spotted owl, but also the listed peregrine falcon, western snowy plover, marbled murrelet, northern bald eagle, and Columbia white-tailed deer, plus twenty species that are candidates for listing.[39]

Plants

Protection of listed plant species must also be addressed during the HCP process. The ESA does not prohibit the take of listed plants on non-Federal lands unless the taking of those plants would otherwise violate state law. However, before the Service issues a permit, it must satisfy the jeopardy requirements of Section 7. Granting a Section 10 ITP, which requires approval of an HCP, is a federal action, which in turn is prohibited by Section 7 unless listed plant species are not jeopardized. To address this issue, an HCP must include and treat listed plant species just as it treats any listed animal species.[40]

C.2. Regional Habitat Conservation Plans

In contrast to individual HCPs, regional HCPs cover multiple parties. These parties can include private landowners, real estate developers, cities, and counties. For instance, the San Bruno Mountain HCP in northern California is designed to guide the development actions of private landowners, the County of San Mateo, and a number of surrounding cities.[41] The actual holders of the ITP are local governments; these parties in turn regulate the activities of all interested developers.[42]

---

38. *See* Lin, *supra* note 22, at 433. For more detail on the range of individual HCPs possible, *see id.; see also* NWF, *supra* note 35.

39. *See* NWF, *supra* note 35.

40. See HCP Handbook, supra note 21, at 3-17.

41. *See* Lindell L. Marsh & Robert D. Thornton, *The San Bruno Mountain Habitat*

C.2.a. Regional Single-Species Habitat Conservation Plans

Some regional HCPs, though they are binding on multiple parties, focus on only one listed species. In these situations, multiple parties convene to scientifically assess the needs of a single species. In accordance with the Section 10 ITP process, they propose incidental take levels and mitigation or enhancement measures. The Section 10 ITP application is not submitted until all participating parties agree on its terms.

Perhaps the most well-known regional single-species HCP is that for the K-rat in Riverside County in Southern California.[43] Since 1988, landowners, environmental groups, state and local governmental representatives, biological consultants, and other interested parties have been attempting to assemble a long-term K-rat HCP.[44] This process has been highly controversial and protracted.[45] FWS issued a interim short-term HCP for the K-rat in 1990,[46] and FWS approved a long-term HCP and granted an ITP for Riverside County covering an estimated 30,000 acres of occupied habitat in 1996.[47]

C.2.b. Regional Multi-Species Habitat Conservation Plans

Regional Multi-Species Habitat Conservation Plans (MSHCPs) are created by multiple parties and encompass numerous listed and unlisted species. Regional and other large-scale HCPs allow the permittee to address a broad range of activities and to bring them under the "umbrella" of the permit's legal protection. The claim made on behalf of MSHCPs is that they also allow analysis of a wider range of factors affecting listed species, can facilitate the flexibility needed to develop innovative mitigation programs, and can minimize the burden of ESA

Conservation Plan, in Managing Land Use Conflicts 114 (David J. Brower and Daniel S. Carol, eds., 1994).

42. *See* Beatley, *supra* note 4, at 61.

43. *See id.* at 128; Robert D. Thornton, *The Endangered Species Act: Searching for Consensus and Predictability: Habitat Conservation Planning Under the Endangered Species Act of 1973,* 21 Envtl. L. 605, 641 (1991).

44. *See* Beatley, *supra* note 4, at 130; *see, e.g.,* Mark Henry, *It's 1996 and Much Lies Ahead: From Budget Blues to Kangaroo Rats, in* The Press-Enterprise, Jan. 1, 1996, p. B1.

45. See, *e.g.,* Jack McCarthy, *Words All Unkind for Inland K-Rat Plan: Conferees Say, After 9 Years, It Hasn't Worked, in* The Press-Enterprise, Nov. 8, 1997, p. A1.

46. *See* Beatley, *supra* note 4, at 130.

47. National Center for Enviornmental Decision-Making Research, Case Studies—Habitat Conservation plans (visited Oct. 24, 2000) <http://www.ncedr.org/casestudies/hcp/western.html>.

compliance by replacing individual project review by the FWS or NMFS with a comprehensive, area-wide review.

Several MSHCPs have recently been developed for the natural eco-systems and species in San Diego, Los Angeles, Orange, Riverside, and San Bernardino Counties in California. These MSHCPs, created under California's Natural Community Conservation Program (NCCP), are claimed by advocates to represent the most comprehensive open-space and conservation partnerships in the United States.[48] Clark County, Nevada is developing a MSHCP for over 200 species in 13 different ecosystems, spread over 5 million acres.[49]

ESA Federalism—California's Natural Community Conservation Planning (NCCP)

An experiment in the administration of the ESA is underway in California. In cooperation with FWS, state and local govern-ments are developing and administering HCPs in Southern California covering the habitat of the threatened California gnat-catcher. The NCCP operates under a "special rule" issued by the Secretary that allows for take of the species during the prepara-tion process. Such a special rule could be issued in this case be-cause the California gnatcatcher is listed as threatened and not endangered.

For details see MICHAEL JASNY, NATURAL RESOURCES DEFENSE COUNCIL, LEAP OF FAITH (1997).

C.3. Low-Effect Habitat Conservation Plans

Low-effect HCPs are a relatively recent option for landowners who wish to apply for a Section 10 ITP. These plans are available for land uses or activities involving minor or negligible effect on listed species, their habitats, or other environmental resources.[50] Processing requirements for low-effect HCPs are simplified and expedited "to the maximum extent practicable and allowable by law," with a target approval time of three months after the completed Section 10(a) application is submitted to the

---

48. *See Babbitt Praises 'Monumental Conservation Achievement' in San Diego County*, U.S. Newswire, Oct. 23, 1997, *available in* 1997 WL 13913913 (Oct. 23, 1997).

49. *See* Keith Rogers, *Conservation Plan Allows Growth, Protects Wildlife*, Las Vegas Review-Journal, Nov. 17, 1997, at 1B.

50. *See* HCP Handbook, *supra* note 21, at 1-8.

FWS.[51] Low-effect HCPs can be more quickly processed in part because they do not require National Environmental Policy Act analysis.[52]

Though primarily intended to address the needs of small landowners for quicker processing and lower cost, low-effect HCPs have no maximum land area. The only requirement is that the proposed activity have minor or negligible effect on listed species, their habitats, or other environmental resources.

Size Distribution of HCPs*

Size of HCPs	Number of HCPs
Less than 1 acre	44
Between 1-10 acres	64
Between 10-100 acres	56
Between 100-500 acres	37
Between 500-1,000 acres	11
Between 1,000-10,000 acres	17
Between 10,000-100,000 acres	14
Between 100,000-500,000 acres	10
Between 500,000-1,000,000 acres	4
Greater than 1,000,000 acres	2

*as of December 31, 1999

For details see Fed. Reg. 35,242, 35,248 (June 1, 2000).

C.4. Recent Trends

In recent years the number of regional, multi-species HCPs has been increasing. For example, between 1982 and 1994, only three regional HCPs were developed.[53] Between 1994 and 1996, three more regional HCPs were developed and the FWS was considering approval of another

---

51. *FWS: Habitat Conservation Planning is Streamlined Under New Guidelines Announced by Two Services*, M2 Presswire, *available in* 1996 WL 11273915 (Sept. 17, 1996).

52. *See* United States Fish and Wildlife Service, *Habitat Conservation Plans and the Incidental Take Permitting Process* (visited Aug. 19, 1999) <http://www.fws.gov/r9endspp/hcp/ hcpplan.html>. For more information on NEPA and HCPs, see part D.2.d. of this chapter.

53. *See* Barton H. Thompson, Jr. *The Endangered Species Act: A Case Study in Takings and Incentives.* 49 Stan. L. Rev. 305, 318 (1997).

five.[54] Because regional MSHCPs are broad in scope and embody an ecosystem approach, the FWS has a general policy of encouraging the development of these large-scale plans.[55]

The average size of land area covered by HCPs appears to be growing. In 1995, most approved HCPs spanned 1,000 acres or less. However, by 1996, approximately 25 HCPs covered areas larger than 10,000 acres; approximately 25 covered areas larger than 100,000 acres; and 18 covered areas larger than 500,000 acres.[56] As of summer 200, 20 million acres are subject to HCPs across the nation.[57]

D. Processing Section 10 ITPs and the accompanying HCPs

Congress intended habitat conservation planning to be flexible and adaptable to the unique needs of individual species and ecosystems. While the specifics of each plan differ, the process by which HCPs are developed can be generalized for all plans.[58] In 1996, the Fish and Wildlife Service and the National Marine Fisheries Service developed an official *Habitat Conservation Planning Handbook* (HCP Handbook) which serves as a useful step-by-step guide to the habitat conservation planning process. Although the HCP Handbook was developed primarily for internal agency guidance, it is available for public evaluation and use.[59]

The HCP planning process consists of four phases: (i) the HCP development phase; (ii) the formal permit processing phase; (iii) the issuance phase; and (iv) the post-issuance phase. Although issuance is not considered a formal phase by the FWS and NMFS, we choose to separate it here to highlight the issuance criteria, and the fact that applicants may submit the Section 10 application several times before the ITP is issued. Each of the phases is discussed more fully on the pages that follow.

---

54. *See id.*

55. *See* HCP Handbook, *supra* note 21, at i; Lin, *supra* note 22, at 395.

56. *See* M2 Presswire, *supra* note 51; HCP Handbook, *supra* note 21, at i.

57. USFWS, Endangered Species Habitat Conservation Planning (visited Oct. 24, 2000) <http://endangered.fws.gov./hcp/index.html>.

58. *See* Beatley, *supra* note 4, at 20.

59. *See* HCP Handbook, *supra* note 21, at 1-1; the FWS augmented the HCP Handbook in June, 2000, *see* HCP Handbook Addendum, *supra* note 33.

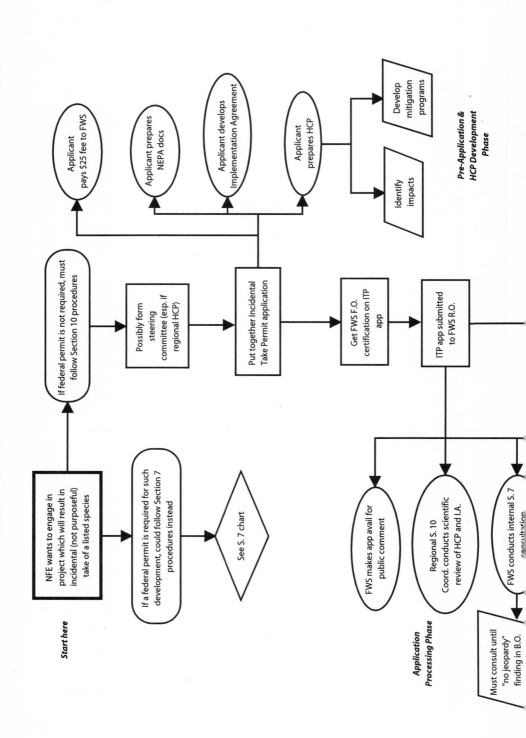

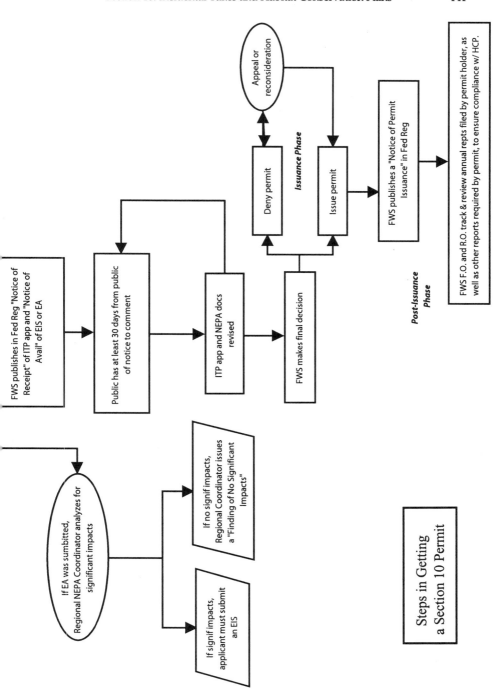

Steps in Getting
a Section 10 Permit

D.1. Habitat Conservation Plan Development Phase
D.1.a. Overview

Habitat conservation planning often begins when developers, local governments, and other resource users conclude that their operations may jeopardize listed species, or species for which listing appears imminent. For example, the Coachella Valley HCP was initiated in the mid-1980s largely because a development company, Sunrise Co., was concerned that its 433-acre, 1300-unit condominium project would jeopardize the threatened Coachella Valley fringe-toed lizard.[60] The official HCP Handbook states that the starting point for the Section 10 ITP process is a determination that a "take" is likely to occur during a proposed non-federal activity and a decision by the landowner or project proponent to apply for a Section 10 ITP.[61] To protect the listed species — and circumvent the potential for lawsuits or criminal prosecution under Section 9 — parties begin procedures necessary for a Section 10 ITP.

During the pre-application phase, the applicant must assess the impacts of the proposed project on endangered species, begin to develop mitigation programs, and assemble the necessary documents to file an application for a Section 10 ITP from the Service.[62]

D.1.b. Committees Formed During the HCP Development Phase

During the HCP development phase, a steering committee may be convened. The steering committee, composed of stakeholders such as landowners, environmentalists, real estate developers, and government officials, oversees the process of creating the HCP. The committee typically includes parties with diverse interests, and is often chaired by a party who is considered to be relatively neutral.[63] Steering committees are not legally required by the Act, and the formation of a steering committee depends entirely upon the desires of the applicants and the agencies.

Typically, steering committees are not used for Section 10 applications based on low-effect HCPs, or on individual (single landowner) HCPs. Where they are used, however, steering committees play a vital role in the HCP process. Steering committees are especially important in the development of regional multi-species HCPs.

---

60. *See* Beatley, *supra* note 4, at 75-76.
61. *See* HCP Handbook, *supra* note 21, at 1-4.
62. *See id.* at 1-5.
63. *See* Beatley, *supra* note 4, at 20.

In addition to a steering committee, a biological or technical committee is often convened in the HCP development phase. This committee designs and begins conducting necessary background studies for the HCP. The biological committee also provides scientific guidance to the steering committee when needed.[64]

Finally, a private consultant or firm is often hired to prepare the plan itself, and participate in the background studies.[65] This person or firm is involved in the entire process, and is responsible for producing the actual habitat conservation plan that is submitted to the Service along with the remainder of the Section 10 ITP application.[66]

D.1.c. Assessing a Project's Impacts on Endangered Species

During the HCP development phase, applicants must assess the project's impacts on endangered species. Ideally, scientifically assessing a project's impacts on endangered species for an HCP includes: (i) delineating the HCP boundaries or plan area; (ii) collecting and synthesizing biological data for species to be covered by the HCP; (iii) identifying activities proposed in the plan area that are likely to result in incidental take; and (iv) quantifying anticipated take levels.[67] Each of these steps can require months or years of study, and the outcomes can generate significant controversy and delay in processing of the HCP. For this reason, many HCPs fail to include crucial information about the biology of the species, the quality of the habitat, or the size of affected populations.

D.1.d. Developing and Initiating Mitigation Programs

One of the most important tasks to be undertaken during the HCP development phase is the development of mitigation measures for the species targeted in the HCP. The general standard for mitigation programs is that they must use "the best scientific and commercial data available."[68] Some broad types of mitigation strategies outlined in the HCP Handbook include: (1) avoiding the impact (to the extent practicable); (2) minimizing the impact; (3) rectifying the impact; (4) reducing or eliminating the impact over time; (5) and compensating for the impact by setting aside or creating new habitat.[69]

---

64. *See id.*
65. *See id.*
66. *See id.*
67. *See* HCP Handbook, *supra* note 21, at 3-10.
68. *Id.* at 3-20, 16 U.S.C. § 1539.
69. *See id.* at 3-19.

HCPs often feature more than one of these types of mitigation strategies. The HCP Handbook offers an illustration of the various strategies in a logging example. According to the Handbook, harm to the HCP's species of concern can be "(1) avoided by relocating project facilities within the project area; (2) minimized through timing restrictions and buffer zones; (3) rectified by restoration and revegetation of disturbed project areas; (4) reduced or eliminated over time by proper management, monitoring, and adaptive management; and (5) compensated by habitat restoration or protection at an onsite or offsite location."[70]

Mitigation for habitat loss, described by the FWS as option (5) above, is commonly found in HCPs. One way that HCPs can mitigate habitat loss is to authorize the acquisition of existing habitat.[71] For example, the Coachella Valley HCP for the fringe-toed lizard involved the outright acquisition of thousands of acres of lizard habitat as part of the habitat mitigation strategy. The short-term Eastern Riverside HCP for the K-rat provided that for each acre of occupied habitat lost outside of reserve sites, an acre of habitat within reserves had to be protected.[72] The proposed Metropolitan-Bakersfield HCP and Balcones Canyonlands Conservation Plans also include habitat acquisition as part of their mitigation.[73]

A second way to offset habitat loss is to protect existing habitat through conservation easements or other legal instruments.[74] For example, the proposed San Diego HCP for the songbird least Bell's vireo involves habitat buffers combined with local land use controls in riparian areas.[75] In an individual HCP issued to a company in Sacramento for the San Joaquin kit fox, Western burrowing owl, and California red-legged frog, an offsite mitigation area of 192 acres will be provided through conservation easement. As another example, the proposed Marina HCP in Southern California for the Smith's blue butterfly and involves land development restrictions.[76]

Third, HCPs can attempt to provide for the enhancement or restoration of former habitats.[77] For example, the San Bruno Mountain HCP, the

---

70. *Id.* at 3-20.

71. *See id.* at 3-22.

72. *See* Beatley, *supra* note 4, at 131.

73. *See id.* at 28; NWF, *supra* note 35.

74. *See* HCP Handbook, *supra* note 21, at 3-22.

75. *See* Beatley, *supra* note 4, at 122-127.

76. *See id.* at 30.

77. *See* HCP Handbook, *supra* note 21, at 3-22.

San Diego HCP and the Coachella Valley HCP discussed above all feature habitat restoration as part of their mitigation strategies.[78]

Fourth, HCPs can authorize the prescriptive management of habitats to achieve specific biological characteristics.[79] For example, the Red Oak Timber HCP for the red-cockaded woodpecker in Louisiana specified that the company create thirty artificial "cavity inserts" for the woodpeckers to nest in. As another example, the Clark County (Nevada) HCP for the Mojave Desert tortoise states that the permittee must build tortoise barriers along roads, among other mitigation measures.[80] And finally, HCPs can provide for the creation of new habitats.[81]

D.1.e. Monitoring Measures

The Federal Regulations for Section 10 of the Act also require that HCPs specify how the permit applicants plan to ensure that their HCP is functioning successfully.[82] Monitoring measures can include, for example, yearly reports to the FWS (as in the for the northern spotted owl), yearly submittal of maps which show all of the incidental takes under the plan (as in the Coachella Valley HCP for the desert fringe-toed lizard), or financial auditing conducted after the sale of mitigation "permits" (as in the Balcones Canyonlands MSHCP for the golden-cheeked warbler, brown pelican, bald eagle, peregrine falcon, whooping crane, piping plover, and several other species).[83] The HCP Handbook explains how monitoring measures should be developed and how the results of monitoring efforts should be reported.[84] The HCP Handbook Addendum clarifies the types of monitoring required for every HCP and provides flexible guidance on the customized development, implementation, reporting, and funding of an HCP monitoring program.[85]

---

78. See Beatley, *supra* note 4, at 28.
79. See HCP Handbook, *supra* note 21, at 3-22.
80. See NWF, *supra* note 35.
81. See HCP Handbook, *supra* note 21, at 3-22.
82. See 50 C.F.R. §§ 17.22(b)(1)(iii)(B); 222.22(b)(5)(iii).
83. See NWF, *supra* note 35.
84. See HCP Handbook, *supra* note 21, at 3-26 to 3-27, 6-25 to 6-26.
85. See HCP Handbook Addendum, *supra* note 33, at 35,253.

D.2. Permit Application Processing Phase
D.2.a. Overview

Once the Section 10 ITP application is submitted, the FWS or NMFS Regional Office reviews the documents and makes them available for public comment. In addition, the FWS or NMFS Regional Section 10 coordinator performs a scientific review of the HCP and draws up an Implementation Agreement.[86]

D.2.b. Implementation Agreements

The Implementation Agreement (IA), which is a document signed by the permit applicant and the Service, states exactly how the HCP will be implemented. FWS notes that IAs are not required for low-effect HCPs, but an IA may be developed if the permit applicant or the Service requests one.[87] The Service recommends IAs for regional and large-scale HCPs that address significant portions of a species range or involve numerous activities or landowners, for HCPs with long-term mitigation and monitoring programs, and for HCPs where habitat protection programs are complicated or have other special features.[88]

Implementation Agreements have been cited as important in assuring both the landowners and the Service that the provisions set forth in the HCP will be upheld. An IA is a contract that "defines the obligations, benefits, rights, authorities, liabilities, and privileges of all signatories and other parties to the HCP" and "specifies the responsibilities of the FWS, NMFS, or other state and Federal agencies in implementing or monitoring the HCP's conservation program."[89] Some observers believe that IAs are crucial in bolstering so-called "No Surprises" agreements between the FWS and permit applicants.[90] Similarly, an IA by its terms can legally bind landowners and their successors, as would be the case for an IA that grants a conservation easement in perpetuity.

D.2.c. Section 7 Consultation

During the permit application processing phase, the FWS must simultaneously conduct an internal (intra-agency) Section 7 consultation

---

86. *See* HCP Handbook, *supra* note 21, at 2-5.

87. *See id.* at 3-36.

88. *See id.*

89. *Id.* at 3-37. "No Surprises" is described in part E.3.d. of this chapter.

90. *See* Eric Fisher, *Habitat Conservation Planning Under the Endangered Species Act: No Surprises & the Quest for Certainty*, 67 U. Colo. L. Rev. 371 (1996).

between the FWS Regional Director and the FWS Ecological Services office. This internal consultation is necessary because Section 7 applies to any proposed federal action, and FWS issuance of a Section 10 ITP is such an action.[91]

D.2.d. National Environmental Policy Act (NEPA)

Because the issuance of an ITP constitutes federal agency action, the requirements of the National Environmental Policy Act (NEPA)[92] potentially apply to the permit application processing phase. NEPA has a very different function than the ESA. It is a procedural statute that requires consideration and disclosure of the environmental consequences of major federal actions significantly affecting the quality of the human environment. Unlike the ESA, NEPA does not mandate any particular outcome; it merely provides procedural safeguards and public participation to ensure the careful consideration of environmental impacts by agency decisionmaking.

The NEPA process can substantially impact the speed and complexity of the HCP planning, and may provide more opportunity for third-party involvement in the ITP permitting process than the ESA itself. It also can provide an additional legal hurdle for potential challengers of the ITP.

In processing an ITP, the Service must comply with NEPA in one of three ways. First, the Service may determine that the permitted activity constitutes the type of activity that will not cause any significant environmental impacts and is, therefore, "categorically excluded" under NEPA. For example, low-effect HCPs with negligible effects on federally listed and candidate species and their habitats may qualify for categorical exclusion.[93]

If the Service cannot conclude with certainty that an ITP will not have a significant impact, it must prepare an environmental assessment (EA). Based on the analysis in the EA, the Service may either (1) determine that the ITP will not have "significant" impacts on the species and issue and Finding of No Significant Impact (FONSI) or (2) conclude that the ITP may have significant environmental impacts and then prepare a more thorough analysis in the form of an environmental impact statement (EIS).

---

91. *See supra*, Chapter Three (Requirements for Federal Agencies).

92. 42 U.S.C. § 4321 *et. seq.*

93. *See* HCP Handbook, *supra* note 21, at 5-2.

As one moves along the continuum from categorical exclusion to EA to EIS, the detail, time, and expense of the required analysis increases, as does the opportunity for public participation in the process. Moreover, lawsuits challenging the Service's determination that an ITP is categorically excluded, or its decision to prepare an EA rather than a full-blown EIS, can increase costs substantially and allow potential challengers some increased legal leverage in negotiating concessions. Even where an EIS is prepared, challengers may be able to overturn a permit decision under NEPA by showing that the EIS is inadequate.

Agencies and applicants can avoid having to prepare a full EIS by relying on mitigation provided for in the HCP to make up for the impact of the applicant's proposed actions.[94] In the Ninth Circuit, mitigation does not even have to completely offset the impact in order for the Service to issue a FONSI.[95] Federal regulations state that mitigation of impacts to a less-than-significant level is sufficient to avoid EIS requirements.[96]

D.2.e. Public Notice and Participation

Once these processing steps have been satisfied, the FWS publishes in the Federal Register a "Notice of Receipt" of the Section 10 ITP application and a "Notice of Availability" of the EIS or EA. The public must have at least 30 days from publication of the notice to comment on the documents. In its HCP Handbook Addendum, FWS extends the minimum comment period to 60 days for most HCPs (low-effect HCPs, amendments, and individual permits issued under a programmatic HCP remain eligible for the shorter 30-day period), and up to 90 days for large-scale, regional or "exceptionally complex" HCPs.[97] FWS must consider the opinions of persons with expertise that is germane to the application.[98] The permit application and NEPA documents are then revised to incorporate public comments, and the FWS publishes an additional notice in the Federal Register, if necessary. Persons objecting to the application can request an advance warning that

94. See HCP Handbook, *supra* note 21, at 5-3.

95. See Friends of Endangered Species v. Jantzen, 760 F.2d 976, 987 (9th Cir. 1985), relying solely on ambiguous precedent in Preservation Coalition, Inc. v. Pierce, 667 F.2d 851, 860 (9th Cir. 1982).

96. See Forty Most Asked Questions concerning CEQ's National Environmental Policy Act, 46 Fed. Reg. 18,026, 18,038 (1981).

97. See HCP Handbook Addendum, supra note 21, at 35,256.
98. See 50 C.F.R. § 17.22(a)(2)(v).

the permit will issue if FWS plans to proceed with the permit contrary to the objections.[99]

D.3. Issuance

Although issuance is not considered a formal phase by the FWS and NMFS, it is included here to highlight the issuance criteria and to recognize that applicants may submit the Section 10 ITP application several times before it is issued. Often the central reason for a non-issuance decision from the FWS or NMFS is an inadequate HCP.

In its HCP Handbook, the Service has articulated the following criteria for issuance of an ITP.[100]

Scientific issuance requirements:

(i)   the HCP's mitigation is adequate for the take;

(ii) the mitigation is established before the take;

(iii) the preserves are biologically viable; and

(iv) there is no adverse modification of critical habitat and no "jeopardy."

Financial issuance requirements:

(i)   funding must be available for permit monitoring; and

(ii) funding must be available for perpetual management of preserves.

Legal issuance criteria:

(i)   the State has authority to charge fees;

(ii) local entities have authority to charge fees; and

(iii) local entities have authority to manage preserve lands.

D.4. Post-Issuance Phase

It should be noted, however, that the Service frequently faces the position that the HCP Handbook is not legally enforceable by third parties. Therefore, the ITP requirements set forth in Section 10 itself constitute the minimum legal issuance criteria.

---

99. *See id.* § 17.22(c).

100. *See* HCP Handbook, *supra* note 21, at 7-1 to 7-5.

D.4.a. Reconsideration and Appeals of Rejections

If a Section 10 ITP is not granted, an applicant can request reconsideration. This request must be in writing, signed by the applicant or a representative. If, after reconsideration, the FWS persists in its denial of the ITP, it must issue its denial in writing within 45 days of the request, state the reasons for denial, identify the evidence that supports the denial, and identify the appeal process to the applicant.[101]

HCPs are negotiated at the level of the field office and are approved at the level of the regional office. If a regional office disapproves of an HCP, an appeal can be made only to the regional office. Appeals will be considered by officials superior in rank to those who issued the denial.

Deal Killers

Any of the following will block the issuance of an ITP:

• The applicant has been convicted of a crime relevant to the activity for which the application is filed, if this indicates a lack of responsibility.

• The applicant lied or failed to disclose necessary information in the application.

• The applicant has failed to show "responsibility" or valid justification for the permit.

• Authorization would violate the "jeopardy" standard.

• The applicant is not qualified to conduct the proposed activities.

For details see 50 C.F.R. § 13.21 (1997).

Upon a second denial, applicants can appeal to the director of the regional office. A denial at this stage ends administrative options for the applicant, who would then have to go the courts. Court review asks only whether the administrative action was "arbitrary and capricious, an abuse of discretion, or otherwise not in accordance with law."[102]

Because reconsideration and appeals are handled at the same regional office that issued the original decision, it may be difficult to get a decision reversed. Applicants may want to revise their application at this time and resubmit, instead of appealing the decision. When an applica-

---

101. *See* 50 C.F.R. § 13.29(d) (1997); HCP Handbook, *supra* note 21, at 6-26 to 6-27.
102. Friends of Endangered Species, 760 F.2d at 981-985.

tion is revised, it becomes a new application, and the entire process begins anew.

The fact that administrative appeals are limited to the same regional level that rejected the original application, coupled with limited judicial review, suggests it is much more important to rely on communication with the agencies during the HCP negotiation process than to hope for a judicial reversal of an agency denial.

D.4.b. Changing an HCP—The Amendment Process

An HCP can be changed after the ITP has been issued. A minor change requires only minimal processing, while a major change requires the same procedures as an entirely new HCP.

Some examples of minor changes include correcting records of land ownership, making minor revisions to the survey, monitoring, or reporting protocols, or making minor corrections to reserve boundaries that result in no net loss of reserve land or do not otherwise alter the effectiveness of the HCP.[103] To be considered minor, a change must not result in a quantifiable change in net effect to the species. Presumably, however, a change resulting in net benefit to the species without a major restructuring of the plan would also be considered minor.

Even if it is made formally, an amendment will typically involve less in the way of documentation than a new application. For example, the NEPA analysis that is required for the amendment may draw upon the original NEPA analysis.

Alternatively, an HCP can be amended administratively, so long as:

- the permittee and the agency agree on the amendment;
- the changes constitute what the original HCP defines as "minor amendments";
- the original HCP establishes procedures for incorporating minor amendments;
- those procedures allow for public comment;
- the amendments are consistent with those procedures;
- a written record of the amendments is prepared; and
- the net effect on the species does not differ significantly from that of the original HCP.[104]

---

103. *See* HCP Handbook, *supra* note 21, at 3-33.
104. *See id.*

D.4.c. Legal Options for Outside Parties

One important advantage for a permittee in obtaining an HCP is that legal liability for violating the ESA is transferred from the permittee to the issuing agencies, so long as the permittee is in full compliance with the terms of the permit. This transfer of liability means that private parties cannot sue the permittee under the citizen-suit provision of the ESA. Rather, the primary option available to outside parties is a lawsuit against the agency challenging the ITP and HCP on its face or as it is being implemented. Unfortunately for potential challengers, wide discretion given to FWS and NMFS in the HCP process makes such lawsuits difficult.

A facial challenge to the ITP will usually be focused on the document's failure to meet the permitting criteria of 16 U.S.C. § 1539(a)(2)(B). Of these, the most important are the requirements that (1) the permittee "minimize and mitigate" the impacts of the take "to the maximum extent practicable," (2) the permitter ensure adequate funding for the HCP, and (3) the take will not appreciably reduce the likelihood of survival and recovery of the covered species (essentially, a "no jeopardy" finding). Two successful challenges to ITPs have begun to establish judicial precedent on what is required to satisfy these criteria.

In *Sierra Club v. Babbitt*, environmentalists successfully challenged the administrative record used to defend FWS approval of HCPs for the Alabama beach mouse.[105] The court ruled the administrative record did not show that the level of funding for off-site mitigation of the mouse habitat destroyed by the planned activity was sufficient to minimize the effect on the species to the maximum extent practicable, and that the reliance on speculative additional sources of funds was insufficient to make up for the deficiency in the HCP.[106]

In *National Wildlife Fed. v. Babbitt*,[107] the court invalidated an ITP based on the regional, multi-species Natomas Basin HCP. The court found that the plan failed to minimize and mitigate the take impacts to the maximum extent possible, failed to ensure adequate funding and failed to ensure the survival and recovery of listed species. The court also found that FWS violated NEPA by failing to prepare an EIS.

Sierra Club and *National Wildlife Fed.* suggests the requirement that applicants mitigate impacts to the maximum extent practicable is a standard sufficiently strong to persuade judges to overrule agency decisions. This may also be possible as more HCPs are developed,

---

105. 15 F. Supp.2d 1274 (S.D. Ala. 1998).

106. *See id*. at 1283-85.

107. Civ. S-99-274 DFL JFM, Aug. 15, 2000.

creating more opportunities to compare mitigation levels. Environmentalists may argue that stronger mitigation in similar HCPs shows that the "maximum extent practicable" standard was not meant; agency defendants would likely argue that the comparisons are inapt and distinguishable.

The other lesson outside parties may take from *Sierra Club* is that internal conflict within FWS or NMFS may be used in court to overrule an administrative decision. The judge in that case discusses how the FWS field office severely criticized the HCP proposal, and concludes the criticism was both correct and for the most part ignored by the agency's regional office when it approved the HCP.[108]

The NEPA process can also create legal options for outside parties,[109] and state environmental laws may create legal options not available at the federal level. For example, the environmental laws in Washington state, under the state's Landowner Landscape Plans, may give stakeholders, such as environmental groups, access to HCP planning negotiations, even though they have no such right under federal law.[110] State and local laws and regulations are not preempted by the federal permit.[111] Even if an action is permissible under the ESA, outside parties could use state or local regulation to block an action.

Finally, environmentalists may challenge HCP regulations as being facially invalid, attacking policies like the "jeopardy standard" for approving HCPs or the "No Surprises" rule[112] as violations of the ESA. A successful legal challenge to those regulations could drastically change the legal landscape.

D.4.d. Monitoring, Permit Violations, Suspensions, and Revocations

After the ITP is issued, FWS or NMFS regional and field offices are supposed to track and review annual reports filed by the permit holder, as well as other reports required by the permit, to ensure compliance with the permit conditions and the HCP.[113] One emerging issue in Section 10 implementation is whether the Service is actually fulfilling its oversight and monitoring obligations in this regard.

---

108. *See generally, id.*
109. *See* part D.2.d. of this chapter (NEPA).
110. Telephone interview with Sibyl Ackerman, National Wildlife Federation (Jan. 14, 1998).
111. *See* HCP Handbook, *supra* note 21, at 7-5.
112. *See* part E.3.a. of this chapter (Jeopardy Standard) and part E.3.d. of this chapter (No Surprises).
113. *See* HCP Handbook, *supra* note 21, at 6-31; 50 C.F.R. §§ 13.27-28 (1997).

Technical or unintentional violations of the HCP or IA provisions may (apparently at agency discretion) result in no more than the sending of a notice of non-compliance to the permit holder. Presumably, a correction of the violation will end the issue, while continuation could result in permit suspension or revocation. Defining what is technical or inadvertent is a matter of agency discretion.

Permit suspension and revocations can occur if a permittee does not comply with permit conditions or "applicable laws and regulations," or if a permittee fails to pay any fees owed to the government.[114] The difference between suspension and revocation appears to be at agency discretion. Revocations and appeals of revocations are handled administratively in the same manner as appeals of denials of the original HCPs at the regional office level.

With use of multi-party permits on the rise, enforcement between and among the parties makes implementation more complex. A multi-party permit may be violated by a single party if, for instance, multiple parties undertake obligations and then one party reneges (for example, a local government might fail to contribute to approve a development as promised). In this situation, in order to avoid permit violation, it is the responsibility of the non-reneging parties to force compliance by the reneging party or otherwise insure that the responsibilities of the reneging party are met. In litigation, such a case would likely turn on contractual interpretation of the IA to determine whether the non-reneging party(s) has a cause of action against the reneging party. One published case involved this scenario on the San Bruno Mountain. In particular, after a developer and a number of local government agencies negotiated and received an HCP, one government agency denied the developer's development in the form it had been described in the HCP. The judge did not reach a decision because he abstained to await a state court decision; however, the judge, in dicta, spoke about some of the issues in contract law terms.[115] Following the litigation, the parties undertook three years of further negotiations which resulted in a new, smaller development proposal, an amended HCP, and an enforceable agreement whereby the government agencies effectively guaranteed approval of the development.

The lesson at San Bruno Mountain and other places is that all parties to an HCP should ensure that the IA clearly defines the responsibilities, both in regards to the HCP and in regards to any related dealings, of each party. The negotiation phase is the best phase for avoiding

---

114. HCP Handbook, *supra* note 21, at 6-31.

115. *See* Southwest Diversified, Inc. v. City of Brisbane, 652 F. Supp. 788 (N.D. Cal. 1986).

confusion: parties can attempt to clarify their responsibilities and clearly delineate the circumstances that would qualify as violations. Where a local government entity is the permittee, it should also ensure that any obligation to issue development approval is expressly contingent on all parties' compliance with the conditions of a legally valid HCP.

E.   Habitat Conservation Plans in Practice: Issues and Conflicts

Habitat conservation planning typically demands considerable time, energy, financial resources, patience, and careful coordination of all parties involved. The process can be far from easy or expeditious. This section highlights some of the major points of conflict surrounding HCPs, including those related to the procedural, scientific, and legal aspects of the planning process.

E.1.   Procedural Conflicts related to Habitat Conservation Plans
E.1.a.   Delays

Among the most common criticisms developers raise against the Section 10 ITP application process is that it can take several years to complete.[116] For financial and other reasons, developers often want to go forward with their projects long before they receive approval from the FWS on their Section 10 ITP. There are numerous causes of delay, including the need for more scientific information, negotiation difficulties between different stakeholders, public controversy, and negotiators' schedules, as well as internal agency obstacles.[117] Environmentalists, it should be noted, may strategically use delay tactics in order to reach alternative solutions, improve the science being used, or in general, achieve a better result for the environment.

Delays Due to Scientific Uncertainty. One important cause of delay is scientific uncertainty, which typically persists throughout the HCP planning process. One survey of people involved in HCP planning found that insufficient biological knowledge was the most frequently cited cause of delay.[118] Sometimes scientific tests in preparation for HCPs take several months or years to complete. For example, the San Bruno HCP

116. *See* Lin, *supra* note 22, at 433; Thornton, *supra* note 43, at 606; Lindell L. Marsh, *Conservation Planning Under the Endangered Species Act: A New Paradigm for Conserving Biological Diversity,* 8 Tul. Envtl. L.J. 97, 110 (1994).

117. *See* Lin, *supra* note 22, at 398-408; Marsh, *supra* note 116, at 110; Thornton, *supra* note 43, at 648.

118. *See* Lin, *supra* note 22, at 398.

was not initiated until two years of biological studies had been performed.[119]

Even after tests are completed, scientific uncertainty can remain. This can slow down the process of HCP approval, especially when scientists hired by the developers disagree with scientists in environmental groups or universities, or scientists at the FWS or NMFS. When this kind of disagreement exists, delays can be caused by conflicts over issues such as habitat area, mitigation measures, and amount of projected take. At times, inaccurate science may prevail in the final draft of an HCP, to the detriment of the species.[120]

Multi-species HCPs can take an especially long time, often largely for scientific reasons. One of the reasons cited for the delay of the MSHCP is a lack of sufficient scientific information. One company, the Simpson Timber Company, decided to develop multiple single-species HCPs — instead of one multi-species HCP — because of scientific delays. It developed an HCP for the northern spotted owl in 1992 and delayed several years in creating HCPs for the marbled murrelet and other species for which more scientific information was needed. The Simpson Timber Company chose not to develop a multi-species HCP because the accompanying delay would have been "incompatible with the company's immediate harvesting needs."[121] At least with a spotted owl HCP, the company could harvest on one part of their property, while it waited for the other HCPs to be completed.[122]

In its HCP Handbook Addendum, the Service encourages use of adoptive management in HCPs as a tool for addressing scientific uncertainty with more efficiency and effectiveness.[123]

Delays Due to Conflicts in Negotiations. As mentioned in section D.1.b, above, steering committees are often composed of representatives of diverse and conflicting community interests. Especially if the committee decides to make decisions by consensus, negotiations can become protracted and contentious.[124] However, this kind of decision-making approach ultimately may be crucial in easing tensions and overcoming the initial level of distrust and conflict inherent in this type of collaborative project.[125]

---

119. *See* Thornton, *supra* note 43, at 650.

120. *See* discussion *infra* part E.2.b.

121. Lin, *supra* note 22, at 399.

122. *See id.*

123. *See* HCP Handbook Addendum, supra notes 33, at 35,252.

124. *See id.* at 401; Thornton, *supra* note 43, at 631.

125. *See* Lin, *supra* note 22, at 401.

Even when a steering committee succeeds in agreeing on certain provisions, the plans can be blocked by parties outside the steering committee. For example, one observer, Albert Lin, recounts a major setback in the proposed Balcones Canyonlands regional HCP in Texas. After the steering committee decided to issue a bond to finance the comprehensive regional HCP, the bond issue was blocked by an unusual coalition of builders, landowners, environmentalists, and grassroots activists.[126]

However, if the committee decides to vote by majority, then the decision-making process can be stalled by bad science, which might result from vote-trading or from ignoring minority views. If minority views happen to be more scientifically accurate than the views of the majority, the FWS might reject the HCP based on inadequate scientific information, and further delay the Section 10 process. Lin tells of one HCP in Utah, in progress since 1990, which had been rejected by the FWS twice, primarily because the steering committee had not adequately considered biological information.[127]

Another observer, Robert Thornton—who was involved in the development of the San Bruno Mountain HCP—points out that one way of expediting steering committee negotiations is for the committee to adopt a memorandum of understanding. This memorandum would reflect the primary purposes of the negotiation process, the HCP's goals, and the committee's goals and procedures. The steering committee for the Kern County, California, HCP developed such a memorandum.[128] Thornton states that

> [u]nless there is a written understanding at the beginning of the process setting forth what the parties intend to achieve, there is a considerable risk that the effort will fail. Inevitably, the individual representatives of parties to the HCP process will change during the course of the effort. A written understanding of the HCP's objectives is critical to maintaining cohesiveness throughout these changes and to the endeavor's success.[129]

The failure of key parties to negotiate can stall the HCP process by introducing ambiguity, limiting options, and reducing the resources available for the HCP.[130] Should those parties choose to join later—or worse yet, try to obstruct the process—more delay and protracted dis-

---

126. See id.
127. See id. at 401-02.
128. See Thornton, supra note 43, at 631.
129. Id.
130. See Lin, supra note 22, at 407.

cussions would result. In other cases, an HCP simply cannot go forward without the participation of certain parties, and the other participating parties have to wait and renegotiate until the hesitant parties finally decide to join. In the Clark County (Nevada) HCP for the desert tortoise, for example, six cities containing desert tortoise habitat did not participate in the process, delaying HCP development.[131] Another potential source of delay is a local government decision to renegotiate the HCP, even after approval by the FWS or NMFS. Failure to involve the appropriate tribal governments in a timely manner could also delay or jeopardize an HCP. In the HCP Handbook Addendum, FWS recommends timely involvement of affected Native American Tribes during HCP development. If an applicant chooses to ignore this advice, the FWS will consult with the affected Tribes and "advocate the incorporation of measures that will conserve, restore, or enhance Tribal trust resources."[132]

Delays Due to Public Controversy. Still another source of delay is public controversy. Public opinions span the spectrum of views with regard to the tension between endangered species protection and real estate development or resource use. Public controversy, involving members from all sides of the endangered species debate, has stalled HCP development processes across the country.

Because regional HCPs tend to affect large numbers of people over a vast area, these HCPs often are beleaguered with public controversy. One vivid example of this is the Riverside County (CA) habitat conservation planning process for the K-rat, which took nearly a decade to complete and has been subject to ongoing litigation.[133] The K-rat HCP planning process takes place in one of the "last undeveloped segments of the Los Angeles metropolitan area, and the area has been receiving substantial growth pressures in recent years."[134] The Riverside County Habitat Conservation Agency, which manages the K-rat HCP planning process, is composed of nine governmental representatives in the County, including the County itself. A profile of the K-rat conservation plan appears in the box on page 159.

One newspaper article published on January 1, 1996 encapsulates the difficulty of the K-rat HCP process, as seen from the pro-development perspective:

> Frustration over the K-rat has led to a near-revolt against the
> Endangered Species Act. The county has tried to protect the

---

131. *See* Beatley, *supra* note 4, at 134.

132. *See* HCP Handbook Addendum, supra note 21, at 35,256.

133. *See id.* at 128; Henry, *supra* note 44.

134. Beatley, *supra* note 4, at 128.

animal, but, after years of debate and millions of dollars, officials are fed up and demand closure on the divisive issue, which has tied up the development of private property in western Riverside County.[135]

The plan that the HCP planning committee chose ended up costing an additional $1.1 million in litigation involving fourteen lawsuits. The money came from mitigation fees that were supposed to be directed towards habitat development and other mitigation measures.[136]

Another example is the regional multi-species Metropolitan-Bakersfield HCP, which took three years of planning, and another four years to go from draft to approval. Albert Lin described the delay in his survey of HCP experiences:

> The agreement on the draft HCP was particularly fragile because of public controversy, and the attempts of some parties to change the agreement resulted in charges of lack of good faith, which snowballed into poor communication and refusal to communicate between the applicants, affected interests, and state and federal agencies. The communication difficulties were exacerbated when some parties undertook unilateral negotiations without the participation of other key actors, arousing resentment and creating further delay.[137]

Delays Due to Procedural Requirements of Other Laws. According to the Fish and Wildlife Service, the factor most likely to extend the processing time of an HCP after it has been submitted is the level of analysis required under the National Environmental Policy Act (NEPA).[138] The length of time depends on whether an Environmental Impact Statement, Environmental Assessment (EA), or a categorical exclusion is appropriate.[139] A low-effect HCP is categorically excluded from NEPA analysis and has a target processing time of 3 months; an EA has a target of 3-5 months; and an EIS of less than 10 months.[140]

NEPA preparation differs from HCP preparation in that the agency and not the applicant is responsible for preparing the relevant docu-

---

135. Henry, *supra* note 44.

136. *See* McCarthy, *supra* note 45.

137. Lin, *supra* note 22, at 400.

138. For more information on NEPA, see part D.2.d. of this chapter.

139. *See* U.S. Fish & Wildlife Serv., *Habitat Conservation Plans and the Incidental Take Permitting Process* (visited Oct. 24, 2000) <http://www.fws.gov/r9endspp/hcp/hcpplan.html>.

140. *See id.*

mentation. However, an applicant may, within certain limitations, prepare draft Environmental Assessment analyses in order to speed the
process. This can benefit the applicant and the government by expediting
the application process and issuance of the permit. When this is done, the

Basics of an HCP: Stephen's Kangaroo Rat Long-Term Conservation Plan, Riverside County, California

PERMIT NUMBER: #805414

PERMIT ISSUED: 5/3/96

REGION: 1

FWS FIELD OFFICE: Carlsbad

STATE: CA

COUNTY: Riverside

PERMITTEE: Riverside County Habitat Conservation
Agency, Cities of Moreno Valley, Lake Elsinore, Riverside, Hent,
Perris, Corona, Murrieta, and Temecula.

PERMITTED SPECIES: Stephens' Kangaroo Rat

LISTED SPECIES THAT HCP PURPORTS TO COVER: Stephens'
Kangaroo Rat

SPECIES OF CONCERN THAT HCP PURPORTS TO COVER:
None

DATE ASSISTANCE INITIATED: 1995

SIZE: 533,954 acres (30,000 acres occupied by Stephens'
Kangaroo Rat).

DURATION 30 years.

RENEWABLE? Yes

NO SURPRISES? Yes

SAFE HARBOR AGREEMENT? No

10(a)(2)(A) HCP MANDATORY SPECIFICS: (i) Impact which
will likely result from such taking: Over 50% of Stephens'
Kangaroo Rat habitat will be destroyed.

For summaries of HCPs, see <http://www.nwf.org/
smartgrowth/learnhcp.html>. *For details of all HCPs to date, see*
<http://www.fws.gov/r9endspp/hcp/hcptable.pdf>.

Service will: (1) provide the preparer with appropriate guidance concerning document preparation; and (2) review the document within 30

days and take ultimate responsibility for its scope, adequacy, and content.[141]

Delays Due to FWS. In some cases, developers accuse the Fish and Wildlife Service of delaying the HCP planning process. Among the major concerns are: understaffing of the FWS and staff turnover, multiple rejections of draft HCPs by the FWS field office, and inadequate FWS guidance in the development of the HCP.[142] These types of delays can be a major source of frustration. One HCP planner described his experience with the FWS as follows: "Fish and Wildlife tell us that they are responsible for enforcing the ESA. But then they won't tell us what they want. They want us to come up with the plan and then they'll say if they like it."[143] Developers may also find that proposed HCPs that attempt to commit the bare minimum in environmental protection are the plans that are most likely to be delayed.

E.1.b. Costs

Section 10 of the ESA expressly requires that HCPs demonstrate adequate funding of planned mitigation before receiving approval.[144] Because some HCPs anticipate significant land acquisition or perpetual management of preserve lands, or both, the funding obligation can be significant. The only two court decisions overturning an HCP approval turned, in part, on the issue of adequate mitigation funding.

There are additional cost issues as well, such as the costs of developing the HCP and acquiring necessary scientific information. Cost distribution may be of primary interest to some parties and be subject to intense negotiation.

Lack of money to initiate planning, as well as disputes among negotiating parties over how mitigation measures will be funded, can also be barriers to the development of an HCP.

For the applicant, the cost of developing an HCP can vary widely. Depending on the nature and amount of assistance provided by the local FWS office, a small landowner wanting to build a single house on a lot with endangered species habitat may expend several hundred or several thousand dollars for legal and technical advice. Developing larger HCPs can cost in excess of several hundred thousand dollars.

---

141. *See id.*
142. *See* Lin, *supra* note 22, at 400, 402-404.
143. *Id.* at 404.
144. *See* 16 U.S.C. § 1539(a)(2)(A)(ii).

Implementation costs may appear relatively low at the individual level. For the individual developer participating in a countywide HCP, such costs, which are generally passed on to new home buyers, have ranged from $250 to $5,500 per acre.[145] However, total implementation costs can add up and become a focus of dispute and delay. The cost of establishing land preserves under the Coachella Valley HCP, which does not include planning costs, totaled an estimated $25 million, and other HCPs may ultimately cost far more.[146]

The Service will not issue a permit unless the applicant clearly has the financial capability to carry out mitigation measures described in the plan.[147] The Service is especially likely to scrutinize finances when the species take will occur before the mitigation. Finances are also important as potential deal-breakers when there are multiple parties negotiating the plan and when mitigation or monitoring must be long-term or permanent.

When the plan envisions mitigation happening before the take, concern over finances become less crucial. An example of this would be relocating an affected species prior to beginning the development activities. The Service will instead condition the permit on completion of the mitigation. Financial inability to carry out the mitigation will automatically eliminate the ability to use the permit.

The more common kind of plan has mitigation and monitoring activities that extend after the take has occurred. Some need perpetual funding mechanisms to support long-term management of mitigation plans or monitoring.[148]

In some cases where the developer proposes mitigation to occur after take of the species, the best way to avoid rejection of proposed plans because of financial weaknesses is for the applicant to provide letters of credit controlled by the government until the mitigation activities have been carried out. For other plans, typically smaller plans, the mitigation problem is solved with a cash payment into a mitigation fund prior to commencement of the plan activities.

Another type of financial problem for applicants is demonstrating the ability to fund solutions to long-term problems created by the increased development and human contact with habitat. Some successful

145. See Beatley, *supra* note 4, at 39.

146. See id. at 94, 206 (low figure); Travis County Transportation and Natural Resources, (*Balcones Canyonlands Conservation Plan* (visited Aug. 19, 1999) <http://www.co.travis.tx.us/tnr/bccp/> (high figure).

147. See part E.4. of this chapter.

148. See HCP Handbook, *supra* note 21, at 3-34.

permits provide funding to control predators or competitors of listed species, to address nuisance or exotic vegetation pollution, and to educate and inform the local community about the listed species.[149] The flagship San Bruno HCP has a funding mechanism for controlling invasive, non-native weeds.[150]

According to the HCP Handbook, an HCP or its Implementation Agreement cannot contractually commit the federal government to expending resources without stating the expense is subject to the Anti-Deficiency Act,[151] which states that the government can only expend appropriated funds.[152] In other words, the FWS and other federal agencies cannot commit to future expenditures or support for which funds are not already available; they can only commit to make the expenditure if future Congresses provide the money. This requirement applies to all federal discretionary spending, including HCPs.[153]

A favored method for funding perpetual mitigation and monitoring is through payment of development fees into an interest-bearing account, and using only the interest and not the principal to fund the program.[154] A theoretical problem with requiring the payment of development fees, or, by extension, with other restrictions on the use of land due to the ESA restrictions on taking species, is that such restrictions may constitute a regulatory taking of the land which is prohibited without compensation.[155]

Struggles over which party will pay what share of the costs of an HCP can substantially delay HCPs in the pre-application phase as parties negotiate with each other and as representatives wait either for approval for commitments they have made, or for authority to negotiate further.

Substantial delays can also result from the requirement for adequate funding of the HCP. An agency may, in the pre-application phase, inform the parties that they need more funding or more reliable funding for what they propose, delaying the HCP as the parties negotiate that issue. Alternatively, an HCP submitted for approval may be rejected by the agency regional office because of inadequate funding, resulting in more delay as the HCP is renegotiated and resubmitted.

---

149. *See id.* at 3-17.
150. *See* Friends of Endangered Species, 760 F.2d at 979.
151. HCP Handbook, *supra* note 21, at 3-34.
152. *See generally,* Anti-Deficiency Act, 31 U.S.C. § 1341.
153. *See id.*
154. *See id.* at 3-35.
155. *See generally,* Thompson, *supra* note 53. *See also,* part E.3.b. of this chapter (Takings of Property Challenges); section F.1. of Chapter Four (Takes and Due Process Rights).

E.2.   Scientific Issues Related to Habitat Conservation Plans
E.2.a. Background

Inadequate scientific information can delay HCP approval and forms the basis of controversy over whether HCPs truly provide adequate protection for listed species. As discussed above, the need to collect more scientific information for a particular HCP can often cause delay and much frustration for property owners and others involved in the planning. Still, the alternative to performing more scientific studies — approving a habitat conservation plan without adequate science — can prove disastrous for an endangered species.

The initial assessment of the first comprehensive study of the scientific integrity of approved HCPs (the Kareiva study) was completed in 1997.[156] The study collected 206 HCPs from various FWS offices and other sources. After reviewing all 206, the reviewers chose 44 HCPs to study in-depth.[157] The scientists analyzed the plans' scientific design only, not their implementation or enforcement.[158]

E.2.b. Scientific Findings of In-Depth Study

The results of the study show that authors of HCPs in general tend to make good use of existing scientific data, but are significantly hampered when little scientific data exists prior to the beginning of an HCP development effort.[159]

On the positive side, the study found that two-thirds of the plans "reliably determined a population's health before implementation."[160] In addition, about half of the plans "made a reasonable guess as to the harm the landowners would cause species," though the study did not evaluate what happened in actuality. And, about half of the HCPs evaluated adequately assessed "primary threats, such as habitat loss" to the target species.[161]

On the negative side, the study showed that "nearly two-thirds of the studies were deemed 'insufficient' in determining how the actions allowed by an HCP would affect species' viability as a whole, rather than

---

156. Carol Kaesuk Yoon, *Many Habitat Conservation Plans Found to Lack Key Data*, The N.Y. Times, Dec. 23, 1997, at F3.

157. *See* National Center for Ecological Analysis and Synthesis, *National Center for Ecological Analysis and Synthesis* (visited Aug. 19, 1999) <http://www.nceas.ucsb.edu>.

158. *See* Charles Mann & Mark Plummer, Noah's Choice: The Future of the Endangered Species Act 243 (1995).

159. *See generally, id.*

160. *See id.*

161. *Id.*

merely the local population in the plan."[162] Moreover, 60 percent of the HCPs were either inadequate or unclear as to monitoring, because either the plans "were poorly crafted," or the scientists "couldn't tell from the documents whether the monitoring was sufficient." In addition, poor understanding of the natural history of target species was prevalent in many HCPs.[163] The study leader says, "For a large portion of these plans, maybe half of them, they lack the data to do anything remotely scientific. . . . If you don't know this basic biology, it's sort of a delusion to think you're doing anything to help these species."[164]

Among the most disturbing findings related to two Utah prairie dog HCPs, which featured management strategies that were known, by scientific consensus, to cause actual harm to the species.[165] In these HCPs, property owners were permitted to build on prairie dog habitat if they relocated the animals to public land. However, the study points out, "it has long been scientifically established that relocation fails—only 3 percent of prairie dogs survive such a move. Still, FWS approved the plans because relocation was the agency's own strategy for recovering the species."[166] In some other HCPs, it appeared that virtually no accurate science was utilized in creating mitigation strategies and assessing the impacts of the development on the target species.[167]

The scientists also found some interesting relationships between scientific accuracy and size of the HCP. They determined that "medium-sized HCPs—not the largest ones, which generally are the most elaborately prepared—appeared to have the best scientific grounding." And, "the science underlying multi-species plans seemed as sound as that behind single-species ones," despite the greater complexity of multi-species plans.[168]

E.2.c. Standard of Review for Scientific Methodology

The exact standard of review for HCP scientific methodology is unknown. One of the few HCP-related cases, *Friends of Endangered Species*

---

162. *Id.*
163. *Id.*
164. Leslie Brown, *Study Finds Habitat Plans Lacking; Timber-Cutting Accords Often are Based on Little or No Science, Review Says*, The News Tribune, Dec. 23, 1997, at B4.
165. *See* Charles Mann & Mark Plummer, *Qualified Thumbs Up for Habitat Plan Science*, SCIENCE, Dec. 17, 1997, at 2053.
166. *Id.*
167. *See id.*
168. *Id.*

v. Jantzen,[169] establishes a level of scientific methodology that can withstand legal challenge. In this case, an environmental group sued the FWS, claiming that the permit issuance violated Sections 7 and 10 of the ESA because it jeopardized the continued existence of the mission blue butterfly. The Court upheld FWS approval of the HCP, largely because of its perception of the credibility of the scientific studies conducted in preparation for the plan. Thus, science of similar-level quality in other HCPs would also likely survive judicial scrutiny.

There is no clear case law delineating what scientific methodology is not good enough. The two cases that have found an HCP to be legally inadequate have both focused on the lack of an adequate funding mechanism, not the HCPs use of science.[170] Thus, it remains to be seen where the courts will set the bar for review of an HCP's scientific methodology, but it is likely to be quite high under the applicable "arbitrary and capricious" standard.

Relatedly, while the Service has never been found to err in using bad science to reject an HCP proposal, it has been found to have erred in accepting an HCP with insufficient mitigation.[171] The quality of science used in determining proper mitigation may become a significant issue in the future.

Establishing error in the scientific procedure behind an agency action can be potentially disastrous for large-scale HCPs. In *Endangered Species Committee v. Babbitt*,[172] the District Court of the District of Columbia found procedural error in an agency refusal to obtain and publish raw data used in a disputed scientific report. The normal remedy for such error would be to remove the species' threatened listing pending completion of proper procedure; however, such a remedy would have unraveled the regulatory underpinning of California's Natural Community Conservation Program and created turmoil in Southern California land use planning. The Court chose to leave the species' listing, and therefore the HCP requirements, in place pending resolution of the procedural error.[173]

---

169. 596 F. Supp. 518 (N.D. Cal. 1984), *aff'd*, 760 F.2d 976, 982 (9th Cir. 1985).

170. *See* part D.4.c. of this chapter (Legal Options).

171. *See* part D.4.c. of this chapter (Legal Options).

172. 852 F. Supp. 32, 37 (D.D.C. 1994).

173. *See id.* at 41. *See also* City of Las Vegas v. Lujan, 891 F.2d 927 (D.C. Cir. 1989) (preserving an emergency listing decision concerning the desert tortoise awaiting correction of procedural error).

E.3. Legal Issues Related to Habitat Conservation Plans
E.3.a. Jeopardy Standard versus Recovery Standard for Approving HCPs

FWS maintains that it prefers HCPs to promote the recovery of a species, but that it is not required by Section 10 to do more than assure survival of the species.[174] This could mean any plan that does not jeopardize a species' existence is permissible, and even that HCPs inconsistent with recovery plan objectives are permissible, although "discouraged."[175] Environmental groups have consistently rejected this interpretation.[176]

A lawsuit to mandate that HCPs meet a recovery standard remains a possibility. If such a suit were successful, HCPs may have to become consistent with recovery plans, and no Section 10 ITPs could be issued for species that do not have recovery plans.[177] Alternatively, HCPs might be required to result in a net benefit to the species in question.

E.3.b. Takings of Property Challenges

As the use of Sections 9 and 10 has grown in the last decade, an active public and scholarly debate has emerged over whether the ESA is vulnerable in some situations to Constitutional "takings" challenges under the 5th and 14th Amendments.[178] Under the takings clause, "Private property [shall not] be taken for public use without just compensation."[179]

Although there is no judicial precedent for property owners to win a takings challenge to ESA regulation under Section 9, at least one observer believes that takings jurisprudence may influence habitat conservation planning at the margin.[180] In an attempt to escape a possible takings challenge, HCPs may be altered. For example, under *Lucas v. South Carolina Coastal Council*,[181] if a regional HCP requires habitat to be purchased and converted to a land preserve, the "best" habitat scenario for the species (for instance, large and continuous tracts of land) might be at odds with the need to avoid depriving particular landowners of all eco-

---

174. *See* HCP Handbook, *supra* note 21, at 3-20.

175. *See id.*

176. *See, e.g.,* Michael Jasny, Natural Resources Defense Council, Leap of Faith 34 (1997).

177. Telephone interview with Sybil Ackerman, National Wildlife Federation (Portland, Oregon) (Jan. 14, 1998).

178. *See* section F.1. of Chapter Four (Takes and Due Process).

179. U.S. Const. amend. V.

180. *See* Thompson, *supra* note 53, at 338. *See also,* section F.1. of Chapter Four.

181. 505 U.S. 1003 (1992).

nomically viable use of their lands. Other case law might require altering a scheme of development fees such that the fees must be "proportional" to the harm that the development inflicts on the target species.[182] Such changes might become particularly problematic in regional, multi-species HCPs if the fees for development are assessed asymmetrically on different parties or groups, according to their relative impact.

E.3.c. Assurances: The "Safe Harbor" Policy

According to a 1997 study, the highest concentrations of endangered and threatened species in the United States occur on private lands.[183] Many ecologists believe that successful preservation of these species relies on preserving their habitats. To address this concern, the Clinton Administration developed a "Safe Harbor" policy[184] that is designed to encourage landowners to take voluntary actions to protect or enhance populations of endangered species on their property. The policy is implemented throughout the development of Safe Harbor agreements between the Service and private landowners. Under such an agreement, a landowner voluntarily agrees to alter his property to benefit or attract endangered species in exchange for the assurance that FWS or NMFS will permit future takes above a pre-determined baseline. The FWS and NMFS, in their HCP Planning Handbook, explain that the purpose of the Safe Harbor approach is to "reduce the disincentives (for example, fear of regulatory restrictions) that often cause landowners to avoid or prevent land use practices that would otherwise benefit endangered species."[185]

Sections 9 and 10 only state that private landowners cannot take listed species without mitigation; they do not impose an affirmative duty to enhance or restore habitat or endangered populations if no take is presently occurring. This means that if landowners do not voluntarily enhance or restore their property to attract listed species, they are not violating any part of the Act. Without the Safe Harbor provision, therefore, landowners would have few economic incentives to voluntarily create habitat for endangered species. In fact, without a Safe Harbor provision, many landowners consider it undesirable to encourage listed species to colonize their land, because of concern that the Section 9 prohibi-

182. See Thompson, supra note 53, at 338.

183. See U.S. General Accounting Office, supra note 1.

184. 64 Fed. Reg. 32706 (June 17, 1999). The final Safe Harbor policy relies upon the "enhancement of survival" provisions of 16 U.S.C. § 1539(a)(1)(A), rather than the HCP provisions of 16 U.S.C. § 1539(a)(1)(B), but the two are closely related.

185. HCP Handbook, supra note 21, at 3-41.

tion on take would actually bring further restrictions on their use of their property.

Safe Harbor agreements are available to all landowners—a landowner need not have a Section 10 ITP to have a Safe Harbor agreement. Similarly, not all Section 10 ITPs include Safe Harbor agreements.

Candidate Conservation Agreements

In June, 1997, FWS and NMFS proposed a policy and regulations for Candidate Conservation Agreements (CCAs). The CCA policy can be regarded as a cousin to the Safe Harbor policy: its goal is to protect unlisted species by providing incentives for non-federal landowners and land managing agencies to restore, enhance, or maintain habitats for those species.

Under the final policy for CCAs, FWS or NMFS assist participating property owners in developing CCAs, and assure those landowners that if the covered species are eventually listed, they will not be required to more than they agreed to in the CCA.

CCAs are intended to encourage landowners to manage their property in such a way that, if such management were adopted on a broad scale by similarly situated landowners, threats to species would be removed, with the result that there would be no need to list those species as threatened or endangered under the ESA. Readers should consult the Federal Register for the current status of the CCA proposal.

For details see Safe Harbor Agreements and Candidate Conservation Agreements With Assurances, 64 F.R. 32706 (1999) (50 C.F.R. § 13.23 et seq. & § 17.22 et seq.)

Some environmentalists are concerned about how Safe Harbor and HCP agreements may interact. One concern is that the possibly temporary protection afforded by Safe Harbor agreements may give a false sense of security and justify too much habitat loss through HCPs.[186] Another concern, sometimes called "double dipping," involves combining HCPs with Safe Harbor agreements.[187] This setup raises the question whether a landowner should be able to use the lower baseline created by

---

186. *See* Mary Minette & Tim Cullinan, A Citizen's Guide to Habitat Conservation Plans (1997) at 26-27.
187. *See* Mueller, *supra* note 35.

the take allowed under the HCP, rather than having to enhance the habitat above the pre-HCP baseline before gaining the benefits of Safe Harbor.[188] Finally, it would be inappropriate for FWS to consider a landowner's offer of a Safe Harbor as a factor when deciding whether to approve an HCP, as the potential mitigation benefits could disappear at any time.

E.3.d. Assurances: The "No Surprises" Rule

The "No Surprises" policy of the Service says that if unforeseen circumstances occur that make the commitments of the permit holder appear to be insufficient to protect the listed species, the permittee will not be required to commit additional land or monies beyond what was negotiated.[189] The Service may not seek additional mitigation of land under these "unforeseen circumstances,"[190] unless any such additional mitigation will be compensated for by the government. Note that under unforeseen conditions, it is possible that different actions will be required of the permittee, so long as the permittee is not required to set aside additional land for preservation or pay additional funds for conservation.[191]

The No Surprises policy also applies to unlisted species when they are treated in the HCP as if they were listed species and where the conditions for the listed species would have satisfied Section 10 criteria if the species had been listed.[192]

Despite the fact that the government is required to compensate for additional mitigation measures under "unforeseen circumstances," the landowners avoid any requirements to act not covered by the HCP. The agencies bear the burden of proof to show that unforeseen circumstances exist, which is primarily determined by the level of biological peril to species covered by the HCP in question and the degree to which the welfare of the species is tied to a particular HCP. An HCP covering an ecologically insignificant portion of a species' range might not be covered by unforeseen circumstances.[193]

No Surprises applies to all Section 10 ITPs issued on or after March 25, 1998.[194] ITPs issued before that date must rely on assurances provided

---

188. *See* Minette & Cullinan, *supra* note 186, at 27.
189. 50 C.F.R. §§ 17.22(b)(5-6); 17.32(b)(5-6); 222.22(g-h).
190. *Id.*
191. *See* HCP Handbook, *supra* note 21, at 3-30.
192. *See id.*
193. *See id.* at 31.
194. 50 CFR §§ 17.22(b)(5); 17.32(b)(5); and 222.22(g).

in the specific ITPs themselves, if any were made.[195] As in all other permissions created by the Section 10 ITP, No Surprises only applies to species covered by the HCP, so if a different endangered species is found on the property and was not included in the HCP, the No Surprises policy would not prevent the Service from requiring additional measures to prevent take of this different species.

No Surprises is supposed to apply to unforeseen circumstances, with foreseeable, changed circumstances to be accounted for in the HCP. This raises the question of what results when a circumstance occurs that was not described in the HCP but was demonstrably foreseeable. Environmentalists would argue that because responsibility for preparing the HCP lies with the applicant, the burden for "covering all the bases" also lies with the applicant and therefore an unanticipated but foreseeable circumstance partially or wholly invalidates a Section 10 ITP, and does not come under the No Surprises provision. No cases have decided this issue.

The No Surprises policy may be the most controversial of the recent administrative reforms of the ESA, because once a Section 10 ITP is granted, the Service loses much of its ability to further protect a species if it turns out the original mitigation is insufficient. Many environmental groups strongly criticize this feature as inconsistent with adaptive management, which emphasizes a recognition of scientific uncertainty and flexible change in management practices as new information develops.[196] Some environmental groups contend that No Surprises is actually illegal, contradicting congressional intent to preserve the government's power to regulate in favor of a listed species. A successful legal challenge on this issue would limit or possibly eliminate No Surprises as a feature of the ESA.[197] In reaction, the Service (and environmental groups, to the extent they can exert influence) might push for stronger mitigation methods or methods, like performance standards, that incorporate flexibility. Another possibility for reducing the environmental impact of No Surprises is to create a source of funding to buy habitat improvement concessions from landowners. In the meantime, FWS claims that responsible use of both the No Surprises policy and adaptive management should afford listed and unlisted species more protection through the HCP process.[198]

---

195. See id.

196. See, e.g., National Wildlife Federation, *Habitat Conservation Plans* (visited Aug. 19, 1999) <http://www.nwf.org/endangered/hcp/h1hcpsaf.html>.

197. A lawsuit filed in 1998 may eventually decide this issue. See Spirit of the Sage Council v. Babbitt, No. 98-1873 (D.D.C. filed July 29, 1998).

198. See HCP Handbook Addendum, *supra* note 33, at 35,244.

E.3.e. Transferability

As of June 17, 1999, Section 10 ITPs can be traded or sold. However, for a transfer to be allowed, a number of conditions must be met as outlined in the regulations.[199] Also, note that Safe Harbor Agreements are not automatically transferred along with the ITP. Instead, the new owner must become a signatory to the original Safe Harbor Agreement.[200]

E.3.f. HCPs and Critical Habitat Designation

It is conceivable that the establishment of an HCP might eliminate the legal requirement for an agency to designate critical habitat for a species, if, for example, the HCP process begins before listing occurs and if the HCP process is likely to benefit the species more than designating critical habitat would. The case that comes closest to addressing this issue is *Natural Resources Defense Council v. U.S. Dept. of Interior*,[201] which suggests that agencies need not designate critical habitat if there is no situation in which the habitat designation would provide benefit to the species additional to that provided by the HCPs.[202] This case is not fully determinative, however, since the state-run HCP at issue did not require federal involvement in managing habitat, which would be the case in a typical HCP.

E.4. Economic Issues and Habitat Conservation Plans

FWS is not supposed to consider economic factors in determining whether an HCP should be disallowed because it jeopardizes a listed species' survival. While the requirement that impacts be mitigated to the maximum extent practicable has an implicit economic component, concern has arisen over some evidence suggesting disparate treatment of large, economically powerful landowners relative to small landowners.[203] Insofar as the FWS has considerable administrative discretion, wealthy property owners may exercise their presumably greater political influence to affect HCP design and approval, thus transferring a disproportionate share of the regulatory burden to property owners with less economic and political means, and to state and local governmental lands.

---

199. *See* 50 C.F.R. § 13.25.

200. *See* Announcement of Final Safe Harbor Policy, 64 Fed. Reg. 32717, 32725 (1999).

201. 113 F.3d 1121 (9th Cir. 1996). *See also,* part D.2.b. of Chapter Two (The Tide Turns).

202. *See* 113 F.3d at 1125.

203. *See, e.g.,* Thompson, *supra* note 53, at 321.

To the extent that the HCP process favors applicants who apply before the habitat destruction reaches its worst point, economically powerful applicants may use their superior resources to become aware of the need to apply early and to apply successfully.

F. Review of Incidental Takes

For all incidental takes, whether permitted under Section 7[204] or Section 10,[205] the Secretary's biological findings and the Secretary's decision whether to issue a permit are both evaluated under the arbitrary and capricious standard.[206] Thus, in order to prevail on a claim alleging that a Section 10 conservation plan does not minimize and mitigate incidental takes, or that the plan jeopardizes a species, a plaintiff must demonstrate that the Secretary acted arbitrarily and capriciously in approving an incidental take permit.[207] This means the relevant issue is not whether the conservation plan in fact minimizes and mitigates incidental takes, but rather whether as a matter of law the Secretary has abused his or her discretion in making a finding on whether a conservation plan fulfills this Section 10 requirement. Likewise, in order to prevail on a claim that approval of a permit violates Section 7(a)(2) by failing to consider the best scientific data available, a plaintiff must demonstrate that the Secretary acted arbitrarily and capriciously.[208]

One issue that deserves careful thought by would-be challengers to an HCP and ITP is what happens if the challenge succeeds? If a court invalidates a multi-party HCP that brings all developers in the region under its umbrella, some developers may elect to go forward not withstanding the absence of a valid ITP and assume the risk of enforcement by FWS. Because FWS may refuse to take such enforcement action, the challengers' only legal remedy may be a Section 9 "take" suit directly against the developer. Such suits impose a heavy evidentiary burden on plaintiffs and, therefore, are rarely successful. As a result, challengers may actually find that they are in a worse position after successfully challenging a multi-party or regional HCP because the mandatory mitigation and funding requirements contained in the HCP are no longer enforceable.

---

204. 16 U.S.C. § 1536(b)(4).

205. *See id.* § 1539(a).

206. *See* Bennett v. Spear, 117 S. Ct. 1154, 1167-69 (1997) (Section 7), Friends of Endangered Species v. Jantzen, 760 F.2d 976, 982-84 (9th Cir. 1985) (Section 10).

207. *See* Friends of Endangered Species, 760 F.2d at 982-84.

208. *See id.* at 984-85.

CHAPTER SIX

International Aspects of the ESA

A. Introduction

Extinction of species and loss of habitat are occurring not just in the United States, but across the globe. Protecting domestic biodiversity is of little value in the long run unless biodiversity is also protected on an international scale. Species and ecosystems do not recognize national boundaries. Efforts to conserve a migratory shorebird in Delaware will be meaningless unless its wintering habitat in Argentina and its breeding habitat in Canada are also conserved. In enacting the ESA, Congress recognized that global efforts were necessary to address conservation problems, and that the United States had an obligation to provide international leadership by passing strong legislation to protect its own species.[1]

The ESA provides this needed leadership and other more direct methods of protecting international biodiversity. The ESA permits the Secretary to list species even if they are not found in the United States.[2] Currently, of the 1,743 ESA listings, 565 are not found in the United States.[3] The ESA encourages the contribution of U.S. resources, including money and personnel, toward the conservation of species and habitat in other nations.[4] It also requires the Secretary to enforce and implement provisions of various international treaties aimed at protecting wildlife.[5]

B. Section 8 Programs
B.1. International Cooperation and Enforcement

Section 8 of the ESA attempts to protect endangered species through international cooperation. Its purpose is to develop international programs "[a]s a demonstration of the commitment of the United States to

---

1. *See, e.g.,* H.R. Rep. No. 93-412, at 4-6 (1973).

2. *See* 16 U.S.C. § 1533(b).

3. U.S. Fish and Wildlife Service, *Box Score Listing and Recovery Plans as of April 30, 1999* (visited Aug. 19, 1990) <http://www.fws.gov/r9endspp/boxscore.html>. The FWS does not designate critical habitat, develop recovery plans, or regulate take of species outside the United States.

4. *See* 16 U.S.C. § 1537.

5. *Id.* § 1537(a).

the worldwide protection of endangered species and threatened species. . . ."[6] It gives the Secretary broad discretion to assist foreign countries and individuals with species conservation, but does not require that the Secretary undertake any specific actions. FWS has developed a few programs that provide financial and technical assistance in developing countries. However, much untapped potential remains for Section 8 programs.

For instance, Section 8(a) authorizes the United States to provide financial assistance to countries developing local programs that conserve ESA listed species.[7] The funds spent on these efforts must be foreign currencies owned by the United States that cannot be converted into U.S. dollars.[8] The currencies are accumulated through the sale of agricultural commodities under the Agricultural Trade Development and Assistance Act of 1954, and through repayment of loans by foreign governments.[9] The governments can pay for these products and services with local currencies, kept on deposit and required to be spent in the home countries.[10] However, the ESA's authorization to use these foreign currencies is limited by the Supplemental Appropriation Act of 1953.[11] This Act requires that Congress appropriate money for each program that will spend foreign currency.[12] So, before any of the foreign currencies can be spent on endangered species programs, Congress must authorize the expenditure. Congress may not wish to appear partial to foreign endangered species programs over domestic programs. However, because these currencies cannot be converted into U.S. dollars and must be spent in the foreign country, Congress could appropriate the currency for endangered species programs without affecting domestic appropriations.

Congress authorized FWS to begin using "excess foreign currencies" in 1976.[13] At that time, five countries had "excess" currencies available—

---

6. *Id.*

7. *Id.*

8. *See* Office of Int'l Affairs, U.S. Fish and Wildlife Serv., The Special Foreign Currency Program.

9. *See id.*

10. Letter from Irene James, FWS Office of International Affairs, to Stephanie Easley, Stanford Environmental Law Society (May 29, 1998).

11. 16 U.S.C. § 1537(a).

12. 31 U.S.C. § 1306(a).

13. *See* Letter from Irene James, *supra* note 10. The foreign currencies collected by the U.S. are used for embassy maintenance costs, expenses incurred by U.S. officials, economic development in the host country, and to purchase military equipment and supplies. *See id.* When foreign currencies on deposit represent more than the two-year supply of funds for these purposes, the U.S. Treasury Department designates them as "excess" currencies. *See id.*

FWS Special Foreign Currency Program

The FWS Foreign Currency Program's activities are concentrated in three countries: India, Pakistan, and Egypt. India has some of the most well-known endangered species, such as the snow leopard, tiger, Asian elephant, great Indian bustard, and Siberian crane. FWS has supported a multitude of short-term activities and 37 major research conservation projects since the program began. Each project included training for local personnel and has been a stepping stone for advanced degrees for Indian personnel. The project has resulted in the publication of over 300 scientific papers, the training of hundreds of Indians in both the United States and India. FWS also facilitated a series of pilot workshops to train teachers, produced conservation education materials, and transferred over 5,000 scientific papers and other publications to organizations in India.

The foreign currency programs in Pakistan and Egypt, though smaller than the India program, have also produced results for conservation and education. These programs focus on education and attempt to catalyze other in-country conservation actions. In Pakistan, activities included international workshops on snow leopards, environmental education, wetlands conservation, raptor identification, and Convention on International Trade in Endangered Species (CITES) implementation. The program has facilitated field studies of monitor lizards, ibex, marine turtles, marine mammals and many other species, as well as the development of student wildlife clubs.

In Egypt, the program focuses on basic training, institutional development, and the collection of biological data. The program's activities fostered new wildlife legislation, the establishment of new agencies and organizations to manage wildlife, and led to the establishment of national parks and protected areas. It also produced educational materials, transferred technical information, and assisted Egypt in more effectively carrying out its responsibilities under international environmental conventions.

See Letter from Irene James, FWS OFFICE OF INT'L CONSERVATION (May 29, 1998); OFFICE OF INT'L CONSERVATION, U.S. FWS, THE SPECIAL FOREIGN CURRENCY PROGRAM.

India, Pakistan, Egypt, Guinea, and Burma.[14] Guinea and Burma had small amounts of currencies available but were not particularly interested in participating in the program. Instead, the United States developed programs with India, Pakistan and Egypt, which together are home to over 100 ESA-listed species.[15] These countries wanted to cooperate with the United States and had sufficient amounts of excess currencies to sustain long-term programs.

The foreign currency programs are administered by the FWS, Office of International Affairs. The program focuses on developing cooperation with local institutions that conserve endangered species and their habitats.[16] FWS has coordinated federal, state, university, and private organizations' expertise to provide maximum benefits at a relatively low cost to a variety of threatened and endangered species. Since 1976, the ESA authority has allowed FWS to channel over $12 million in excess foreign currencies into the three countries.[17] The FWS has managed to accomplish this, while only spending approximately $325,000 of its own funds, and an additional $1 million from other U.S. cooperators.[18]

Section 8(b) encourages foreign programs that conserve listed species, and allows the Secretary to help the State Department develop bilateral or multilateral conservation agreements.[19] The Office of International Affairs participates with other agencies in administering such agreements. One example of such an agreement is The Protocol on Cooperation and Exchanges in the Field of Conservation of Nature. This agreement, between China's Ministry of Forestry and the U.S. Department of Interior, was signed in 1986. The Protocol has provided a framework for exchange of scientists and scientific data, and for training Chinese authorities to better implement the Convention on International Trade in Endangered Species (CITES).[20]

The last part of Section 8(b) pertains to foreign persons that collect fish, wildlife, or plants from the wild for importation into the United States.[21] This small, unused provision allows the Secretary to assist such persons in developing conservation practices designed to enhance the collected species and its habitat.[22] This provision applies to all species

---

14. *See id.*

15. *See id.*

16. *See id.*

17. *See id.*

18. *See id.*

19. *See* 16 U.S.C. § 1537(b).

20. See section C of this chapter (Section 8A: International Agreements).

21. *See* 16 U.S.C. § 1537(b)(3).

22 *See id.*

collected for import into the United States; it is not limited to species listed on the ESA.

Section 8(c) authorizes the Secretary of Interior, after consultation with the Secretary of State, to make FWS employees available to foreign countries and international organizations. The employees work on-site in the country to develop personnel resources and programs which promote conservation of fish, wildlife, and plants, and to provide training in fish, wildlife, or plant management, research, and law enforcement.[23]

B.2. Sea Turtle Protection

The Conservation of Sea Turtles provision, added to Section 8, attempts to protect endangered sea turtles by reducing the unintentional killing of sea turtles in the nets of commercial shrimping operations.[24] This provision directs the Secretary of State to negotiate international agreements that require all countries importing shrimp into the United States to use sea turtle protections in their shrimping operations.[25] The U.S. government must certify that each shrimp-importing country has adopted a regulatory scheme for the shrimp industry that reduces incidental take of sea turtles to levels comparable to those required by the United States.[26] All shrimp and shrimp products from non-certified countries are prohibited from importation.[27]

C. Section 8A: International Agreements
C.1. CITES

ESA Section 8A implements two international conventions. The first is CITES.[28] Signed in 1973, CITES is the most significant international agreement regulating trade in wildlife.[29]

23. See id. § 1537(c).

24. Pub. L. No. 101-162, Title VI, § 609, Nov. 21, 1989, 103 Stat. 1037, reprinted in 16 U.S.C. § app. 1537.

25. See id.

26. Id. § 609(b)(2).

27. This provision of the ESA became the subject of a high-profile dispute between the United States and various foreign countries that viewed it as a measure intended to protect the U.S. shrimp industry from foreign competition. In an October 1998 decision, the World Trade Organization ruled in favor of the foreign countries. World Trade Organization, WT/DS58/AB/R, 12 October 1998 (98-0000). The United States government continues to support the validity of the law. For details, see World Wildlife Fund for Nature, Dispute Settlement in the WTO: A Crisis for Sustainable Development (visited Oct. 24, 2000) <http:// www.panda.org/resources/publications/sustainability/wto-98/fifth.htm>.

28. 16 U.S.C. § 1537(a).

29. Convention on International Trade in Endangered Species of Wild Fauna and Flora, March 3, 1973, 27 U.S.T. 1087, 993 U.N.T.S. 243.

The international wildlife trade is worth billions each year. CITES attempts to protect species in the wild from over-exploitation through international trade; it does not regulate take or domestic trade of listed species. In the United States, the protections of CITES are implemented by the ESA. CITES and ESA share definitions, penalties and requirements. CITES does not supersede import or export requirements of other wildlife laws. Requirements of all laws, including ESA, under which a species is listed, must be met prior to any trade of a species.

CITES Administration

Each party country is required to have a designated Management Authority (MA) review applications for CITES permits and certificates (CITES art. IX).

The United States's MA is the U.S. Fish and Wildlife Service, Office of Management Authority, 4401 N. Fairfax Drive, Arlington, Virginia 22203, telephone 1-800-358-2104. This office processes all CITES permit applications, as well as import and export permit applications for most other federal wildlife laws, including the ESA, Wild Bird Conservation Act, and the Marine Mammal Protection Act.

CITES is administered internationally by the United Nations Environmental Programme through the CITES Secretariat, located in Geneva, Switzerland. (CITES Secretariat, 15, chemin des Anémones, CH-1219 Châtelaine-Genève, Suisse. Tel. (4122) 979 9139/40, e-mail: cites@unep.ch)

For details see: <http:www.wcmc.org.uk/CITES/english/ index.html>.

C.1.a. CITES Organization and Listing

CITES aims to protect wild species threatened by international trade and to monitor species in trade to prevent over-exploitation. CITES listings focus on species that are common in trade. Many species are listed on both ESA and CITES, but CITES lists far more species than ESA, and does not list endangered and threatened species that are not exchanged in commerce. CITES organizes protected species into three categories or appendices, with different degrees of protection for each category.

- **Appendix I** species are the most vulnerable and include species "threatened with extinction which are or may be threatened by trade." Appendix I species cannot be traded for primarily commercial purposes.
- **Appendix II** consists of species that may become threatened with extinction unless strict trade regulations are enacted. Appendix II species may be traded for primarily commercial purposes after certain findings are made by the exporting country.
- **Appendix III** lists species at the request of a range country to help that country protect the species within its jurisdiction. Appendix III species can be traded for all purposes from all countries except the listing country.

Initially, CITES listed approximately 1,500 species in Appendix I and II. CITES now has over 30,000 listed species, sub-species and populations.[30] Every two years, representatives of all the CITES party countries attend a Conference of the Parties (COP). Changes in Appendix I and II listings are primarily done at the COP. Any party country may propose a change in an Appendix I and II listing for any species, whether native to that country or not. Changes in Appendix I and II listing are adopted by a two-thirds vote of parties at the COP. If a listing change is required between COPs, CITES has a procedure for a postal vote of the parties.[31]

Appendix III listings and delistings are made unilaterally by a party country. Because Appendix III does not require a vote of the parties, listings may be made at any time.

A loophole exists for countries that do not agree with a CITES listing. Under Article XV, any party can exempt itself from implementing a CITES listing for a particular species by entering a reservation for that species. The reservation must be made within 90 days of the close of the COP when the species listing amendment was made or when the country becomes a CITES party. These reservations allow countries to continue unrestricted trade in a species that the parties have voted to protect. For instance, Japan and Norway have entered multiple reservations for Appendix I whale species. Switzerland entered reservations on 14 Appendix I listings including the gray wolf, European river otter, Tibetan antelope, and the scarlet macaw. Switzerland, along with Liechtenstein, also entered reservations for many Appendix II parrot, parakeet, and conure species.

---

30. Nearly 25,000 of these are Appendix II plant species.
31. See CITES, *supra* note 29, art. XV(2).

The reservation process permits countries to unilaterally allow unrestricted and unmonitored trade in a species that requires CITES protection. However, this loophole is important in CITES politics; the general view is that it is better to have a country implement CITES for most species even if it enters reservations on some. For example, when Saudi Arabia became a CITES party in 1996, it entered reservations on 16 Appendix I falconiformes species, including the critically imperiled California condor. Even with all these reservations, it is probably more preferable to have Saudi Arabia as a CITES party than otherwise.

Of course, CITES is most effective when the parties do not enter reservations. It is especially difficult to justify a reservation for a non-native species that the range country wants to protect. One of the current criticisms of CITES is that it punishes range countries for not stopping poaching and illegal trade, but does not address the consumer demand for those species in the importing countries. Allowing wealthy developed nations to import species without restrictions when the range states have not entered reservations adds to this tension.

The United States has never entered a reservation on any species. However, FWS does solicit comments on potential reservations.[32]

The CITES parties have also developed numerous committees and working groups. These groups convene both at the COP and between the biannual meetings. They address a broad range of issues including conservation needs of particular taxa, CITES implementation problems, and logistics.

CITES Listing is Effective

In 1990 Jack Ivey and William "Rusty" Wallace were indicted for conspiracy to buy bobcat hides imported from Mexico in violation of CITES and for several counts of smuggling the species. The defendants argued that because bobcat was not listed on the Convention when it was signed in 1973, but added to Appendix II in 1977, the species was actually not listed on CITES in the United States. The 5th Circuit found this argument unconvincing, noting "it would be contrary to the purpose of the act to view the Convention as a static document without the ability to add species as they become endangered or remove animals that are no longer endangered."

For details see United States v. Ivey, 949 F.2d 759, 764 (5th Cir. 1991).

C.1.b. Opportunities for Public Participation

Non-governmental organizations play an important role in CITES administration and determinations. The text of the treaty allows non-governmental organizations to participate in the COPs as observers.[33] Observers may attend all plenary sessions, comment on the proposals, join in debates, and otherwise participate in the COP. However, they cannot vote.[34]

Any non-governmental organization may apply for observer status. Observers must be "technically qualified in protection, conservation, or management of wild fauna and flora."[35] Individuals not affiliated with any organization may not be observers. Organizations based in the United States apply to the FWS, Office of Management Authority to obtain observer status. International organizations must apply directly to the CITES Secretariat.

FWS advertises its CITES process both in the Federal Register and on its web site to solicit public comment.[36] Prior to each COP, FWS publishes the U.S. position on CITES listing changes in the Federal Register.[37] FWS also publishes the COP's agenda, the U.S. position on resolutions scheduled for vote, and the dates of pre-COP public meetings. After the COP, FWS publishes the results on the COP and holds at least one public meeting to discuss the changes adopted by the parties.[38]

C.1.c. Convention Interpretation

CITES is an unusual treaty.[39] With 143 signatory nations, its membership is significant in number and diversity. The parties' representatives are also unusual. CITES negotiators and government representatives tend to be scientific and technical experts rather than diplomats.[40] CITES is not a "framework" treaty with general guiding principles and hazy implementation. It is a command and control

---

32. *See, e.g.,* 62 Fed. Reg. 31,054, 31,060 (1997).

33. CITES, *supra* note 29, art. XI(7).

34. *Id.*

35. *Id.*

36. U.S. Fish and Wildlife Service, *CITES* (last modified Aug. 18, 1999) <http://international.fws.gov/cites/cites.html>.

37. 50 C.F.R. §§ 23.32-.35.

38. 62 Fed. Reg. 41,408 (1997).

39. *See generally* Environmental Resources Management, Study on How to Improve the Effectiveness of the Convention on International Trade in Endangered Species of Wild Fauna and Flora, Reference 3717 (1996).

40. *See id.*

convention. It specifically describes its requirements and procedures in the text of the treaty. This structure allows CITES to stay focused to identify wild species likely to be threatened by overexploitation and to develop strategies to reduce those threats. However, CITES does have some flexibility, and it has evolved significantly in the last 25 years.

CITES can be changed by amendment to the text of the Convention. Amendments can be made by a two-thirds majority vote at an "extraordinary meeting of the Conference of the Parties."[41] This process is expensive, politically unwieldy and has only been used twice. Instead, the Conference of the Parties uses "resolutions" passed at COPs by a two-thirds majority vote to interpret the Convention. Parties have used resolutions to recommend conservation actions far beyond trade restrictions. Dozens of resolutions have been passed on a broad range of topics — from a 1976 resolution encouraging natural history museums and herbaria to inventory their holdings of endangered species, to a 1992 resolution to recognize the benefits of trade in wildlife, to the 1997 adoption of several recommendations dealing with the threats that invasive exotic species in trade pose to native ecosystems.[42] Resolutions are not binding on the parties, but they provide a catalyst for domestic conservation actions by the parties.

CITES Article XIV states that the parties can, of course, enact "stricter domestic measures" to protect CITES and non-CITES species. Resolutions can identify species that require such "stricter domestic measures" and suggest more effective measures.

Resolutions have helped CITES evolve from a trade monitoring treaty to a much broader conservation tool. As it matures and conservation needs change, CITES is expanding to protect species from new pressures.[43] CITES cannot monitor trade in a vacuum; the parties must also work on developing conservation strategies for listed species. The sophisticated strategy adopted at COP 10 to monitor trade in elephant ivory was evidence of CITES evolution.[44] This growing sophistication will help as CITES continues to expand its reach. Currently, the parties are considering how to use CITES to regulate timber and commercially fished species. These taxa are subject to enormous trade pressures and powerful economic lobbying efforts but historically have not been regulated by CITES listings.

---

41. CITES, *supra* note 29, art. XVII(1).
42. *See* Environmental Resources Management, *supra* note 39, at Reference 3717.
43. *See id.*
44. *See id.*

The parties are also grappling with very controversial environmental issues. For instance, much debate has arisen among the parties about "sustainable use." This catch phrase of 1990s environmentalism does not have a standard meaning and is used inconsistently in international treaties. Sustainable use may mean entirely different things to a country with a wealth of natural resources, low per capita income, and a developing economy, than to a rich, developed country with few natural resources left. The debate on how, if at all, to incorporate sustainable use into CITES has been raging for years. The CITES parties will have to continue to rely on science in determining the outcome of the debates.

C.1.d. Recent Developments at COP 10

The most recent meeting of the Conference of the Parties was COP 10, held in Harare, Zimbabwe in June 1997. Many major changes were made to CITES listings. Highlights include:

- Down-listing of three populations of African elephant to Appendix II in March 1999 if certain conditions are met (see African elephant case study on page 185).
- Listing all of the world's species of sturgeons in CITES Appendix II (other than the four species which are already included in Appendix I or Appendix II) in response to trade pressure.
- Appendix II listing of three medicinal plants, including the U.S. native goldenseal.
- Defeat of the United States/Bolivia cosponsored proposal to list bigleaf mahogany, a heavily traded tropical timber species. However, a compromise was developed where all bigleaf mahogany range states will make recommendations for trade management, and Brazil, the most vocal range state opponent, along with Mexico and Bolivia, will list bigleaf mahogany on Appendix III. Bolivia listed bigleaf mahogany on Appendix III in March 1998, and it has been listed in Costa Rica since 1995.
- Defeat of Cuba's proposal to transfer the "Cuban population" of hawksbill sea turtles (*Eretmochelys imbricata*) from Appendix I to Appendix II. The proposal would have allowed the hawksbill trade only between Cuba and Japan.

- Defeat of five proposals sponsored by Japan and Norway to down-list, from Appendix I to Appendix II, specific whale stocks subject to the International Whaling Commission commercial whaling moratorium.[45]

C.1.e. The African Elephant—A CITES Case Study

Historically, the African elephant ranged throughout the African continent, absent only in parts of the Sahara and other desert regions. The African elephant was extinct in North Africa by the nineteenth century, but the elephant population was still reasonably well distributed in its remaining historic range. These populations have, however, declined steadily over the last century due to the high demand for ivory, loss of habitat, and decertification.

The African elephant was placed on CITES Appendix II in 1977. To stem the continuing illegal trade of poached ivory, the Ivory Export Quota System was developed in 1985. The System required that each ivory exporting state determine the number of elephant tusks it could export each year, and mark each tusk with its country of origin and a unique code number. A database was created to assist customs agents in determining which countries could legally export ivory within their quota, and also ensure that a country accepting ivory for import ascertained that a valid export permit had been granted for that ivory. The problem, however, was that each country determined its own quota and could allow over-harvest of elephants or trade of illegally taken tusks.[46] These measures failed to stem the trade in poached ivory or the decline in elephant populations.

At the 1989 meeting of the COP, the elephant was moved to Appendix I, and all trade in ivory was banned. This move was supported by Eastern African countries, led by Kenya, but opposed by some Southern African states[47] which promptly entered reservations for the elephant listing, arguing that their elephant populations were properly managed and not in decline. This issue arose again in 1992, when the Southern African countries attacked the complete ban on ivory trade. They argued that countries with effective wildlife utilization and management programs should be allowed to earn revenue from the

---

45. *See* U.S. Fish and Wildlife Serv., *The Official U.S. CITES ONLINE Cover, International Affairs* (visited Aug. 19, 1999) < http://www.fws.gov/r9dia/cop10/dbtestim.html>.

46. *See* Raymond Bonner, At the Hand of Man 96 (1993).

47. These included Botswana, Malawi, Namibia, South Africa, Zambia and Zimbabwe. *See* Official Documents, Seventh Meeting of the Conference of the Parties, Lausanne (Switzerland), October 9-20, 1989.

beneficial use of wildlife.[48] However, faced with major opposition, these countries withdrew their proposal.

At COP 10 in 1997, three countries proposed to have their elephant populations down-listed from Appendix I to Appendix II, to allow raw ivory (uncarved elephant tusks) to be traded commercially. The United States opposed the down-listing. The parties voted to transfer the elephant populations of Zimbabwe, Botswana and Namibia to Appendix II, effective on March 18, 1999 if the CITES Standing Committee certified that certain conditions have been met.[49] This is not a typical Appendix II listing. Ivory can only be exported to Japan, and initially only legally held ivory can be traded.[50] The parties also imposed very stringent conditions on this limited trade: the three countries were to establish or strengthen mechanisms to re-invest ivory trade revenue into elephant conservation; they committed to international cooperation in law enforcement; and they instituted a mechanism to halt trade immediately in the event of non-compliance, escalation of poaching, or illegal trade in elephant products due to resumption of trade.[51] Further, they had to establish an international reporting and monitoring system for poaching and for legal and illegal trade, and to ensure that Japan, the only country allowed to import the ivory, could not re-export it. Moreover, ivory trade could not occur before March 1999, and then, only if the CITES Standing Committee certified that improvements had been made in instituting the requisite mechanisms for control.[52]

The requirements for ivory trade in Botswana, Namibia and Zimbabwe attempted to deal with a general shortcoming of CITES, namely its failure to deal with supply and demand of wildlife products and the lack of provisions for cooperation between nations.[53] Previously, each country acted on its own but it is now recognized that cooperation between range states in dealing with trade in endangered species could contribute significantly to the achievements of CITES' objectives.

---

48. See Eighth Meeting of the Conference of the Parties, Kyoto (Japan), March 2-13, 1992. See also David S. Favre, *Debate within the CITES Community: What Direction for the Future?*, 33 Nat. Resources J. 875, 903-904 (1993).

49. See *Proposals Concerning Export Quotas for Specimens of Species in Appendix I or II*, Convention in International Trade in Endangered Species of Wild Fauna and Flora, Tenth Meeting of the Conference of the Parties, Harare, June 9-20, 1997, UN Doc 10.89 [hereinafter COP 10]. Prop. 10:25,26,27.

50. Legally held ivory includes ivory confiscated from poachers and ivory acquired as a result of natural elephant mortality and management activities. COP 10 Proposals Concerning Export Quotas for Specimens of Species in Appendix I or II; Prop. 10:25,26,27

51. See COP 10, *supra* note 49.

52. See COP 10, *supra* note 49.

53. See Favre, *supra* note 48, at 888 (arguing that demand creates value for wildlife products and creates incentives for illegal takings thereof).

More attention still needs to be focused on the demand side. The continuing demand for wildlife products provides incentives for illegal killing and trading in those species.[54] However, the limited reopening of the African elephant ivory trade, with its many restrictions, demonstrates how far CITES has evolved as a trade monitoring tool and an international conservation mechanism.

C.1.f. CITES Permit Requirements

CITES does not regulate activities within a country. CITES documents are required only when CITES-protected materials are shipped from one country to another or are taken from the high seas and imported into a country. Exporting, for CITES purposes, is shipping CITES-protected materials from the country where the wildlife originated to another country. CITES shipments can be re-exported: exported to an intermediary country that imports the material and then re-exports it to another country. The Management Authority is required to issue a CITES re-export certificate before the material may be re-exported.

Import permits are issued by the importing country. Import permits must be obtained prior to shipping of Appendix I material. Each of the three CITES Appendices has different permit requirements.

- **Appendix I** species are subject to the most restrictive require-ments. Both an import and export permit must be issued be-fore the material is shipped. The importing country issues a CITES import permit after it determines that: 1) the trade is not for primarily commercial purposes, and 2) in the case of living specimens, the proposed recipient can suitably house and care for the species. The exporting country must verify that an im-port permit has been issued before it issues an export permit (or re-export certificate). If the wildlife was taken from waters outside the jurisdiction of any country, the importing country must issue an import permit prior to importation.[55]
- **Appendix II** species can be traded for commercial purposes if certain criteria are met. Trade requires only an export permit (or re-export certificate) issued by the exporting country. If the species is taken from waters outside the jurisdiction of any

---

54. *See, e.g.,* David Harland, Killing: International Law and the African Elephant 36 (1994) (noting that Asian countries continue to demand ivory and are responsible for 88 percent of the global consumption of raw ivory).
55. 50 C.F.R. § 23.12.

country the importing country must issue an import permit prior to importation.[56] The exporting country can limit the export of Appendix II species "in order to maintain that species throughout its range at a level consistent with its role in the ecosystems in which it occurs" and at levels well above where the species may require Appendix I listing.[57]

- **Appendix III** species exported (or re-exported) from a country where that species is listed require an export permit (or re-export certificate). If the species is exported from a country where it is not listed, a certificate of origin (or re-export certificate) must be obtained prior to exportation.[58]

Prior to issuing any CITES permit, the issuing government must determine that the import, export, or re-export will not be detrimental to the survival of the species. In the United States, the FWS, Office of Scientific Authority, makes the "no detriment" finding. The Office of Management Authority considers the following factors in determining whether or not to issue a CITES permit or certificate after a no detriment finding is made:[59]

- Whether the species was lawfully acquired;
- Whether living wildlife or plant species imported into the United States will be prepared, shipped and handled to minimize the risk of injury, damage to health, or cruel treatment;
- Whether the material qualifies for a CITES exemption.

In the United States, CITES permit applications (form 3-200) are obtained from the FWS, Office of Management Authority (OMA). The current application fee is $25. FWS can deny a CITES permit application if the applicant: 1) made false statements in connection with the application; 2) violated other wildlife laws; 3) had a previous permit revoked; or 4) failed to disclose material information, pay fees, submit required reports, or provide the required justification and showing of responsibility.[60] FWS can suspend or revoke CITES permits if the permittee does not comply with the conditions of the permit, or if the

---

56. *Id.*
57. *See* CITES, *supra* note 29, art. IV(3).
58. 50 C.F.R. § 23.12(b)(2).
59. *See id.* § 23.15(d).
60. *See id.* § 13.21.

wildlife or plant species declines so that continuation of the permitted activity would be detrimental to the species.[61]

While FWS has no deadline to make a determination on a permit request, FWS recommends that applicants allow at least 60 days for review. If a permit application is denied, the applicant can make an administrative appeal within 45 days.

If the applicant is unsatisfied with the administrative appeal, he or she can challenge the permit decision in federal court. Courts can overrule a FWS decision if they find the decision was arbitrary and capricious, an abuse of discretion, or contrary to law.[62] Typically, courts will not substitute their judgment for that of the agency in administrative decisions, but courts will not infer findings that are not in the administrative record. FWS should expressly make any findings required by CITES in the administrative record.[63]

C.1.g. State Tagging Programs

Export of some native, Appendix II species (bobcat, lynx, river otter, Alaskan brown bear, Alaskan gray wolf, and American alligator) is regulated through tagging programs administered by the states, not FWS. The FWS Office of Scientific Authority makes the "no detriment" finding based on data collected by each state. FWS then issues each state a number of tags for each species. The tags are distributed by the state to individual exporters. Each hide, pelt or other product of these species must have a tag attached before it is exported.

In 1981, the D.C. Court of Appeals held that the Office of Scientific Authority's no detriment findings for these species must be based on reliable estimates of the species population and data showing the total number to be killed in each state.[64] The court's opinion stated the importance of reliable data.

> We do not see how, without adequate information on total bobcat population and the number to be killed in a particular season, the Scientific Authority can make a valid determination of no detriment. For example, the Scientific Authority set a quota for the 1978-1979 season of 2,000 bobcats to be killed in

---

61. See id. §§ 13.27-28.
62. See Underwater Exotics, Ltd. v. Secretary of the Interior, 1994 WL 80878 (D.D.C. February 28, 1994); World Wildlife Fund v. Hodel, 1988 WL 66193 (D.D.C. June 17, 1988) (citing Administrative Procedure Act, 5 U.S.C. § 706)).
63. See World Wildlife Fund, 1988 WL 66193, at *2-3.
64. See Defenders of Wildlife, Inc. v. Endangered Species Scientific Authority, 659 F.2d 168 (D.C. Cir. 1981), cert. denied, 454 U.S. 963 (1981).

Wyoming. If Wyoming had a total population of only 2,500 bobcats, the killing of 2,000 would have a devastating impact upon the survival of the species there. . . . Unless the total bobcat population is known . . . it is impossible to predict the effect upon bobcat survival of the killing of a specified number.[65]

The court went on to note that "[a]ny doubt whether the killing of a particular number of bobcats will adversely affect the survival of the species must be resolved in favor of protecting the animals and not in favor of approving the export of their pelts."[66]

This decision was legislatively overturned by the 1982 amendments to the ESA. FWS is no longer required to base its no detriment finding on estimates of a state's population, and the Secretary is explicitly forbidden from requiring that states estimate population sizes of CITES species.[67]

C.1.h. Imports into the United States

In a few instances, CITES species may enter the United States without permits. However, in most cases the imports will require some other kind of CITES document that shows which exemption applies. CITES species that are shipped through the United States do not require permits if the shipment remains in Customs' custody.[68] (ESA listed species in transit through the United States require permits, whether or not the shipments entered the country for customs purposes.[69]) A limited exception allows shipments, without permits, of wildlife or plants accompanying personal baggage or part of a shipment of the household effects of persons moving their residences to or from the United States.[70] This exception does not apply to Appendix I species acquired outside the United States or Appendix II species taken from the wild in a foreign country.[71] However, the foreign country involved may require CITES documents for such shipments, and it may be difficult to prove that the species was not taken from the wild. It is preferable to obtain CITES documents for such shipments to avoid possible delay or confiscation of the material. CITES species are considered to be imported for CITES

---

65. 659 F.2d at 177.

66. 659 F.2d at 178.

67. *See* 16 U.S.C. § 1537(c)(2).

68. *See* 50 C.F.R. § 23.13(b).

69. *See id.* § 17.21(b).

70. *See id.* § 23.13(d).

71. *See id.*

purposes if they enter the United States as part of an unscheduled airline flight landing.[72]

Shipments of CITES-listed species cannot be imported into the United States without proper export permits, even if the exporting nation is not a CITES signatory.[73] Trade in CITES-listed species with a non-party country requires documentation. The non-party nation must have the "competent authorities" issue "comparable documentation" which "substantially conform" to CITES requirements.[74] Of course, non-party countries can trade with each other without permits or monitoring requirements.

All CITES permits must be presented to FWS personnel at a designated port of entry or exit.[75] The designated ports are: Atlanta, Baltimore, Boston, Chicago, Dallas/Ft. Worth, Honolulu, Los Angeles, Miami, New Orleans, New York, Newark, Portland (Oregon), San Francisco, and Seattle. If a permittee cannot transport the wildlife through a designated port, FWS can grant exceptions to use border ports.[76] A wildlife declaration form (form 3-177) must be filed with the FWS inspector at the time of importation or exportation. CITES documents must be physically endorsed at export, and all shipments are subject to inspection.

C.1.i.　Trade Monitoring

Each party country is required to submit an annual report of its trade in CITES-listed species to the CITES Secretariat.[77] The report must include the number and type of permits and certificates granted, the countries involved, and the quantities and types of specimens traded.[78] This data is used to determine pressure on traded species, evaluate CITES listing changes, and identify possible illegal shipments. However, many parties do not produce their annual reports on time or at all. The CITES Secretariat has made efforts in recent years to encourage timely reporting, and as a result, more countries are producing their annual reports on time.[79]

72. *See* United States v. 3210 Crusted Sides of Caiman Crocodilus Yacare, 636 F. Supp. 1281 (S.D. Fla. 1986).

73. *See* U.S. v. Ivey, 949 F.2d 759, 764 (5th Cir. 1991); 50 C.F.R. § 23.14(b).

74. CITES, *supra* note 29, art. X.

75. 50 C.F.R. § 23.15(e)(1).

76. *See id.* § 14.16.

77. CITES, *supra* note 29, art. VIII(7)(a).

78. *See id., supra* note 29, art. VIII(6)(b).

79. *See* Environmental Resources Management, *supra* note 39, at Reference 3717.

Most monitoring of trade in CITES-listed species is done by two independent non-profit organizations. The World Conservation Monitoring Center (WCMC), established by the World Conservation Union, the
World Wide Fund for Nature, and the United Nations Environment Programme, manages CITES trade data under a contract with the Secretariat. The WCMC database has a record of every CITES transaction reported in each country's annual CITES trade report.[80] The second organization, the Trade Records Analysis of Fauna and Flora in Commerce
(TRAFFIC), is a joint effort of the World Wide Fund for Nature and the
World Conservation Union. TRAFFIC assists the Secretariat with ana-
lyzing CITES trade data.

Copies of the United States annual reports before 1990 are available
from the U.S. Department of Commerce, National Technical Information
Service, 5285 Port Royal Road, Springfield, Virginia 22161, (703) 605-
6000, orders@ntis.fedworld.gov. Information about more recent annual
reports can be obtained from the Office of Management Authority.

C.1.j. CITES International Enforcement

CITES does not have an international enforcement mechanism.
Concerns about national sovereignty and security make some CITES
parties leery of any international effort to combat the illegal wildlife
trade. At COP 10, the United States proposal to establish a CITES
committee to study the illegal wildlife trade was rejected by the parties.
However, the nature of wildlife smuggling on an international scale
makes it difficult for individual countries to study and combat the illegal
wildlife trade. For now, each party country is responsible for
"appropriate measures to enforce the provision of the present
Convention and to prohibit trade in specimens in violation thereof."[81]

Each party country issues its CITES permits unilaterally, based on
the findings of its Scientific and Management authorities as provided by
the Convention. Generally, these findings are not reviewable by other
parties, and no enforcement mechanism is in place that might prevent
the issuance of CITES documents based on invalid scientific determinations. The CITES Steering Committee has recommended enforcement of
trade sanctions against countries that allow trade in endangered species.

80. Information on the WCMC databases can be obtained from the World Conservation
Monitoring Centre, 219 Huntingdon Road, Cambridge, CB3 0DL, United Kingdom
(telephone: +44 (0)1223 277314; fax: +44 (0)1223 277136, Web home page:
http://www.WCMC.org.uk).
81. CITES, *supra* note 29, art. VIII (1).

However, each country is responsible for implementing such sanctions domestically.

Party countries differ widely in their desire and ability to enforce CITES. Many parties are limited by insufficient national legislation implementing CITES, minimal communication with other parties, and a lack of trained enforcement personnel.[82]

C.1.k. Domestic Enforcement

CITES violations within the United States are investigated by the FWS. Penalties for CITES violations are set by the ESA. Maximum penalties for criminal violations of Section 8A are a $25,000 fine, six months in prison, or both.[83] Civil penalties can be up to $25,000 for each violation.[84] The penalties double if the species being imported or exported is also listed on the ESA.[85] Specimens traded in violation of CITES are subject to seizure and forfeiture. The Federal Sentencing Guidelines provide for an increase of four levels if the violation involves a CITES Appendix I species, and an increase of two levels when an offense was committed for pecuniary gain or commercial purposes.[86]

C.1.l. The Lacey Act

The Lacey Act imposes penalties for the possession, importing, or exporting of fish or wildlife taken, possessed, transported or sold in violation of any United States state or foreign law.[87] The purpose of the Lacey Act with respect to international wildlife is to reduce poaching of endangered species in their range countries.[88] It allows U.S. courts to penalize U.S. importers who violate the CITES requirements or other wildlife laws in foreign countries.

Courts will interpret foreign wildlife laws in determining Lacey Act violations. In *United States v. 2,507 Live Canary Wilnger Parakeets (Brotogeris vresicolorus)*,[89] the Southern District of Florida invalidated a Peruvian export permit for a forest-dwelling CITES-listed bird species. The court used a Peruvian law prohibiting the export of any forest-dwelling

---

82. *See* Shennie Patel, Note, *The Convention on International Trade in Endangered Species: Enforcement and the Last Unicorn*, 18 Hous. J. Int'l L. 157, 186 (1995).

83. 16 U.S.C. § 1540(b).

84. *Id.* § 1540(a).

85. *Id.* §§ 1540(a)-(b).

86. U.S. Sentencing Guidelines § 2Q2.1.

87. 16 U.S.C. § 3372.

88. *See* S. Rep. No. 526, 91st Cong., 1st Sess. 4 (1969), *reprinted in* 1969 U.S.C.C.A.N. 1413, 1416.

89. 689 F. Supp. 1106 (S.D. Fla. 1988).

court used a Peruvian law prohibiting the export of any forest-dwelling species to invalidate the Peruvian CITES export permit signed by the proper authority.[90]

Penalties for CITES violations charged under the Lacey Act violations include fines up to $20,000, five years' imprisonment, and forfeiture of the illegal wildlife and vehicles and equipment used in the violation.[91] Unlike the ESA, the Lacey Act includes felony as well as misdemeanor charges.[92] The government can prove conspiracy violations of the Lacey Act without showing the defendant violated any substantive provision of the Lacey Act.[93]

C.1.m. International CITES Enforcement through the Pelly Amendment

The Pelly Amendment to the Fisherman's Protection Act of 1967[94] (Pelly Amendment) contains a powerful trade sanction that allows the United States to restrict imports of all fish and wildlife products from countries that violate international fishery or endangered and threatened species protections.[95] The Pelly Amendment requires the Secretary to "certify" to the President that nationals of a foreign country are engaging in trade which diminishes the effectiveness of an international program to protect endangered or threatened species.[96] The certifications are made in response to petitions from non-governmental organizations, or government agencies. The President then has discretionary power to direct the Secretary of the Treasury to prohibit the importation of all fish or wildlife products from the offending country.[97]

Pelly Amendment certifications have been made dozens of times. Actual sanctions were imposed for the first time in April 1994. President Clinton prohibited importation of wildlife and wildlife products from Taiwan in response to Taiwan's trade in rhinoceros and tiger parts in violation of CITES. The Court of International Trade held that sanctions

---

90. See id. at 1114-15 ("Colorable compliance with the CITES requirements is not a defense to the Lacey Act").

91. 16 U.S.C. § 3373(d).

92. 16 U.S.C. §§ 3373(d)(1)(B), 3373(d)(2).

93. See 16 U.S.C. § 3373(d)(2); United States v. Groody, 785 F. Supp. 875 (D. Mont. 1991).

94. 22 U.S.C. § 1978.

95. Id. § 1978(a)(4).

96. Id. §§ 1978(a)(1)-(2).

97. Id. § 1978(a)(4).

could be imposed against a country that imported wildlife products in violation of CITES whether the species was native or exotic to that country.[98]

The imposition of actual trade sanctions by the United States proved an effective catalyst for stronger domestic enforcement of CITES in importing countries. Taiwan, China, Singapore, South Korea, Japan and Hong Kong announced new efforts to curtail trade in endangered species soon after the sanctions began.[99] The United States lifted the Pelly sanctions in May 1995, when an interdepartmental panel recognized Taiwan's attempts to curtail illegal trade in rhinoceros and tiger parts.[100] The Pelly sanctions cost Taiwan an estimated $25 million in lost trade.[101]

C.2. Convention on Nature Protection and Wildlife Preservation in the Western Hemisphere

C.2.a. Provisions and Administration

In 1982, Congress amended Section 8A of the ESA to direct the Secretary of Interior, acting in cooperation with the Secretary of State, to implement a second international treaty, the Convention on Nature Protection and Wildlife Preservation in the Western Hemisphere (WHC).[102] WHC entered into force in 1942 and is open to signature by all "American Governments."[103] Current WHC signatories are: Argentina, Bolivia, Brazil, Chile, Colombia, Costa Rica, Cuba, the Dominican Republic, Ecuador, El Salvador, Guatemala, Haiti, Mexico, Nicaragua, Panama, Peru, Surinam, Trinidad and Tobago, United States, Uruguay, and Venezuela.

WHC's purpose is to protect and preserve native plant and animal species in their natural habitat. In furtherance of this purpose, WHC imposes four requirements on party countries:

- First, parties must establish and maintain a national system of protected areas for species conservation, public recreation and education.
- Second, parties must implement domestic legislation to protect

---

98. *See* Florsheim Shoe Co. v. United States, 880 F. Supp. 848 (Ct. Int'l Trade 1995).

99. *See* Julie Cheung, *Implementation and Enforcement of CITES: An Assessment of Tiger and Rhinoceros Conservation Policy in Asia*, 5 Pac. Rim L. & Pol'y J. 125, 138 (1995).

100. *U.S. Announces Decision to End Trade Sanctions over Wildlife*, Reuters News Service, July 1, 1995, *available in* LEXIS, World Library, Curnws File.

101. *See id.*

102. 16 U.S.C § 1537(e).

103. Convention on Nature Protection and Wildlife Preservation in the Western Hemisphere, Oct. 12, 1940, art. XI, para. 2, 56 Stat. 1354, 161 U.N.T.S. 193 [hereinafter "WHC"].

all the country's flora and fauna, both inside and outside the national protected areas, and control trade in protected species.

- Third, parties should develop international agreements for cooperation in scientific research and share scientific knowledge resulting from such efforts.
- Fourth, parties must adopt measures to protect migratory birds and to prevent extinction of any migratory bird species.[104]

With its broad provisions for preserving biological diversity and the membership of ecologically important nations, WHC would appear to be a powerful conservation treaty. However, the United States, like most WHC signatories, has not fully implemented the four WHC provisions.[105] Because of the treaty's weak structure and lack of enforcement, WHC is regarded as a "paper" treaty that is thus far largely unimplemented.[106]

The largest obstacle to implementation is WHC's lack of administrative structure. The treaty has no secretariat, conferences, or reporting requirements. Parties are not required to keep any records regarding WHC implementation, and enforcement is not monitored.

C.2.b. U.S. Implementation

President Roosevelt signed the WHC in 1941. However, its first implementing legislation was enacted as part of the 1973 ESA. The United States has not fully implemented WHC domestically. However, some of the WHC's provisions are accomplished by other laws. For instance, none of the United States's National Parks and Wildlife Refuges were designated as WHC "protected areas," but they attempt to serve the same purposes. The United States has used its WHC authority to export conservation money and expertise to other American nations.

In the 1982 ESA Amendments, Congress designated the Secretary of the Interior, in cooperation with the Secretary of State, as the United States's WHC representative.[107] In 1983, FWS created the Western Hemisphere Program to implement the WHC. The program's focus is on providing training and information to other American countries. The Program provides master's-degree level certification programs in Costa

---

104. *Id.* arts. II-VII.

105. *See generally* Kathleen Rogers & James A. Moore, *Revitalizing the Convention on Nature Protection and Wild Life Preservation in the Western Hemisphere: Might Awakening a Visionary but "Sleeping" Treaty Be the Key to Preserving Biodiversity and Threatened Natural Areas in the Americas?*, 36 Harv. Int'l L.J. 465 (1995).

106. *See id.* at 466.

107. 16 U.S.C. § 1537(e)(1).

Rica, Brazil, Venezuela, and Argentina. The program also provides separate practical training for reserve managers in Mexico and Brazil. To improve access to natural resource information, particularly unpublished local reports and documents, the program developed regional "BIODOC" clearing houses in Costa Rica, Venezuela, Brazil and Argentina. The small grants program supports locally organized, community-based conservation and education projects. All WHC programs are undertaken with regional partners, such as schools, local governments, and non-governmental organizations, to ensure that the programs are catalysts for local conservation.

Interest is strengthening in the WHC. In 1994, the Director of the U.S. Fish and Wildlife Service proposed the establishment of a permanent WHC office to facilitate inter-regional communications and coordination, developing multilateral cooperative agreements, and implementation of new WHC initiatives. That office was not established, but as NAFTA and other free trade agreements affect the environment of the Western Hemisphere, a revitalized WHC could be an excellent means for regional conservation and cooperation in the hemisphere.[108]

D. International Applications of Other ESA Provisions
D.1. Listing, Critical Habitat Designation, and Recovery Plans

Under Section 4 of the ESA, the Secretary may list species even if they are not found in the United States and should consider listing species identified by foreign governments as in danger of extinction, as well as species which foreign nations or international agreements protect from unrestricted commerce.[109] Listing determinations for non-U.S. species are made using the same criteria as for domestic species, including efforts by foreign countries to protect the species.[110] The Secretary is required to give actual notice of proposed listing changes to each foreign country where the species is believed to occur.[111]

The Secretary does not designate critical habitats for species with ranges completely outside the United States. A 1976 opinion by the Assistant Solicitor of Interior for Fish and Wildlife concluded that the ESA

---

108. *See* Rogers & Moore, *supra* note 105, at 488.

109. 16 U.S.C. § 1533(b)(1)(B).

110. *Id.* § 1533(b)(1)(A). See also Chapter Two, section C.1 (The Substance of Listing: Listing Factors).

111. *Id.* § 1533(a)(5)(B).

does not require designation for such species. In 1978, FWS and the National Marine Fisheries Service issued regulations which adopted the position that "critical habitat may not be determined in foreign countries."[112]

The Service also does not prepare recovery plans for listed foreign species. The recovery priority guidelines note that priority for preparing and implementing recovery plans goes to species with the greatest potential for recovery success.[113] FWS has greater ability to promote recovery of domestic species through restrictions on take and habitat protection, so recovery plans for domestic species are given a higher priority than plans for foreign species. The Service does prepare recovery plans for migratory species which spend some part of their life cycle in the United States.

D.2. Section 7's Jeopardy Standard

Currently, the Secretary does not require Section 7 consultations for federal actions carried out in foreign countries.[114] From 1978 to 1986, FWS regulations explicitly required federal agencies to consult with the Secretary under Section 7(a)(2) to ensure that any action authorized, funded, or carried out in a foreign country was not likely to jeopardize the continued existence of any threatened or endangered species.[115] In 1986, ESA regulations were changed to eliminate the consultation requirement for extraterritorial federal actions.[116]

In 1986, Defenders of Wildlife, Friends of Animals and Their Environment, and the Humane Society sued the Secretary of Interior challenging the limit on Section 7 consultation. The federal district court dismissed the suit ruling that environmental groups did not meet standing requirements.[117] The Eighth Circuit reversed the standing ruling.[118] On remand, the district court granted summary judgment for the plaintiffs, explaining that the plain language of the ESA was inclusive, covering all federal actions, whether domestic, on the high seas, or within foreign countries.[119] The Eighth Circuit affirmed, citing the plain language of the statute and the legislative intent of the Act as a whole to the worldwide

---

112. 42 Fed. Reg. 4869 (1977); 43 Fed. Reg. 870 (1978).

113. 48 Fed. Reg. 3098, 43,104 (1983).

114. See Chapter Three (Section 7: Requirements for Federal Agencies).

115. 43 Fed. Reg. 874 (1978).

116. *See* 50 C.F.R. § 402.01(a).

117. *See* Defenders of Wildlife v. Hodel, 658 F. Supp. 43 (D. Minn. 1987).

118. *See* Defenders of Wildlife v. Hodel, 851 F.2d 1035 (8th Cir. 1988).

119. *See* Defenders of Wildlife v. Hodel, 707 F. Supp. 1082 (D. Minn. 1989).

conservation of endangered species.[120] On certiorari, a plurality of the Supreme Court dismissed the suit without deciding the Section 7 question, ruling that the plaintiffs failed to satisfy standing requirements.[121]

Although the extraterritorial application of Section 7 was not decided by the Supreme Court and the Eighth Circuit found that consultations were required for all federal actions outside the United States, current ESA regulations require Section 7 consultations only for federal actions within the United States or on the high seas.[122]

D.3. Section 9 Prohibitions
D.3.a. Endangered Species

Section 9 also prohibits import or export of all species listed as endangered, including exclusively foreign species without a permit.[123] Permits are only issued for "scientific purposes" and for activities that "enhance the propagation or survival" of the species.[124] FWS regulations explicitly allow threatened species to be imported for "zoological exposition."[125] However, FWS has allowed endangered species to be imported for zoological exposition by finding that the importation will "enhance the propagation or survival" or the species. In one case, FWS allowed importation of two endangered giant pandas for a temporary exhibit at the Toledo Zoological Gardens by finding the importation enhanced the survival of the species.[126] FWS made this finding in part because the zoo promised a minimum of $300,000 in equipment and vehicles, and future joint activities with a panda reserve in China.[127] Two other very limited exemptions exist for Alaskan natives or "undue economic hardship" caused by a new ESA listing.[128]

Section 9 also prohibits anyone subject to United States jurisdiction from transporting, receiving, delivering, carrying, shipping, selling, or offering endangered species for sale in foreign commerce.[129] The ESA broadly defines foreign commerce to include: transactions between persons in foreign countries; transactions between a person in the United

---

120. *See* Defenders of Wildlife v. Lujan, 911 F.2d 117 (8th Cir. 1990).

121. *See* Lujan v. Defenders of Wildlife, 504 U.S. 555 (1992).

122. 50 C.F.R. § 402.01.

123. 16 U.S.C. § 1538(a)(1)(A). See also Chapter Four (Section 9: Protecting Members of Listed Species).

124. *See id.* § 1539(a)(1)(A).

125. 50 C.F.R. § 17.32.

126. World Wildlife Fund v. Hodel, 1988 WL 66193, at *1.

127. *See id.*

128. 16 U.S.C. §§ 1539(b), 1539(e).

129. *Id.* §§ 1538(a)(1)(E)-(F).

States and a person in a foreign country; or between persons in the
United States, where the fish and wildlife are moving in any country
outside the United States.[130] Section 9 also prohibits those subject to
United States jurisdiction from taking endangered fish and wildlife
species in the United States, the territorial sea of the United States, or
upon the high seas.[131] The prohibition does not extend to takings in
foreign countries. However, a species so taken cannot be imported into
the United States except with an ESA permit for scientific purposes or to
enhance the propagation or survival of the affected species.[132]

D.3.b. Threatened species

The ESA does not give threatened species the same protections
as endangered species. Instead, ESA Section 4(d) requires that the Secretary issue regulations deemed "necessary and advisable" to conserve
threatened species.[133] Section 9 prohibits the violation of those regulations.[134]

FWS regulations allow threatened species to be imported for: scientific purposes; enhancement of propagation or survival of the species; to
avoid economic hardship; zoological exhibition; educational purposes; or
"special purposes consistent with the purposes of the Act."[135]

Current FWS regulations apply most of Sections 9's other prohibitions to threatened species.[136] However, these prohibitions may be weak-
ened by "special rules" that apply to specific threatened species.[137] The
FWS has promulgated a special rule that allows importation of trophies
of some threatened mammal species for personal use. African elephants,
and the threatened populations of Southern Africa leopards and Argali
sheep are covered under the rule.[138]

The National Marine Fisheries Service does not have a blanket regulation protecting threatened species. Instead, special rules are issued on a
species by species basis.[139]

---

130. *Id.* § 1532(9).
131. *Id.* §§ 1538(a)(1)(B)-(C).
132. *See id.* § 1539(a)(1)(A).
133. *Id.* § 1533(d).
134. *See id.* § 1538(a)(1)(G).
135. 50 C.F.R. § 17.32.
136. *See id.* § 17.31 (wildlife and fish), § 17.71 (plants).
137. *See id.* § 17.31(c).
138. *See id.* § 17.40(e), (f), (j).
139. See Chapter Four, section B.4.a (Regulations Pertaining to Threatened Species).

E. Other International Endangered Species Protections

In addition to the programs enacted under Section 8 and Section 8A of the ESA, the United States has an extensive collection of conservation laws and international agreements that protect foreign (and domestic) wildlife. While a complete discussion of these laws is outside the scope of this book, it should be noted that they intersect with and supplement the ESA in many ways.[140]

---

140. For further discussion of international wildlife laws and their intersection with the ESA, see P. Van Heijnsbergen, Legal Protection Of Wild Fauna & Flora (1997).

CHAPTER SEVEN

Section 11: Bringing Suit

A. Introduction

To provide for enforcement of the Endangered Species Act (ESA), the drafters included a mechanism for citizen watchdogs to bring suit. According to the Supreme Court, the ESA's citizen suit provision is "an authorization of remarkable breadth."[1] Under the citizen suit provisions, any person with standing may seek to compel the Secretary to list species deemed threatened or endangered, or designate critical habitat for listed species; or secure injunctions against violators of the ESA.[2] The ESA expressly grants to "any person"[3] the right to commence legal action against any other person (including the United States or any other Government entity) allegedly in violation of the ESA. In addition, the ESA permits persons to sue the Secretary for failure to enforce ESA taking prohibitions or for failure to perform any non-discretionary duty under ESA Section 4 (such as listing, critical habitat designation, and recovery planning).[4] To encourage citizen suits, the ESA eliminates the traditional amount-in-controversy and diversity-of-citizenship requirements for federal jurisdiction over citizen suit claims. It also provides for the recovery of legal costs in some citizen suits, and allows the Government to take the place of plaintiffs in some cases.[5] The ESA, by implementing the Convention on International Trade in Endangered Species (CITES), also indirectly provides private persons with judicially enforceable rights under that international treaty.[6]

---

1. Bennett v. Spear, 520 U.S. 154, 164 (1997).

2. *See, e.g.,* Martha Phelps, Comment, *Candidate Conservation Agreements Under the Endangered Species Act: Prospects and Perils of an Administrative Experiment,* 25 B.C. Envtl. L. Rev. 175, 186 (1997).

3. 16 U.S.C. § 1540(g)(1).

4. *See id.* § 1540(g). See also Chapter Two (Section 4: Listing, Critical Habitat Designation, and Recovery Plans).

5. *See* 16 U.S.C. § 1540(g)(1).

6. *See* Defenders of Wildlife v. Endangered Species Scientific Auth., 659 F.2d 168, 174-75 (D.C. Cir. 1981). For a discussion of CITES, see also Chapter Six (International Aspects of the ESA).

The ESA contains only two express limitations on private enforcement; it bars citizen suits when: (1) the Secretary is pursuing civil penalties against an alleged violator, or (2) when the United States is pressing criminal charges.[7]

Plaintiffs: Can Animals Sue?

Section 11 allows "any person" to commence a civil suit to enjoin violations of the ESA. The ESA broadly defines "person" as any

> individual, corporation, partnership, trust, association, or any other private entity; or any officer, employee, agent, department, or instrumentality of the Federal Government, of any State, municipality, or political subdivision of a State, or of any foreign government; any State, municipality, or political subdivision of a State; or any other entity subject to the jurisdiction of the United States.

Courts have expanded this definition, and many cases demonstrate that animal plaintiffs have successfully sued. For instance in *Palila v. Hawaii Dept. of Land and Natural Resources*, the Ninth Circuit noted that the palila bird "has legal status and wings its way into federal court as a plaintiff in its own right." In other cases, however, such as *Hawaiian Crow v. Lujan*, animal plaintiffs have not been so lucky. In *Hawaiian Crow*, environmentalists sought to include the endangered alala as one of the plaintiffs suing for implementation of the alala's recovery plan. The *Hawaiian Crow* court held that a bird protected by the ESA was not a person within the meaning of the ESA's citizen suit provision, noting that "all of the relief sought in this action can be obtained by the [environmental groups] suing, regardless of whether the bird itself remained as a named plaintiff." The court distinguished the raft of previous cases in which animal plaintiffs had been named by showing that no defendant had ever directly challenged the inclusion of an animal plaintiff, dismissing the language in *Palila* as dictum.

For details see 16 U.S.C. § 1532(13); Hawaiian Crow, 906 F. Supp. 549, 552 (D. Haw. 1991); Palila, 852 F.2d 1106 (9th Cir. 1991).

---

7. *See* 16 U.S.C. § 1540(g)(2).

B. Categories of Statutory Causes of Action

While the ESA's provisions clearly encourage citizen suits, many de-
fenses can bar a court from reaching the merits of a citizen's claim. For
instance, defendants can argue that a claim is not reviewable under the
citizen suit provisions of the ESA because it does not fall within one of
the categories of causes of action provided by the statute. Under the ESA,
a person may bring a cause of action for three enumerated purposes:
(1) to enjoin the actions of any person or governmental entity who is
allegedly in violation of the ESA or its implementing regulations; (2) to
compel the Secretary to enforce the prohibitions regarding the taking of
any endangered species or threatened species within any state; or (3) to
compel the Secretary to perform any non-discretionary duty under
Section 1533, requiring the Secretary to list animal species that are
"threatened" or "endangered" and designate their "critical habitat."[8]

In *Bennett v. Spear*,[9] the Supreme Court considered the types of claims
that fall within the first category (enjoining the actions of any person or
governmental entity who is allegedly in violation of the ESA or its
implementing regulations). Justice Scalia defined this category as:

> a means by which private parties may enforce the substantive
> provisions of the ESA against regulated parties—both private
> entities and Government agencies—but it is not an alternative
> avenue [to be used in lieu of the third category] for judicial re-
> view of the Secretary's implementation of the statute.[10]

The Court concluded that alleged maladministration of the ESA by
the Secretary could not be considered, for the purposes of the first category, a violation of the ESA or its implementing regulations. Therefore,
the term *violation*, according to the Court, most likely does not refer to the
failure by the Secretary or other federal officers and employees to adequately perform their duties in administering the ESA.[11] Accordingly,
where plaintiffs complained that the U.S. Fish and Wildlife Service's
jeopardy determination was not supported by scientific evidence, the
Bennett court held the petitioner's claim was not subject to judicial review
under the ESA's citizen suit provisions, but could only be challenged
under the Administrative Procedure Act.

---

8. *See* 16 U.S.C. § 1540(g)(1)(A)-(C).

9. 520 S. Ct. 154 (1997).

10. *Id.* at 173.

11. This interpretation has been applied to other environmental statutes as well. For
example, in Battaglia v. Browner, 963 F. Supp. 689, 691 (N.D. Ill. 1997), the court held that
the term "violation" in the citizen suit provision of the Comprehensive Environmental
Response, Compensation and Liability Act (CERCLA) does not encompass failure on the
part of the U.S. EPA administrator to perform her duties.

C. Standing

Despite broad language allowing "any person" to sue under the ESA, simply qualifying as a person does not automatically grant one standing to sue.[12] A plaintiff suing under the citizen suit provision is still required to demonstrate that she has standing — a personal stake in the outcome of

---

Bringing Suit: the Administrative Procedure Act and the ESA

Even where plaintiffs are precluded from suing under the ESA (for example, their claim does not fit into one of the three cause-of-action categories listed in the Act), plaintiffs still may be able to sue under the Administrative Procedure Act (APA), which authorizes courts to "set aside agency action, findings, and conclusions found to be . . . arbitrary, capricious, an abuse of discretion, or otherwise not in accordance with law." The APA provides a right to judicial review of a "final agency action for which there is no other adequate remedy in a court" with only two exceptions where: "(1) statutes preclude judicial review; or (2) agency action is committed to agency discretion by law." Thus, where a plaintiff is suing a federal agency over a final agency action, the APA provides a popular alternative to the ESA. In fact, in *Bennett*, the Supreme Court explicitly stated that the plaintiffs' claims which could not be brought under the ESA could be brought under the APA.

Some of the requirements listed in this chapter for suing under the ESA will differ for suits brought under the APA. For example, the requirements of ripeness and finality — essentially, the parameters surrounding *when* a suit may be brought — are somewhat more strict when suing under the APA in some cases. For example, a plaintiff often must demonstrate that she has been reasonably diligent in pursuing relief through the administrative process before she can sue under the APA. On the other hand, suing under the APA has no 60-day notice requirement. Plaintiffs suing under the APA will also face different rules for recovering attorney fees and damages.

For details see 5 U.S.C. §§ 551-59, 701-06; Bennett, 117 S. Ct. 1154, 1160-61 (1997).

---

12. *See, e.g.,* Defenders of Wildlife v. Hodel, 851 F.2d 1035, 1039 (8th Cir. 1988).

a controversy. Establishing standing is not always easy. The Supreme Court has stated that "when the plaintiff is not himself the object of the government action or inaction he challenges, standing is not precluded, but it is ordinarily 'substantially more difficult' to establish."[13]

The Supreme Court has set forth the three following constitutional requirements for establishing standing, based on the "case or controversy" requirements of Article III of the U.S. Constitution: (1) actual injury, (2) connection between the plaintiff's injury and the defendant's conduct, and (3) a likelihood of redressability. These, along with the nonconstitutional "zone of interests" requirement, are discussed in the following section.

C.1. Actual Injury

First, the plaintiff must show that she, herself, has suffered a specific "actual or imminent" injury. General grievances, which cannot be distinguished from those shared by members of the general public, cannot provide a basis for standing. The injury must be demonstrated by the "invasion of a legally protected interest which is (a) concrete and particularized, [and] . . . (b) actual or imminent not 'conjectural' or 'hypothetical.'"[14] For example, in *Lujan v. Defenders of Wildlife*, the plaintiffs challenged certain federal agency actions that would have had the effect of endangering certain species in other countries. The plaintiffs argued that they had standing because they had traveled, and would travel overseas again, to the habitats of the potentially affected species. The Court held that "'some day' intentions—without any description of concrete plans, or indeed any specification of when the some day will be—do not support a finding of the 'actual or imminent' injury [required]."[15]

In other cases, the actual injury requirement has been applied with different results. For instance, in *Bennett*, the Supreme Court held that the petitioner ranch operators and irrigation districts had demonstrated "injury in fact" when they argued that under restrictions imposed by an allegedly faulty biological opinion, the amount of available water for ranching and farming would be reduced. The Court did not require the petitioners to demonstrate that they would actually receive less water if the biological opinion were to take effect.[16] In *Idaho Farm Bureau Federation v. Babbitt*,[17] the Ninth Circuit found that a group of intervenors,

13. Lujan v. Defenders of Wildlife, 504 U.S. 555, 562 (1992) (citations omitted).
14. *Id.* at 560 (citations omitted).
15. *Id.* at 564 (citations omitted).
16. *See* 520 U.S. at 167-68.
17. 58 F.3d 1392 (9th Cir. 1995).

appealing a district court order directing the FWS to delist a snail species, passed the injury-in-fact requirement where some of the intervenors lived in the state where the snail was found; some of the intervenors visited the specific area in which the species was found; and the intervenors "maintain[ed] a factual and scientific understanding of the [endangered species], its habitat, and threats to the species."[18]

Additionally, in *Mountain States Legal Foundation v. Glickman*, the D.C. Circuit found that an economic injury can be a basis for injury in fact, holding that "government acts constricting a business's supply of its main raw material clearly inflict the constitutionally necessary injury."[19]

C.2. Connection Between Plaintiff's Injury and Defendant's Conduct

A second requirement of standing is the demonstration of a causal connection between the plaintiff's injury and the defendant's conduct. The injury must be "fairly traceable" to the challenged action of the defendant.[20] The plaintiff must "establish that, in fact, the asserted injury was the consequence of the defendant's actions, or that prospective relief will remove the harm."[21] For example, in *Florida Key Deer v. Stickney*,[22] a Florida district court found that environmental groups had standing to bring an action against the Federal Emergency Management Agency (FEMA) in part because the action complained of—FEMA's failure to comply with the ESA's Section 7(a)(2) consultation requirements—was a fairly traceable cause of the plaintiffs' injury.[23] The court held that "[p]laintiffs must only show that there is a 'substantial likelihood' that the actions of FEMA in administering and implementing [agency actions] in Key deer habitat in any way facilitates, encourages, or makes [new] development more likely than would [otherwise] be the case."[24]

C.3. Likelihood of Redressability

To establish standing, plaintiffs must also demonstrate that there is a significant likelihood that the injury will be redressed by the relief the

---

18. *Id.* at 1338-99.

19. 92 F.3d 1228, 1233 (D.C. Cir. 1996).

20. The Supreme Court distinguished this requirement from a requirement of "an injury as to which the defendant's actions are the very last step in the chain of causation." *Bennett v. Spear*, 520 S. Ct. at 168-69.

21. *Warth v. Seldin*, 422 U.S. 490, 505 (1975).

22. 864 F. Supp. 1222 (S.D. Fla. 1994).

23. *See id.* at 1224.

24. *Id.* at 1226 (citations omitted).

plaintiff seeks. In *Lujan v. Defenders of Wildlife*,[25] the Supreme Court found that the plaintiffs failed to demonstrate redressability. In *Lujan*, plaintiffs challenged the Department of Interior and Department of Commerce's joint regulation interpreting Section 7(a)(2) to require consultation by federal agencies for only those actions taken in the United States or on the high seas. Justice Scalia declared that even if the Secretary could be ordered to revise his regulations to require consultation for foreign projects, it would not necessarily remedy the plaintiffs' alleged injury (inability to visit endangered species during foreign travel) unless the agencies funding the overseas project were bound by the Secretary's regulation, "which is very much an open question."[26]

Similarly, in *Pacific Northwest Generating Coop v. Brown*,[27] the court held that plaintiffs representing the interests of high-volume hydropower users lacked standing to challenge plans to augment flows of water over certain hydropower dams to improve salmon migration. According to the court, the causal link between the plaintiffs' projected injury (increased costs associated with augmenting flow over the dam) and the asserted violations of the ESA was attenuated at best. The Ninth Circuit agreed with the district court's findings that plaintiffs had failed to demonstrate that the remedies requested — consultations and a ban on take of the listed species — would enable the listed species to rebound to such an extent that flow augmentation and spill releases would no longer be necessary to aid the survival of juvenile salmon.

The Tenth Circuit's analysis was similar in *Glover River Organization v. United States Department of the Interior*,[28] where the court held that plaintiffs, who opposed the listing of the leopard darter because they feared such listing would preclude construction of certain dams, lacked standing. The court found that no facts supported the existence of a substantial nexus between the relief plaintiffs requested (not listing the species) and the elimination of plaintiffs' alleged injuries (threatened future flood damage in the absence of dams). In other words, the plaintiffs did not present sufficient proof "that there [was] a substantial likelihood that absent the listing of the leopard darter one or more flood control projects helpful to plaintiff would be undertaken."[29]

The redressability requirement is not without loopholes, however. In 1992, the Supreme Court introduced an exception:

---

25. 504 U.S. 555 (1992).

26. *Id.* at 568.

27. 822 F. Supp. 1479, 1502-06 (D. Or. 1993), *aff'd*, 38 F.3d 1058, 1064 (9th Cir. 1993).

28. 675 F.2d 251 (10th Cir. 1982).

29. *Id.* at 254.

[U]nder our case law, one living adjacent to the site for proposed construction of a federally licensed dam has standing to
challenge the licensing agency's failure to prepare an environmental impact statement, even though he cannot establish with
any certainty that the statement will cause the license to be
withheld or altered, and even though the dam will not be completed for many years.[30]

Cass Sunstein has pointed out that one so situated can proceed "without meeting all the normal standards of redressability
and immediacy."[31]

C.4. Zone of Interests Requirement

In addition to these constitutional requirements of standing, courts
have often spoken of the prudential requirement that a plaintiff
demonstrate that her injury is within the "zone of interests" protected or
regulated by the statute at issue.[32] In other words, the plaintiff's interests
and the interests protected by the statute under which the plaintiff is
suing must be somewhat aligned.

In *Bennett*, the Supreme Court clarified the requirements for standing
under the ESA. In that case, the Court unanimously held that the gener-
ous citizen-suit language in the ESA — granting standing to "any person"
to commence a civil action under the ESA — negates the prudential zone
of interests requirement. The Court held that plaintiffs seeking to *prevent*
application of environmental restrictions, as well as those seeking to
force implementation of such restrictions, have standing to sue under the
ESA.[33] According to one commentator, the Court held in short that
"[g]overnment agencies' accountability to the law and access to the federal courts to review ESA issues should not be cabined by whether the
plaintiff wears environmentalist stripes on its sleeve."[34]

D. Ripeness

To determine whether a claim is ripe, a court will "evaluate both the fit-

---

30. Lujan v. Defenders of Wildlife, 504 U.S. at 573 n.7.

31. *See* Cass Sunstein, *What's Standing After* Lujan? *Of Citizen Suits, "Injuries," and Article
III*, 91 Mich. L. Rev. 163, 225 (1992) (quoting Lujan).

32. *See* Mountain States Legal Foundation v. Glickman, 92 F.3d 1228, 1232 (D.C. Cir. 1996)
(stating that "[o]n any given claim, the injury that supplies constitutional standing must be
the same as the injury within the prudential ['zone of interests' test]").

33. *See* Bennett v. Spear, 520 U.S. 154 (1997).

34. Murray D. Feldman, Bennett v. Spear: *Supreme Court Confirms Standing to Challenge
Excessive Government Regulation Under Endangered Species Act*, Advocate, June 1997, at 20,
24.

ness of the issues for judicial decision and the hardship to the parties of withholding court consideration."[35] An administrative action is "fit for judicial review" if the agency action challenged is final (that is, the administrative agency has given its last word on the matter), and the issues raised are "purely legal."[36] According to the Supreme Court, two conditions must be satisfied for agency action to be final. First, the action must mark the "consummation" of the agency's decision making process, and second, the action must be one by which "rights or obligations have been determined," or from which "legal consequences will flow."[37]

In general, "courts will not entertain a petition where pending administrative proceedings or further agency action might render the case moot and judicial review completely unnecessary."[38] However, the requirement that an agency take some concrete step is not absolute if the agency has adopted a plan that will likely result in some future harm. For instance, in *Seattle Audubon Society v. Espy*, the Ninth Circuit allowed plaintiffs to challenge an owl management plan adopted by the Forest Service even though the Service had not yet authorized any timber sales under the plan. The Court rejected the defendant's ripeness claim, recognizing that "individual timber sales are driven by an underlying owl-management plan."[39] Also, as held in *American Forest & Paper Ass'n v. U.S.E.P.A.*, the Fifth Circuit follows the rule that if the questions presented are purely legal and there are no facts to consider or awaiting development, then a case may also be found to be ripe for review.[40]

E.   Notice Requirements

Persons wishing to exercise their right to file a citizen suit must provide both the Secretary and any alleged violator with written notice of the violation 60 days prior to commencing court action.[41] The purpose of this provision is to allow the government to review the situation and decide whether it should bring the suit itself, or, if the government is the target of the lawsuit, to give the government a chance to act. Absent strict com-

---

35. Abbott Labs. v. Gardner, 387 U.S. 136, 149 (1967). *See also* American Forest and Paper Ass'n v. United States Environmental Protection Agency, 137 F.3d 291 (5th Cir. 1998).

36. Bennett v. Spear, 520 U.S. at 177-78.

37. *Id.*

38. Sierra Club v. United States Nuclear Regulatory Commission, 825 F.2d 1356, 1362 (9th Cir. 1987).

39. 998 F.2d 699, 703 (9th Cir. 1993).

40. *See* 137 F.3d 291, 296-97 (5th Cir. 1998).

41. *See* 16 U.S.C. § 1540(g)(2)(A)(i).

pliance with the 60-day notice requirement, a court generally cannot assume jurisdiction over an ESA claim.

In the leading case in the Ninth Circuit, *Save the Yaak Committee v. Block*,[42] plaintiffs filed suit 38 days after sending a formal notice of their intention to do so. *Save the Yaak* illustrates the strict application of the 60-day notice requirement. In this case, the court interpreted the ESA's notice requirement as jurisdictional and thus held that it lacked jurisdiction to consider an ESA claim because the plaintiffs had failed to provide timely notice before filing suit.[43] The court then cited several other deficiencies in the plaintiffs' notice. For instance, the court noted that the letter relied on by the plaintiffs specifically failed to give notice of an ESA violation and specifically failed to mention an intention to file suit. And, even if these weaknesses were not enough to render the plaintiffs' written notice inadequate, the court found the notice to be faulty because it had not been sent to the Secretary of the Interior, as required by the statute. The court implicitly construed "Secretary of the Interior" to mean the actual cabinet official, rather than merely one of his or her subordinates. The plaintiffs had sent a letter to a U.S. Fish and Wildlife Service Regional Director, a subordinate of the Secretary of the Interior.

Perhaps the strictest application of the 60-day notice requirement can be found in the Third Circuit. In *Hawksbill Sea Turtle v. Federal Emergency Management Agency*, the court found the plaintiff's letter to the Secretary of the Interior insufficient notice when jurisdiction over the Hawksbill sea turtle's habitat was shared by both the Secretaries of Commerce and the Interior. The court rejected an argument that the sea turtle could be found both on land and at sea, noting that the court "surely does not know when it crosses from the jurisdiction of the Secretary of Commerce to that of the Secretary of the Interior."[44] The court reasoned that the notice requirement is designed to allow the agency to respond to the plaintiff's concerns. The National Marine Fisheries Service should have had the opportunity to act to satisfy the plaintiff's concerns and avoid the lawsuit.

A challenge under the 60-day notice requirement must be preserved at the time of trial. Although the Ninth Circuit characterizes the 60-day notice requirement as jurisdictional, in *Sierra Club v. Yeutter*, the Fifth Circuit tested that definition and found the requirement not to be

---

42. 840 F.2d 714 (9th Cir. 1988).

43. *See id.* at 721; *see also* Lone Rock Timber Co. v. United States Department of Interior, 842 F. Supp. 433, 440 (D. Or. 1994) (holding that "[t]he 60-day notice is jurisdictional, and failure to comply with that requirement is an absolute bar to bringing an action under this statute").

44. 126 F.3d 461, 464 (3rd Cir. 1997).

Immediate Judicial Review

In limited circumstances, the ESA allows for immediate judicial review of disputes arising under the statute. In the event of "an emergency posing a significant risk to the well-being" of any listed species, any person may bring an action seeking to compel the Secretary to carry out a non-discretionary duty under Section 4. In such a case, the plaintiff must first provide the Secretary with written notice of intent to sue. Immediately upon the Secretary's receipt of this notification, the plaintiff may bring suit. Plaintiffs may also obtain immediate judicial review if the Secretary denies action on a petition to add or remove a species from the lists of threatened and endangered species. Finally, no advance notice is necessary to obtain judicial review of exemptions to Section 7 granted by the Endangered Species Committee.

For details see 16 U.S.C. §§ 1540(g)(2)(C), 1533(b)(3)(C)(iii); City of Las Vegas v. Lujan, 891 F.2d 927 (D.C. Cir 1989); Friends of the Wild Swan v. U.S. Fish and Wildlife Service, 945 F. Supp. 1388 (D. Or. 1996).

"sufficiently jurisdictional" to be raised for the first time on appeal.[45]

The ESA does not specify requirements for the content of the notice. Nevertheless, courts expect notice to be written in such a way that it informs prospective defendants of the nature of the plaintiff's allegations in enough detail to allow defendants to evaluate, and possibly to alter, their conduct. For instance, in *Lone Rock Timber Co. v. United States Department of Interior*, notice which complained of the FWS's failure to issue timely biological opinions and threatened to sue if the FWS did not promptly release those opinions, was not considered sufficient warning of a challenge to the opinions themselves and the process by which those opinions were developed.[46] Although, as *Lone Rock* holds, notice of a procedural challenge will not suffice for notice of an ensuing substantive challenge, notice of one type of substantive challenge may, in some circumstances, allow plaintiffs to bring additional substantive claims. For example, in *Marbled Murrelet v. Babbitt*, the plaintiff environmental group's notice letter, upon which it relied in its complaint, contemplated suit for a violation of ESA Section 9, rather than for violation of Section 7.

45. *See* 926 F.2d 429, 434-36 (5th Cir. 1991).
46. *See* 842 F. Supp. 433, 440 (D. Or. 1994).

The court found that the letter clearly gave notice of an intent to sue under the ESA, and while Section 7 was referenced in only one part of the letter, the letter as a whole provided notice sufficient to afford the opportunity to rectify the asserted ESA violations.[47]

After the ruling in *Bennett* came down in 1997, the Ninth Circuit held, in *American Rivers v. National Marine Fisheries Service*, that if a challenge is made to a final agency action under the APA (as opposed to the ESA), plaintiffs need not comply with the 60-day notice provision.[48] Likewise, unique circumstances can lead a court to soften the strict mandate of the 60-day notice requirement. In *Forest Conservation Council v. Espy*, the plaintiff filed an original complaint alleging the failure to prepare a biological opinion on a Forest Service proposal but did not give the Forest Service or the NMFS notice of intent on a later challenge to the adequacy of the biological opinion. The Ninth Circuit affirmed a lower court ruling which held that the plaintiff should have adhered to the 60-day notice requirement. Nevertheless, due to unique circumstances and a lack of prejudice to the defendant, the plaintiff's case would not be barred despite the lack of proper notice.[49]

F. Injunctions

When a plaintiff prevails in a citizen suit, the typical remedy is injunctive relief. The Supreme Court first established the principle that the ESA forecloses normal equitable analysis in the seminal case of *Tennessee Valley Authority v. Hill*.[50] The Court considered what remedy to grant in light of the "irreconcilable conflict" between the soon-to-be-complete Tellico Dam and ESA Section 7. The court noted that as a "general matter it may be said that '[s]ince all or almost all equitable remedies are discretionary, the balancing of equities and hardships is appropriate in almost any case.'" The court then concluded that, with respect to the ESA, "Congress has spoken in the plainest of words, making it abundantly clear that the balance has been struck in favor of affording endangered species the highest of priorities."[51] In other words, Congress

---

47. *See* 83 F.3d 1068, 1072-73 (9th Cir. 1996). *But see* Building Industry Ass'n of Southern Cal. v. Lujan, 785 F. Supp. 1020 (D.D.C. 1992) (holding that a challenge to an emergency listing is not sufficient notice to challenge a final listing of the same species).

48. *See* 126 F.3d 1118 (9th Cir. 1997).

49. *See* 835 F. Supp. 1202, 1210 (D. Idaho 1993), *aff'd*, 42 F.3d 1399 (9th Cir. 1994) (finding unique circumstances because of the voluminous briefs prepared by both sides and the parties' expeditious progress, and finding lack of prejudice to the defendants because the court had been persuaded to award summary judgment to defendants regardless of the improper notice).

50. TVA v. Hill, 437 U.S. 153 (1978).

51. *Id.* at 193-94.

"foreclosed normal equitable balancing incident to the issuance of injunctive relief."[52] In *Sierra Club v. Marsh*, the Ninth Circuit re-affirmed *TVA*, noting that federal courts are obligated to grant injunctions for substantive violations of the ESA.[53] Injunctions are properly issued as long as the plaintiff shows that a violation of the ESA is "at least likely in the future," or that the violation poses a definitive threat of future harm to protected species.[54]

Future harm to species need not be shown with certainty before a permanent injunction may issue, but mere speculation will not suffice. For example, where plaintiffs argued that a railroad posed the possibility of future accidental grain spills which lured grizzly bears to dangerous areas around railroad tracks, a Montana district court held that the plaintiffs failed to establish the likelihood of irreparable future injury to the bears. The railroad's cleanup efforts substantially minimized the attractiveness of corn spill sites as food sources, and no bears had been hit by trains in the area of corn spills in more than three years. The court found no clear evidence that the railroad operations would result in the deaths of members of a protected species.[55] In contrast, in *Fund for Animals v. Turner*, a district court invalidated a federal regulation and issued an injunction to stop the killing of grizzlies where federal defendants conceded that up to three grizzly bears might be killed in a sport hunt of grizzlies that had been authorized by the regulation.[56]

In *Thomas v. Peterson*, the Ninth Circuit held that an injunction is the proper remedy for ESA procedural violations absent "unusual circumstances."[57] Though the *Thomas* court did not speculate on what unusual circumstances may make an injunction inappropriate, it noted that, in the context of NEPA, unusual circumstances refer to instances where irreparable harm would flow from issuance of an injunction. In a subsequent case, *National Wildlife Federation v. Hodel*,[58] a California District Court considered two unusual circumstances where the issuance of an injunction could conceivably result in harm to the species. The plaintiff attempted to halt the use of lead shotgun pellets to protect bald eagles from lead poisoning. The defendants, however, argued that an injunction

---

52. Arthur D. Smith, *Programmatic Consultation Under the Endangered Species Act: An Anatomy of the Salmon Habitat Litigation*, 11 J. Envtl. L. & Lit. 247, 317 (1996).

53. *See* 816 F.2d 1376, 1383 (9th Cir. 1987).

54. *See* National Wildlife Federation v. Burlington Northern, 23 F.3d 1508, 1511 (9th Cir. 1994).

55. *See id.*

56. *See* 1991 WL 206232 (D.D.C. Sept. 27, 1991).

57. 753 F.2d 754, 764 (9th Cir. 1985).

58. 23 Env't Rep. Cas. (BNA) 1089 (E.D. Cal. 1985).

preventing future use of lead shot would decrease hunting and connected revenue from hunting licenses. The reduction of revenue would, they argued, lead to a cutback on programs to benefit waterfowl, which are a major food source for eagles. The defendants also argued that banning lead shot would create animosity toward federal wildlife agencies and would thus disrupt waterfowl conservation efforts. Despite the defendants' efforts to point out these unusual circumstances, the court found that an injunction was appropriate. The court reasoned that the harm to the species likely to result in the absence of an injunction outweighed the potential harm from a reduction in waterfowl.

G. Attorney Fees

The ESA authorizes courts to award costs of litigation, including reasonable attorney and expert witness fees, to any party to a suit[59] brought under the statute's citizen suit provision where the court determines such an award is appropriate.[60] In determining whether an award of fees is appropriate, courts consider several factors, including whether the applicant is a prevailing party and whether the applicant's lawsuit acted as a catalyst for corrective action.

In determining whether a grant of reasonable attorney fees is appropriate, the court must first consider whether a plaintiff is a prevailing party.[61] The Supreme Court interpreted the citizen suit provision of the Clean Air Act, which is substantially similar to the ESA, in *Ruckelshaus v. Sierra Club.*[62] In that case, the Court rejected a claim that an award of fees could be appropriate where the party seeking fees did not prevail in its case. The court held that, to qualify for reimbursement, a party must be at least "partially prevailing" or achieve "some success, even if not major success."[63] The Court emphasized, however, that more than "trivial success on the merits, or purely procedural victories" were required.[64]

According to the Ninth Circuit, regardless of whether a party has prevailed on every claim, a party may obtain fees if she can show that

---

59. But in Conservation Law Found. of New England, Inc. v. Watt, 654 F. Supp. 706, 707 (D. Mass. 1984), a district court held that a non-party conservation foundation which assisted the state of Massachusetts was entitled to attorney fees for work that was done in a successful claim.

60. *See* 16 U.S.C. § 1540(g)(4).

61. *See* Hensley v. Eckerhart, 461 U.S. 424, 433 (1983).

62. 463 U.S. 680 (1983).

63. *Id.* at 688; *see also* Oregon Natural Resource Council v. Turner, 863 F. Supp. 1277, 1285 (D. Or. 1994) (holding that plaintiffs seeking to recover attorney fees on the theory that the suit was the catalyst for the defendants' development of a recovery plan for an endangered plant failed to establish requisite "prevailing party" status).

64. Ruckelshaus 463 U.S. at 688 n.9.

her lawsuit acted as a catalyst which prompted the opposing party to take action.[65] Accordingly, an Oregon district court made two inquiries in determining whether a lawsuit was the catalyst that prompted the opposing party to take action: (1) whether the suit was causally linked to the relief obtained, and (2) whether the opposing party's response to the lawsuit was required by law. According to the district court, if the relief sought is of the same general type as the relief obtained, the lawsuit demonstrates a causal connection; if the lawsuit was not frivolous, unreasonable or groundless, then the plaintiff will qualify for "prevailing party" status.[66]

G.1. Setting Attorney Fees

After a court decides a fee award is appropriate, it must determine (1) a reasonable number of compensable hours; (2) a reasonable hourly rate; (3) other reasonable expenses; and (4) any additional bonus award. The courts in *Marbled Murrelet v. Pacific Lumber Co.*[67] and *Palila*[68] have discussed several factors relevant to the first two determinations.

If a case contains multiple claims, the Supreme Court has advised that "[w]here the plaintiff has failed to prevail on a claim that is distinct in all respects from his successful claims, the hours spent on the unsuccessful claim should be excluded in considering the amount of a reasonable fee."[69] Accordingly, in *Defenders of Wildlife v. Administrator, Environmental Protection Agency*,[70] a Minnesota district court reduced the fee requested by fifteen percent based on the fact that, in the same case, attorneys spent time on efforts not related to those successful claims furthering the policies of the ESA.

---

65. *See* Sablan v. Department of Finance of the Commonwealth of the Northern Mariana Islands, 856 F.2d. 1317, 1325-27 (9th Cir. 1988).

66. *See* Oregon Natural Resource Council v. Turner, 863 F. Supp. at 1281-82.

67. 163 F.R.D. 308 (N.D. Cal. 1995).

68. 118 F.R.D. 125, 127 (D. Haw. 1987).

69. Hensley v. Eckerhart, 461 U.S. 424, 440 (1983).

70. 700 F. Supp. 1028, 1031 (D. Minn. 1988).

APPENDIX

Endangered Species Act, 16 U.S.C. §§ 1531-1544

(ESA § 2)
§ 1531. Congressional findings and declaration of purposes and policy

(a) Findings

The Congress finds and declares that—
(1) various species of fish, wildlife, and plants in the United States have been rendered extinct as a consequence of economic growth and development untempered by adequate concern and conservation;
(2) other species of fish, wildlife, and plants have been so depleted in numbers that they are in danger of or threatened with extinction;
(3) these species of fish, wildlife, and plants are of esthetic, ecological, educational, historical, recreational, and scientific value to the Nation and its people;
(4) the United States has pledged itself as a sovereign state in the international community to conserve to the extent practicable the various species of fish or wildlife and plants facing extinction, pursuant to—
  (A) migratory bird treaties with Canada and Mexico;
  (B) the Migratory and Endangered Bird Treaty with Japan;
  (C) the Convention on Nature Protection and Wildlife Preservation in the Western Hemisphere;
  (D) the International Convention for the Northwest Atlantic Fisheries;
  (E) the International Convention for the High Seas Fisheries of the North Pacific Ocean;
  (F) the Convention on International Trade in Endangered Species of Wild Fauna and Flora; and
  (G) other international agreements; and
(5) encouraging the States and other interested parties, through Federal financial assistance and a system of incentives, to develop and maintain conservation programs which meet national and international standards is a key to meeting the Nation's international commitments and to better safeguarding, for the benefit of all citizens, the Nation's heritage in fish, wildlife, and plants.

(b) Purposes

The purposes of this chapter are to provide a means whereby the ecosystems upon which endangered species and threatened species depend may be conserved, to provide a program for the conservation of such endangered species and threatened species, and to take such steps as may be appropriate to achieve the purposes of the treaties and conventions set forth in subsection (a) of this section.

(c) Policy

(1) It is further declared to be the policy of Congress that all Federal departments and agencies shall seek to conserve endangered species and threatened species and shall utilize their authorities in furtherance of the purposes of this chapter.

(2) It is further declared to be the policy of Congress that Federal agencies shall cooperate with State and local agencies to resolve water resource issues in concert with conservation of endangered species.

(ESA § 3)
§ 1532. Definitions

For the purposes of this chapter —

(1) The term "alternative courses of action" means all alternatives and thus is not limited to original project objectives and agency jurisdiction.

(2) The term "commercial activity" means all activities of industry and trade, including, but not limited to, the buying or selling of commodities and activities conducted for the purpose of facilitating such buying and selling: Provided, however, That it does not include exhibition of commodities by museums or similar cultural or historical organizations.

(3) The terms "conserve", "conserving", and "conservation" mean to use and the use of all methods and procedures which are necessary to bring any endangered species or threatened species to the point at which the measures provided pursuant to this chapter are no longer necessary. Such methods and procedures include, but are not limited to, all activities associated with scientific resources management such as research, census, law enforcement, habitat acquisition and maintenance, propagation, live trapping, and transplantation, and, in the extraordinary case where population pressures within a given ecosystem cannot be otherwise relieved, may include regulated taking.

(4) The term "Convention" means the Convention on International Trade in Endangered Species of Wild Fauna and Flora, signed on March 3, 1973, and the appendices thereto.

(5)(A) The term "critical habitat" for a threatened or endangered species means —

(i) the specific areas within the geographical area occupied by the species, at the time it is listed in accordance with the provisions of section 1533 of this title, on which are found those physical or biological features (I) essential to the conservation of the species and (II) which may require special management considerations or protection; and

(ii) specific areas outside the geographical area occupied by the species at the time it is listed in accordance with the provisions of section 1533 of this title, upon a determination by the Secretary that such areas are essential for the conservation of the species.

(B) Critical habitat may be established for those species now listed as threatened or endangered species for which no critical habitat has heretofore been established as set forth in subparagraph (A) of this paragraph.

(C) Except in those circumstances determined by the Secretary, critical habitat shall not include the entire geographical area which can be occupied by the threatened or endangered species.

(6) The term "endangered species" means any species which is in danger of extinction throughout all or a significant portion of its range other than a species of the Class Insecta determined by the Secretary to constitute a pest whose protection under the provisions of this chapter would present an overwhelming and overriding risk to man.

(7) The term "Federal agency" means any department, agency, or instrumentality of the United States.

(8) The term "fish or wildlife" means any member of the animal kingdom, including without limitation any mammal, fish, bird (including any migratory, nonmigratory, or endangered bird for which protection is also afforded by treaty or other international agreement), amphibian, reptile, mollusk, crustacean, arthropod or other invertebrate, and includes any part, product, egg, or offspring thereof, or the dead body or parts thereof.

(9) The term "foreign commerce" includes, among other things, any transaction —

(A) between persons within one foreign country;

(B) between persons in two or more foreign countries;

(C) between a person within the United States and a person in a foreign country; or

(D) between persons within the United States, where the fish and wildlife in question are moving in any country or countries outside the United States.

(10) The term "import" means to land on, bring into, or introduce into, or attempt to land on, bring into, or introduce into, any place subject to the jurisdiction of the United States, whether or not such landing, bringing, or introduction constitutes an importation within the meaning of the customs laws of the United States.

(11) Repealed. Pub.L. 97-304, S 4(b), Oct. 13, 1982, 96 Stat. 1420.

(12) The term "permit or license applicant" means, when used with respect to an action of a Federal agency for which exemption is sought under section 1536 of this title, any person whose application to such agency for a permit or license has been denied primarily because of the application of section 1536(a) of this title to such agency action.

(13) The term "person" means an individual, corporation, partnership, trust, association, or any other private entity; or any officer, employee, agent, department, or instrumentality of the Federal Government, of any State, municipality, or political subdivision of a State, or of any foreign government; any State, municipality, or political subdivision of a State; or any other entity subject to the jurisdiction of the United States.

(14) The term "plant" means any member of the plant kingdom, including seeds, roots and other parts thereof.

(15) The term "Secretary" means, except as otherwise herein provided, the Secretary of the Interior or the Secretary of Commerce as program responsibilities are vested pursuant to the provisions of Reorganization Plan Numbered 4 of 1970; except that with respect to the enforcement of the provisions of this chapter and the Convention which pertain to the importation or exportation of terrestrial plants, the term also means the Secretary of Agriculture.

(16) The term "species" includes any subspecies of fish or wildlife or plants, and any distinct population segment of any species of vertebrate fish or wildlife which interbreeds when mature.

(17) The term "State" means any of the several States, the District of Columbia, the Commonwealth of Puerto Rico, American Samoa, the Virgin Islands, Guam, and the Trust Territory of the Pacific Islands.

(18) The term "State agency" means any State agency, department, board, commission, or other governmental entity which is responsible for the management and conservation of fish, plant, or wildlife resources within a State.

(19) The term "take" means to harass, harm, pursue, hunt, shoot, wound, kill, trap, capture, or collect, or to attempt to engage in any such conduct.

(20) The term "threatened species" means any species which is likely to become an endangered species within the foreseeable future throughout all or a significant portion of its range.

(21) The term "United States", when used in a geographical context, includes all States.

(ESA § 4)
§ 1533. Determination of endangered species and threatened species

(a) Generally

(1) The Secretary shall by regulation promulgated in accordance with subsection (b) of this section determine whether any species is an endangered species or a threatened species because of any of the following factors:
(A) the present or threatened destruction, modification, or curtailment of its habitat or range;
(B) overutilization for commercial, recreational, scientific, or educational purposes;
(C) disease or predation;
(D) the inadequacy of existing regulatory mechanisms; or
(E) other natural or manmade factors affecting its continued existence.
(2) With respect to any species over which program responsibilities have been vested in the Secretary of Commerce pursuant to Reorganization Plan Numbered 4 of 1970 —
(A) in any case in which the Secretary of Commerce determines that such species should —
(i) be listed as an endangered species or a threatened species, or
(ii) be changed in status from a threatened species to an endangered species, he shall so inform the Secretary of the Interior, who shall list such species in accordance with this section;
(B) in any case in which the Secretary of Commerce determines that such species should —
(i) be removed from any list published pursuant to subsection (c) of this section, or
(ii) be changed in status from an endangered species to a threatened species, he shall recommend such action to the Secretary of the Interior, and the Secretary of the Interior, if he concurs in the recommendation, shall implement such action; and
(C) the Secretary of the Interior may not list or remove from any list any such species, and may not change the status of any such species which are listed, without a prior favorable determination made pursuant to this section by the Secretary of Commerce.
(3) The Secretary, by regulation promulgated in accordance with subsection (b) of this section and to the maximum extent prudent and determinable —
(A) shall, concurrently with making a determination under paragraph (1) that a species is an endangered species or a threatened species, designate any habitat of such species which is then considered to be critical habitat; and
(B) may, from time-to-time thereafter as appropriate, revise such designation.

(b) Basis for determinations

(1)(A) The Secretary shall make determinations required by subsection (a) (1) of this section solely on the basis of the best scientific and commercial data available to him after conducting a review of the status of the species and after taking into account those efforts, if any, being made by any State or foreign nation, or any political subdivision of a State or foreign nation, to protect such species, whether by predator control, protection of habitat and food supply, or other conservation practices, within any area under its jurisdiction, or on the high seas.

(B) In carrying out this section, the Secretary shall give consideration to species which have been—

(i) designated as requiring protection from unrestricted commerce by any foreign nation, or pursuant to any international agreement; or

(ii) identified as in danger of extinction, or likely to become so within the foreseeable future, by any State agency or by any agency of a foreign nation that is responsible for the conservation of fish or wildlife or plants.

(2) The Secretary shall designate critical habitat, and make revisions thereto, under subsection (a) (3) of this section on the basis of the best scientific data available and after taking into consideration the economic impact, and any other relevant impact, of specifying any particular area as critical habitat. The Secretary may exclude any area from critical habitat if he determines that the benefits of such exclusion outweigh the benefits of specifying such area as part of the critical habitat, unless he determines, based on the best scientific and commercial data available, that the failure to designate such area as critical habitat will result in the extinction of the species concerned.

(3)(A) To the maximum extent practicable, within 90 days after receiving the petition of an interested person under section 553(e) of Title 5 to add a species to, or to remove a species from, either of the lists published under subsection (c) of this section, the Secretary shall make a finding as to whether the petition presents substantial scientific or commercial information indicating that the petitioned action may be warranted. If such a petition is found to present such information, the Secretary shall promptly commence a review of the status of the species concerned. The Secretary shall promptly publish each finding made under this subparagraph in the Federal Register.

(B) Within 12 months after receiving a petition that is found under subparagraph (A) to present substantial information indicating that the petitioned action may be warranted, the Secretary shall make one of the following findings:

(i) The petitioned action is not warranted, in which case the Secretary shall promptly publish such finding in the Federal Register.

(ii) The petitioned action is warranted, in which case the Secretary shall promptly publish in the Federal Register a general notice and the complete text of a proposed regulation to implement such action in accordance with paragraph (5).

(iii) The petitioned action is warranted, but that—

(I) the immediate proposal and timely promulgation of a final regulation implementing the petitioned action in accordance with paragraphs (5) and (6) is precluded by pending proposals to determine whether any species is an endangered species or a threatened species, and

(II) expeditious progress is being made to add qualified species to either of the lists published under subsection (c) of this section and to remove from such lists species for which the protections of this chapter are no longer necessary, in which case the Secretary shall promptly publish such finding in the Federal Register, together with a description and evaluation of the reasons and data on which the finding is based.

(C)(i) A petition with respect to which a finding is made under subparagraph (B)(iii) shall be treated as a petition that is resubmitted to the Secretary under subparagraph (A) on the date of such finding and that presents substantial scientific or commercial information that the petitioned action may be warranted.

(ii) Any negative finding described in subparagraph (A) and any finding described in subparagraph (B) (i) or (iii) shall be subject to judicial review.

(iii) The Secretary shall implement a system to monitor effectively the status of all species with respect to which a finding is made under subparagraph (B)(iii) and shall make prompt use of the authority under paragraph 7 to prevent a significant risk to the well being of any such species.

(D)(i) To the maximum extent practicable, within 90 days after receiving the petition of an interested person under section 553(e) of Title 5, to revise a critical habitat designation, the Secretary shall make a finding as to whether the petition presents substantial scientific information indicating that the revision may be warranted. The Secretary shall promptly publish such finding in the Federal Register.

(ii) Within 12 months after receiving a petition that is found under clause (i) to present substantial information indicating that the requested revision may be warranted, the Secretary shall determine how he intends to proceed with the requested revision, and shall promptly publish notice of such intention in the Federal Register.

(4) Except as provided in paragraphs (5) and (6) of this subsection, the provisions of section 553 of Title 5 (relating to rulemaking procedures), shall apply to any regulation promulgated to carry out the purposes of this chapter.

(5) With respect to any regulation proposed by the Secretary to implement a determination, designation, or revision referred to in subsection (a) (1) or (3) of this section, the Secretary shall—

(A) not less than 90 days before the effective date of the regulation—

(i) publish a general notice and the complete text of the proposed regulation in the Federal Register, and

(ii) give actual notice of the proposed regulation (including the complete text of the regulation) to the State agency in each State in which the species is believed to occur, and to each county or equivalent jurisdiction in which the species is believed to occur, and invite the comment of such agency, and each such jurisdiction, thereon;

(B) insofar as practical, and in cooperation with the Secretary of State, give notice of the proposed regulation to each foreign nation in which the species is believed to occur or whose citizens harvest the species on the high seas, and invite the comment of such nation thereon;

(C) give notice of the proposed regulation to such professional scientific organizations as he deems appropriate;

(D) publish a summary of the proposed regulation in a newspaper of general circulation in each area of the United States in which the species is believed to occur; and

(E) promptly hold one public hearing on the proposed regulation if any person files a request for such a hearing within 45 days after the date of publication of general notice.

(6) (A) Within the one-year period beginning on the date on which general notice is published in accordance with paragraph (5) (A) (i) regarding a proposed regulation, the Secretary shall publish in the Federal Register —

(i) if a determination as to whether a species is an endangered species or a threatened species, or a revision of critical habitat, is involved, either —

(I) a final regulation to implement such determination,

(II) a final regulation to implement such revision or a finding that such revision should not be made,

(III) notice that such one-year period is being extended under subparagraph (B) (i), or

(IV) notice that the proposed regulation is being withdrawn under subparagraph (B) (ii), together with the finding on which such withdrawal is based; or

(ii) subject to subparagraph (C), if a designation of critical habitat is involved, either —

(I) a final regulation to implement such designation, or

(II) notice that such one-year period is being extended under such subparagraph.

(B)(i) If the Secretary finds with respect to a proposed regulation referred to in subparagraph (A) (i) that there is substantial disagreement regarding the sufficiency or accuracy of the available data relevant to the determination or revision concerned, the Secretary may extend the one-year period specified in subparagraph (A) for not more than six months for purposes of soliciting additional data.

(ii) If a proposed regulation referred to in subparagraph (A) (i) is not promulgated as a final regulation within such one-year period (or longer period if extension under clause (i) applies) because the Secretary finds that there is not sufficient evidence to justify the action proposed by the regulation, the Secretary shall immediately withdraw the regulation. The finding on which a withdrawal is based shall be subject to judicial review. The Secretary may not propose a regulation that has previously been withdrawn under this clause unless he determines that sufficient new information is available to warrant such proposal.

(iii) If the one-year period specified in subparagraph (A) is extended under clause (i) with respect to a proposed regulation, then before the close of such extended period the Secretary shall publish in the Federal Register either a final regulation to implement the determination or revision concerned, a finding that the revision should not be made, or a notice of withdrawal of the regulation under clause (ii), together with the finding on which the withdrawal is based.

(C) A final regulation designating critical habitat of an endangered species or a threatened species shall be published concurrently with the final regulation implementing the determination that such species is endangered or threatened, unless the Secretary deems that—

(i) it is essential to the conservation of such species that the regulation implementing such determination be promptly published; or

(ii) critical habitat of such species is not then determinable, in which case the Secretary, with respect to the proposed regulation to designate such habitat, may extend the one-year period specified in subparagraph (A) by not more than one additional year, but not later than the close of such additional year the Secretary must publish a final regulation, based on such data as may be available at that time, designating, to the maximum extent prudent, such habitat.

(7) Neither paragraph (4), (5), or (6) of this subsection nor section 553 of Title 5 shall apply to any regulation issued by the Secretary in regard to any emergency posing a significant risk to the well-being of any species of fish or wildlife or plants, but only if—

(A) at the time of publication of the regulation in the Federal Register the Secretary publishes therein detailed reasons why such regulation is necessary; and

(B) in the case such regulation applies to resident species of fish or wildlife, or plants, the Secretary gives actual notice of such regulation to the State agency in each State in which such species is believed to occur.

Such regulation shall, at the discretion of the Secretary, take effect immediately upon the publication of the regulation in the Federal Register. Any regulation promulgated under the authority of this paragraph shall cease to have force and effect at the close of the 240-day period following the date of publication unless, during such 240-day period, the rulemaking procedures which would apply to such regulation without regard to this paragraph are complied with. If at any time after issuing an emergency regulation the Secretary determines, on the basis of the best appropriate data available to him, that substantial evidence does not exist to warrant such regulation, he shall withdraw it.

(8) The publication in the Federal Register of any proposed or final regulation which is necessary or appropriate to carry out the purposes of this chapter shall include a summary by the Secretary of the data on which such regulation is based and shall show the relationship of such data to such regulation; and if such regulation designates or revises critical habitat, such summary shall, to the maximum extent practicable, also include a brief description and evaluation of those activities (whether public or private) which, in the opinion of the Secretary, if undertaken may adversely modify such habitat, or may be affected by such designation.

(c) Lists

(1) The Secretary of the Interior shall publish in the Federal Register a list of all species determined by him or the Secretary of Commerce to be endangered species and a list of all species determined by him or the Secretary of Commerce to be threatened species. Each list shall refer to the species contained therein by scientific and common name or names, if any, specify with respect to each such species over what portion of its range it is endangered or threatened, and specify any critical habitat within such range. The Secretary shall from time to time revise each list published under the authority of this subsection to reflect recent determinations, designations, and revisions made in accordance with subsections (a) and (b) of this section.

(2) The Secretary shall—

(A) conduct, at least once every five years, a review of all species included in a list which is published pursuant to paragraph (1) and which is in effect at the time of such review; and

(B) determine on the basis of such review whether any such species should—

(i) be removed from such list;

(ii) be changed in status from an endangered species to a threatened species; or

(iii) be changed in status from a threatened species to an endangered species.

Each determination under subparagraph (B) shall be made in accordance with the provisions of subsections (a) and (b) of this section.

(d) Protective regulations

Whenever any species is listed as a threatened species pursuant to subsection (c) of this section, the Secretary shall issue such regulations as he deems necessary and advisable to provide for the conservation of such species. The Secretary may by regulation prohibit with respect to any threatened species any act prohibited under section 1538(a) (1) of this title, in the case of fish or wildlife, or section 1538(a) (2) of this title, in the case of plants, with respect to endangered species; except that with respect to the taking of resident species of fish or wildlife, such regulations shall apply in any State which has entered into a cooperative agreement pursuant to section 1535(c) of this title only to the extent that such regulations have also been adopted by such State.

(e) Similarity of appearance cases

The Secretary may, by regulation of commerce or taking, and to the extent he deems advisable, treat any species as an endangered species or threatened species even though it is not listed pursuant to this section if he finds that—
(A) such species so closely resembles in appearance, at the point in question, a species which has been listed pursuant to such section that enforcement personnel would have substantial difficulty in attempting to differentiate between the listed and unlisted species;
(B) the effect of this substantial difficulty is an additional threat to an endangered or threatened species; and
(C) such treatment of an unlisted species will substantially facilitate the enforcement and further the policy of this chapter.

(f) Recovery plans

(1) The Secretary shall develop and implement plans (hereinafter in this subsection referred to as "recovery plans") for the conservation and survival of endangered species and threatened species listed pursuant to this section, unless he finds that such a plan will not promote the conservation of the species. The Secretary, in developing and implementing recovery plans, shall, to the maximum extent practicable—
(A) give priority to those endangered species or threatened species, without regard to taxonomic classification, that are most likely to benefit from such plans, particularly those species that are, or may be, in conflict with construction or other development projects or other forms of economic activity;
(B) incorporate in each plan—
(i) a description of such site-specific management actions as may be necessary to achieve the plan's goal for the conservation and survival of the species;
(ii) objective, measurable criteria which, when met, would result in a determination, in accordance with the provisions of this section, that the species be removed from the list; and

(iii) estimates of the time required and the cost to carry out those measures needed to achieve the plan's goal and to achieve intermediate steps toward that goal.

(2) The Secretary, in developing and implementing recovery plans, may procure the services of appropriate public and private agencies and institutions, and other qualified persons. Recovery teams appointed pursuant to this subsection shall not be subject to the Federal Advisory Committee Act.

(3) The Secretary shall report every two years to the Committee on Environment and Public Works of the Senate and the Committee on Merchant Marine and Fisheries of the House of Representatives on the status of efforts to develop and implement recovery plans for all species listed pursuant to this section and on the status of all species for which such plans have been developed.

(4) The Secretary shall, prior to final approval of a new or revised recovery plan, provide public notice and an opportunity for public review and comment on such plan. The Secretary shall consider all information presented during the public comment period prior to approval of the plan.

(5) Each Federal agency shall, prior to implementation of a new or revised recovery plan, consider all information presented during the public comment period under paragraph (4).

(g) Monitoring

(1) The Secretary shall implement a system in cooperation with the States to monitor effectively for not less than five years the status of all species which have recovered to the point at which the measures provided pursuant to this chapter are no longer necessary and which, in accordance with the provisions of this section, have been removed from either of the lists published under subsection (c) of this section.

(2) The Secretary shall make prompt use of the authority under paragraph 7 of subsection (b) of this section to prevent a significant risk to the well being of any such recovered species.

(h) Agency guidelines; publication in Federal Register; scope; proposals and amendments: notice and opportunity for comments

The Secretary shall establish, and publish in the Federal Register, agency guidelines to insure that the purposes of this section are achieved efficiently and effectively. Such guidelines shall include, but are not limited to—

(1) procedures for recording the receipt and the disposition of petitions submitted under subsection (b)(3) of this section;

(2) criteria for making the findings required under such subsection with respect to petitions;

(3) a ranking system to assist in the identification of species that should

receive priority review under subsection (a)(1) of this section; and

(4) a system for developing and implementing, on a priority basis, recovery plans under subsection (f) of this section.

The Secretary shall provide to the public notice of, and opportunity to submit written comments on, any guideline (including any amendment thereto) proposed to be established under this subsection.

(i) Submission to State agency of justification for regulations inconsistent with State agency's comments or petition

If, in the case of any regulation proposed by the Secretary under the authority of this section, a State agency to which notice thereof was given in accordance with subsection (b)(5)(A)(ii) of this section files comments disagreeing with all or part of the proposed regulation, and the Secretary issues a final regulation which is in conflict with such comments, or if the Secretary fails to adopt a regulation pursuant to an action petitioned by a State agency under subsection (b)(3) of this section, the Secretary shall submit to the State agency a written justification for his failure to adopt regulations consistent with the agency's comments or petition.

(ESA § 5)
§ 1534. Land acquisition

(a) Implementation of conservation program; authorization of Secretary and Secretary of Agriculture

The Secretary, and the Secretary of Agriculture with respect to the National Forest System, shall establish and implement a program to conserve fish, wildlife, and plants, including those which are listed as endangered species or threatened species pursuant to section 1533 of this title. To carry out such a program, the appropriate Secretary —

(1) shall utilize the land acquisition and other authority under the Fish and Wildlife Act of 1956, as amended [> 16 U.S.C.A. S 742a et seq.], the Fish and Wildlife Coordination Act, as amended [> 16 U.S.C.A. S 661 et seq.], and the Migratory Bird Conservation Act [> 16 U.S.C.A. S 715 et seq.], as appropriate; and

(2) is authorized to acquire by purchase, donation, or otherwise, lands, waters, or interest therein, and such authority shall be in addition to any other land acquisition authority vested in him.

(b) Availability of funds for acquisition of lands, waters, etc.

Funds made available pursuant to the Land and Water Conservation Fund

Act of 1965, as amended [> 16 U.S.C.A. S 4601-4 et seq.], may be used for the purpose of acquiring lands, waters, or interests therein under subsection (a) of this section.

(ESA § 6)
§ 1535. Cooperation with States

(a) Generally

In carrying out the program authorized by this chapter, the Secretary shall cooperate to the maximum extent practicable with the States. Such cooperation shall include consultation with the States concerned before acquiring any land or water, or interest therein, for the purpose of conserving any endangered species or threatened species.

(b) Management agreements

The Secretary may enter into agreements with any State for the administration and management of any area established for the conservation of endangered species or threatened species. Any revenues derived from the administration of such areas under these agreements shall be subject to the provisions of section 715s of this title.

(c) Cooperative agreements

(1) In furtherance of the purposes of this chapter, the Secretary is authorized to enter into a cooperative agreement in accordance with this section with any State which establishes and maintains an adequate and active program for the conservation of endangered species and threatened species. Within one hundred and twenty days after the Secretary receives a certified copy of such a proposed State program, he shall make a determination whether such program is in accordance with this chapter. Unless he determines, pursuant to this paragraph, that the State program is not in accordance with this chapter, he shall enter into a cooperative agreement with the State for the purpose of assisting in implementation of the State program. In order for a State program to be deemed an adequate and active program for the conservation of endangered species and threatened species, the Secretary must find, and annually thereafter reconfirm such finding, that under the State program—
(A) authority resides in the State agency to conserve resident species of fish or wildlife determined by the State agency or the Secretary to be endangered or threatened;
(B) the State agency has established acceptable conservation programs, consistent with the purposes and policies of this chapter, for all resident

species of fish or wildlife in the State which are deemed by the Secretary to be endangered or threatened, and has furnished a copy of such plan and program together with all pertinent details, information, and data requested to the Secretary;

(C) the State agency is authorized to conduct investigations to determine the status and requirements for survival of resident species of fish and wildlife;

(D) the State agency is authorized to establish programs, including the acquisition of land or aquatic habitat or interests therein, for the conservation of resident endangered or threatened species of fish or wildlife; and

(E) provision is made for public participation in designating resident species of fish or wildlife as endangered or threatened;

or that under the State program—

(i) the requirements set forth in subparagraphs (C), (D), and (E) of this paragraph are complied with, and

(ii) plans are included under which immediate attention will be given to those resident species of fish and wildlife which are determined by the Secretary or the State agency to be endangered or threatened and which the Secretary and the State agency agree are most urgently in need of conservation programs; except that a cooperative agreement entered into with a State whose program is deemed adequate and active pursuant to clause (i) and this clause shall not affect the applicability of prohibitions set forth in or authorized pursuant to section 1533(d) of this title or section 1538(a) (1) of this title with respect to the taking of any resident endangered or threatened species.

(2) In furtherance of the purposes of this chapter, the Secretary is authorized to enter into a cooperative agreement in accordance with this section with any State which establishes and maintains an adequate and active program for the conservation of endangered species and threatened species of plants. Within one hundred and twenty days after the Secretary receives a certified copy of such a proposed State program, he shall make a determination whether such program is in accordance with this chapter. Unless he determines, pursuant to this paragraph, that the State program is not in accordance with this chapter, he shall enter into a cooperative agreement with the State for the purpose of assisting in implementation of the State program. In order for a State program to be deemed an adequate and active program for the conservation of endangered species of plants and threatened species of plants, the Secretary must find, and annually thereafter reconfirm such finding, that under the State program—

(A) authority resides in the State agency to conserve resident species of plants determined by the State agency or the Secretary to be endangered or threatened;

(B) the State agency has established acceptable conservation programs, consistent with the purposes and policies of this chapter, for all resident species of plants in the State which are deemed by the Secretary to be endangered or threatened, and has furnished a copy of such plan and program together with all pertinent details, information, and data requested to the Secretary;

(C) the State agency is authorized to conduct investigations to determine the status and requirements for survival of resident species of plants; and

(D) provision is made for public participation in designating resident species of plants as endangered or threatened; or

that under the State program—

(i) the requirements set forth in subparagraphs (C) and (D) of this paragraph are complied with, and

(ii) plans are included under which immediate attention will be given to those resident species of plants which are determined by the Secretary or the State agency to be endangered or threatened and which the Secretary and the State agency agree are most urgently in need of conservation programs; except that a cooperative agreement entered into with a State whose program is deemed adequate and active pursuant to clause (i) and this clause shall not affect the applicability of prohibitions set forth in or authorized pursuant to section 1533(d) or section 1538(a) (1) of this title with respect to the taking of any resident endangered or threatened species.

(d) Allocation of funds

(1) The Secretary is authorized to provide financial assistance to any State, through its respective State agency, which has entered into a cooperative agreement pursuant to subsection (c) of this section to assist in development of programs for the conservation of endangered and threatened species or to assist in monitoring the status of candidate species pursuant to subparagraph

(C) of section 1533(b)(3) of this title and recovered species pursuant to section 1533(g) of this title. The Secretary shall allocate each annual appropriation made in accordance with the provisions of subsection (i) of this section to such States based on consideration of—

(A) the international commitments of the United States to protect endangered species or threatened species;

(B) the readiness of a State to proceed with a conservation program consistent with the objectives and purposes of this chapter;

(C) the number of endangered species and threatened species within a State;

(D) the potential for restoring endangered species and threatened species within a State;

(E) the relative urgency to initiate a program to restore and protect an endangered species or threatened species in terms of survival of the species;

(F) the importance of monitoring the status of candidate species within a State to prevent a significant risk to the well being of any such species; and

(G) the importance of monitoring the status of recovered species within a State to assure that such species do not return to the point at which the measures provided pursuant to this chapter are again necessary.

So much of the annual appropriation made in accordance with provisions of subsection (i) of this section allocated for obligation to any State for any fiscal year as remains unobligated at the close thereof is authorized to be made available to that State until the close of the succeeding fiscal year. Any amount allocated to any State which is unobligated at the end of the period during which it is available for expenditure is authorized to be made available for expenditure by the Secretary in conducting programs under this section.

(2) Such cooperative agreements shall provide for (A) the actions to be taken by the Secretary and the States; (B) the benefits that are expected to be derived in connection with the conservation of endangered or threatened species; (C) the estimated cost of these actions; and (D) the share of such costs to be borne by the Federal Government and by the States; except that—

(i) the Federal share of such program costs shall not exceed 75 percent of the estimated program cost stated in the agreement; and

(ii) the Federal share may be increased to 90 percent whenever two or more States having a common interest in one or more endangered or threatened species, the conservation of which may be enhanced by cooperation of such States, enter jointly into an agreement with the Secretary.

The Secretary may, in his discretion, and under such rules and regulations as he may prescribe, advance funds to the State for financing the United States pro rata share agreed upon in the cooperative agreement. For the purposes of this section, the non-Federal share may, in the discretion of the Secretary, be in the form of money or real property, the value of which will be determined by the Secretary, whose decision shall be final.

(e) Review of State programs

Any action taken by the Secretary under this section shall be subject to his periodic review at no greater than annual intervals.

(f) Conflicts between Federal and State laws

Any State law or regulation which applies with respect to the importation or exportation of, or interstate or foreign commerce in, endangered species or threatened species is void to the extent that it may effectively (1) permit what is prohibited by this chapter or by any regulation which implements this chapter, or (2) prohibit what is authorized pursuant to an exemption or permit provided for in this chapter or in any regulation which implements this chapter. This chapter shall not otherwise be construed to void any State law or regulation which is intended to conserve migratory, resident, or introduced fish or wildlife, or to permit or prohibit sale of such fish or wildlife. Any State law or regulation respecting the taking of an endangered species or threatened species may be more restrictive than the exemptions or permits provided for in this chapter or in any regulation which implements this chapter but not less restrictive than the prohibitions so defined.

(g) Transition

(1) For purposes of this subsection, the term "establishment period" means, with respect to any State, the period beginning on December 28, 1973 and ending on whichever of the following dates first occurs: (A) the date of the close of the 120-day period following the adjournment of the first regular session of the legislature of such State which commences after December 28, 1973, or (B) the date of the close of the 15-month period following December 28, 1973.

(2) The prohibitions set forth in or authorized pursuant to sections 1533(d) and 1538(a)(1)(B) of this title shall not apply with respect to the taking of any resident endangered species or threatened species (other than species listed in Appendix I to the Convention or otherwise specifically covered by any other treaty or Federal law) within any State—

(A) which is then a party to a cooperative agreement with the Secretary pursuant to subsection (c) of this section (except to the extent that the taking of any such species is contrary to the law of such State); or

(B) except for any time within the establishment period when—

(i) the Secretary applies such prohibition to such species at the request of the State, or

(ii) the Secretary applies such prohibition after he finds, and publishes his finding, that an emergency exists posing a significant risk to the well-being of such species and that the prohibition must be applied to protect such species. The Secretary's finding and publication may be made without regard to the public hearing or comment provisions of section 553 of Title 5 or any other provision of this chapter; but such prohibition shall expire 90 days after the date of its imposition unless the Secretary further extends such prohibition by publishing notice and a statement of justification of such extension.

(h) Regulations

The Secretary is authorized to promulgate such regulations as may be appropriate to carry out the provisions of this section relating to financial assistance to States.

(i) Appropriations

(1) To carry out the provisions of this section for fiscal years after September 30, 1988, there shall be deposited into a special fund known as the cooperative endangered species conservation fund, to be administered by the Secretary, an amount equal to 5 percent of the combined amounts covered each fiscal year into the Federal aid to wildlife restoration fund under section 669b of this title, and paid, transferred, or otherwise credited each fiscal year to the Sport Fishing Restoration Account established under 1016 of the Act of July 18, 1984.

(2) Amounts deposited into the special fund are authorized to be appropriated annually and allocated in accordance with subsection (d) of this section.

(ESA § 7)

§ 1536. Interagency cooperation

(a) Federal agency actions and consultations

(1) The Secretary shall review other programs administered by him and utilize such programs in furtherance of the purposes of this chapter. All other Federal agencies shall, in consultation with and with the assistance of the Secretary, utilize their authorities in furtherance of the purposes of this chapter by carrying out programs for the conservation of endangered species and threatened species listed pursuant to section 1533 of this title.

(2) Each Federal agency shall, in consultation with and with the assistance of the Secretary, insure that any action authorized, funded, or carried out by such agency (hereinafter in this section referred to as an "agency action") is not likely to jeopardize the continued existence of any endangered species or threatened species or result in the destruction or adverse modification of habitat of such species which is determined by the Secretary, after consultation as appropriate with affected States, to be critical, unless such agency has been granted an exemption for such action by the Committee pursuant to subsection (h) of this section. In fulfilling the requirements of this paragraph each agency shall use the best scientific and commercial data available.

(3) Subject to such guidelines as the Secretary may establish, a Federal agency shall consult with the Secretary on any prospective agency action at the request of, and in cooperation with, the prospective permit or license applicant if the applicant has reason to believe that an endangered species or a threatened species may be present in the area affected by his project and that implementation of such action will likely affect such species.

(4) Each Federal agency shall confer with the Secretary on any agency action which is likely to jeopardize the continued existence of any species proposed to be listed under section 1533 of this title or result in the destruction or adverse modification of critical habitat proposed to be designated for such species. This paragraph does not require a limitation on the commitment of resources as described in subsection (d) of this section.

(b) Opinion of Secretary

(1)(A) Consultation under subsection (a) (2) of this section with respect to any agency action shall be concluded within the 90-day period beginning on the date on which initiated or, subject to subparagraph (B), within such other period of time as is mutually agreeable to the Secretary and the Federal agency.

(B) In the case of an agency action involving a permit or license applicant, the Secretary and the Federal agency may not mutually agree to conclude consultation within a period exceeding 90 days unless the Secretary, before the close of the 90th day referred to in subparagraph (A) —

(i) if the consultation period proposed to be agreed to will end before the 150th day after the date on which consultation was initiated, submits to the applicant a written statement setting forth —

(I) the reasons why a longer period is required,

(II) the information that is required to complete the consultation, and

(III) the estimated date on which consultation will be completed; or

(ii) if the consultation period proposed to be agreed to will end 150 or more days after the date on which consultation was initiated, obtains the consent of the applicant to such period.

The Secretary and the Federal agency may mutually agree to extend a consultation period established under the preceding sentence if the Secretary, before the close of such period, obtains the consent of the applicant to the extension.

(2) Consultation under subsection (a) (3) of this section shall be concluded within such period as is agreeable to the Secretary, the Federal agency, and the applicant concerned.

(3)(A) Promptly after conclusion of consultation under paragraph (2) or (3) of subsection (a) of this section, the Secretary shall provide to the Federal agency and the applicant, if any, a written statement setting forth the Secretary's opinion, and a summary of the information on which the opinion is based, detailing how the agency action affects the species or its critical habitat. If jeopardy or adverse modification is found, the Secretary shall suggest those reasonable and prudent alternatives which he believes would not violate subsection (a) (2) of this section and can be taken by the Federal agency or applicant in implementing the agency action.

(B) Consultation under subsection (a) (3) of this section, and an opinion issued by the Secretary incident to such consultation, regarding an agency action shall be treated respectively as a consultation under subsection (a) (2) of this section, and as an opinion issued after consultation under such subsection, regarding that action if the Secretary reviews the action before it is commenced by the Federal agency and finds, and notifies such agency, that no significant changes have been made with respect to the action and, that no significant change has occurred regarding the information used during the initial consultation.

(4) If after consultation under subsection (a)(2) of this section, the Secretary concludes that—

(A) the agency action will not violate such subsection, or offers reasonable and prudent alternatives which the Secretary believes would not violate such subsection;

(B) the taking of an endangered species or a threatened species incidental to the agency action will not violate such subsection; and

(C) if an endangered species or threatened species of a marine mammal is involved, the taking is authorized pursuant to section 1371(a)(5) of this title;

the Secretary shall provide the Federal agency and the applicant concerned, if any, with a written statement that—

(i) specifies the impact of such incidental taking on the species,

(ii) specifies those reasonable and prudent measures that the Secretary considers necessary or appropriate to minimize such impact,

(iii) in the case of marine mammals, specifies those measures that are necessary to comply with section 1371(a)(5) of this title with regard to such taking, and

(iv) sets forth the terms and conditions (including, but not limited to, reporting requirements) that must be complied with by the Federal agency or applicant (if any), or both, to implement the measures specified under clauses (ii) and (iii).

(c) Biological assessment

(1) To facilitate compliance with the requirements of subsection (a) (2) of this section, each Federal agency shall, with respect to any agency action of such agency for which no contract for construction has been entered into and for which no construction has begun on November 10, 1978, request of the Secretary information whether any species which is listed or proposed to be listed may be present in the area of such proposed action. If the Secretary advises, based on the best scientific and commercial data available, that such species may be present, such agency shall conduct a biological assessment for the purpose of identifying any endangered species or threatened species which is likely to be affected by such action. Such assessment shall be completed within 180 days after the date on which initiated (or within such other period as is mutually agreed to by the

Secretary and such agency, except that if a permit or license applicant is involved, the 180-day period may not be extended unless such agency provides the applicant, before the close of such period, with a written statement setting forth the estimated length of the proposed extension and the reasons therefor) and, before any contract for construction is entered into and before construction is begun with respect to such action. Such assessment may be undertaken as part of a Federal agency's compliance with the requirements of section 102 of the National Environmental Policy Act of 1969 (> 42 U.S.C. 4332).

(2) Any person who may wish to apply for an exemption under subsection (g) of this section for that action may conduct a biological assessment to identify any endangered species or threatened species which is likely to be affected by such action. Any such biological assessment must, however, be conducted in cooperation with the Secretary and under the supervision of the appropriate Federal agency.

(d) Limitation on commitment of resources

After initiation of consultation required under subsection (a) (2) of this section, the Federal agency and the permit or license applicant shall not make any irreversible or irretrievable commitment of resources with respect to the agency action which has the effect of foreclosing the formulation or implementation of any reasonable and prudent alternative measures which would not violate subsection (a) (2) of this section.

(e) Endangered Species Committee

(1) There is established a committee to be known as the Endangered Species Committee (hereinafter in this section referred to as the "Committee").

(2) The Committee shall review any application submitted to it pursuant to this section and determine in accordance with subsection (h) of this section whether or not to grant an exemption from the requirements of subsection (a) (2) of this section for the action set forth in such application.

(3) The Committee shall be composed of seven members as follows:

(A) The Secretary of Agriculture.

(B) The Secretary of the Army.

(C) The Chairman of the Council of Economic Advisors.

(D) The Administrator of the Environmental Protection Agency.

(E) The Secretary of the Interior.

(F) The Administrator of the National Oceanic and Atmospheric Administration.

(G) The President, after consideration of any recommendations received pursuant to subsection (g) (2) (B) of this section shall appoint one individual from each affected State, as determined by the Secretary, to be a member of the Committee for the consideration of the application for exemption for an agency action with respect to which such recommendations are made, not later than 30 days after an application is submitted pursuant to this section.

(4)(A) Members of the Committee shall receive no additional pay on account of their service on the Committee.

(B) While away from their homes or regular places of business in the performance of services for the Committee, members of the Committee shall be allowed travel expenses, including per diem in lieu of subsistence, in the same manner as persons employed intermittently in the Government service are allowed expenses under section 5703 of Title 5.

(5)(A) Five members of the Committee or their representatives shall constitute a quorum for the transaction of any function of the Committee, except that, in no case shall any representative be considered in determining the existence of a quorum for the transaction of any function of the Committee if that function involves a vote by the Committee on any matter before the Committee.

(B) The Secretary of the Interior shall be the Chairman of the Committee.

(C) The Committee shall meet at the call of the Chairman or five of its members.

(D) All meetings and records of the Committee shall be open to the public.

(6) Upon request of the Committee, the head of any Federal agency is authorized to detail, on a nonreimbursable basis, any of the personnel of such agency to the Committee to assist it in carrying out its duties under this section.

(7)(A) The Committee may for the purpose of carrying out its duties under this section hold such hearings, sit and act at such times and places, take such testimony, and receive such evidence, as the Committee deems advisable.

(B) When so authorized by the Committee, any member or agent of the Committee may take any action which the Committee is authorized to take by this paragraph.

(C) Subject to the Privacy Act [> 5 U.S.C.A. S 552a], the Committee may secure directly from any Federal agency information necessary to enable it to carry out its duties under this section. Upon request of the Chairman of the Committee, the head of such Federal agency shall furnish such information to the Committee.

(D) The Committee may use the United States mails in the same manner and upon the same conditions as a Federal agency.

(E) The Administrator of General Services shall provide to the Committee on a reimbursable basis such administrative support services as the Committee may request.

(8) In carrying out its duties under this section, the Committee may promulgate and amend such rules, regulations, and procedures, and issue and amend such orders as it deems necessary.

(9) For the purpose of obtaining information necessary for the

consideration of an application for an exemption under this section the Committee may issue subpoenas for the attendance and testimony of witnesses and the production of relevant papers, books, and documents.

(10) In no case shall any representative, including a representative of a member designated pursuant to paragraph (3) (G) of this subsection, be eligible to cast a vote on behalf of any member.

(f) Promulgation of regulations; form and contents of exemption application

Not later than 90 days after November 10, 1978, the Secretary shall promulgate regulations which set forth the form and manner in which applications for exemption shall be submitted to the Secretary and the information to be contained in such applications. Such regulations shall require that information submitted in an application by the head of any Federal agency with respect to any agency action include, but not be limited to —

(1) a description of the consultation process carried out pursuant to subsection (a) (2) of this section between the head of the Federal agency and the Secretary; and

(2) a statement describing why such action cannot be altered or modified to conform with the requirements of subsection (a) (2) of this section.

(g) Application for exemption; report to Committee

(1) A Federal agency, the Governor of the State in which an agency action will occur, if any, or a permit or license applicant may apply to the Secretary for an exemption for an agency action of such agency if, after consultation under subsection (a) (2) of this section, the Secretary's opinion under subsection (b) of this section indicates that the agency action would violate subsection (a) (2) of this section. An application for an exemption shall be considered initially by the Secretary in the manner provided for in this subsection, and shall be considered by the Committee for a final determination under subsection (h) of this section after a report is made pursuant to paragraph (5). The applicant for an exemption shall be referred to as the "exemption applicant" in this section.

(2)(A) An exemption applicant shall submit a written application to the Secretary, in a form prescribed under subsection (f) of this section, not later than 90 days after the completion of the consultation process; except that, in the case of any agency action involving a permit or license applicant, such application shall be submitted not later than 90 days after the date on which the Federal agency concerned takes final agency action with respect to the issuance of the permit or license. For purposes of the preceding sentence, the term "final agency action" means (i) a disposition by an agency with respect to the issuance of a permit or license that is subject to administrative review, whether or not such disposition is subject to judicial review; or (ii) if administrative review is sought with respect to such disposition, the decision resulting after such review. Such application shall set forth the reasons why the exemption applicant considers that the agency action meets the requirements for an exemption under this subsection.

(B) Upon receipt of an application for exemption for an agency action under paragraph (1), the Secretary shall promptly (i) notify the Governor of each affected State, if any, as determined by the Secretary, and request the Governors so notified to recommend individuals to be appointed to the Endangered Species Committee for consideration of such application; and (ii) publish notice of receipt of the application in the Federal Register, including a summary of the information contained in the application and a description of the agency action with respect to which the application for exemption has been filed.

(3) The Secretary shall within 20 days after the receipt of an application for exemption, or within such other period of time as is mutually agreeable to the exemption applicant and the Secretary —

(A) determine that the Federal agency concerned and the exemption applicant have —

(i) carried out the consultation responsibilities described in subsection (a) of this section in good faith and made a reasonable and responsible effort to develop and fairly consider modifications or reasonable and prudent alternatives to the proposed agency action which would not violate subsection (a) (2) of this section;

(ii) conducted any biological assessment required by subsection (c) of this section; and

(iii) to the extent determinable within the time provided herein, refrained from making any irreversible or irretrievable commitment of resources prohibited by subsection (d) of this section; or

(B) deny the application for exemption because the Federal agency concerned or the exemption applicant have not met the requirements set forth in subparagraph (A) (i), (ii), and (iii).

The denial of an application under subparagraph (B) shall be considered final agency action for purposes of chapter 7 of Title 5.

(4) If the Secretary determines that the Federal agency concerned and the exemption applicant have met the requirements set forth in paragraph (3) (A) (i), (ii), and (iii) he shall, in consultation with the Members of the Committee, hold a hearing on the application for exemption in accordance with sections 554, 555, and 556 (other than subsection (b) (1) and (2) thereof) of Title 5 and prepare the report to be submitted pursuant to paragraph (5).

(5) Within 140 days after making the determinations under paragraph (3) or within such other period of time as is mutually agreeable to the exemption applicant and the Secretary, the Secretary shall submit to the Committee a report discussing —

(A) the availability of reasonable and prudent alternatives to the agency action, and the nature and extent of the benefits of the agency action and of alternative courses of action consistent with conserving the species or the critical habitat;

(B) a summary of the evidence concerning whether or not the agency action is in the public interest and is of national or regional significance;

(C) appropriate reasonable mitigation and enhancement measures which should be considered by the Committee; and

(D) whether the Federal agency concerned and the exemption applicant refrained from making any irreversible or irretrievable commitment of resources prohibited by subsection (d) of this section.

(6) To the extent practicable within the time required for action under subsection (g) of this section, and except to the extent inconsistent with the requirements of this section, the consideration of any application for an exemption under this section and the conduct of any hearing under this subsection shall be in accordance with sections 554, 555, and 556 (other than subsection (b) (3) of section 556) of Title 5.

(7) Upon request of the Secretary, the head of any Federal agency is authorized to detail, on a nonreimbursable basis, any of the personnel of such agency to the Secretary to assist him in carrying out his duties under this section.

(8) All meetings and records resulting from activities pursuant to this subsection shall be open to the public.

(h) Grant of exemption

(1) The Committee shall make a final determination whether or not to grant an exemption within 30 days after receiving the report of the Secretary pursuant to subsection (g) (5) of this section. The Committee shall grant an exemption from the requirements of subsection (a) (2) of this section for an agency action if, by a vote of not less than five of its members voting in person—

(A) it determines on the record, based on the report of the Secretary, the record of the hearing held under subsection (g) (4) of this section and on such other testimony or evidence as it may receive, that—

(i) there are no reasonable and prudent alternatives to the agency action;

(ii) the benefits of such action clearly outweigh the benefits of alternative courses of action consistent with conserving the species or its critical habitat, and such action is in the public interest;

(iii) the action is of regional or national significance; and

(iv) neither the Federal agency concerned nor the exemption applicant made any irreversible or irretrievable commitment of resources prohibited by subsection (d) of this section; and

(B) it establishes such reasonable mitigation and enhancement measures, including, but not limited to, live propagation, transplantation, and habitat acquisition and improvement, as are necessary and appropriate to minimize the adverse effects of the agency action upon the endangered species, threatened species, or critical habitat concerned.

Any final determination by the Committee under this subsection shall be considered final agency action for purposes of chapter 7 of Title 5.

(2)(A) Except as provided in subparagraph (B), an exemption for an agency action granted under paragraph (1) shall constitute a permanent exemption with respect to all endangered or threatened species for the purposes of completing such agency action—

(i) regardless whether the species was identified in the biological assessment; and

(ii) only if a biological assessment has been conducted under subsection (c) of this section with respect to such agency action.

(B) An exemption shall be permanent under subparagraph (A) unless—

(i) the Secretary finds, based on the best scientific and commercial data available, that such exemption would result in the extinction of a species that was not the subject of consultation under subsection (a) (2) of this section or was not identified in any biological assessment conducted under subsection (c) of this section, and

(ii) the Committee determines within 60 days after the date of the Secretary's finding that the exemption should not be permanent.

If the Secretary makes a finding described in clause (i), the Committee shall meet with respect to the matter within 30 days after the date of the finding.

(i) Review by Secretary of State; violation of international treaty or other international obligation of United States

Notwithstanding any other provision of this chapter, the Committee shall be prohibited from considering for exemption any application made to it, if the Secretary of State, after a review of the proposed agency action and its potential implications, and after hearing, certifies, in writing, to the Committee within 60 days of any application made under this section that the granting of any such exemption and the carrying out of such action would be in violation of an international treaty obligation or other international obligation of the United States. The Secretary of State shall, at the time of such certification, publish a copy thereof in the Federal Register.

(j) Exemption for national security reasons

Notwithstanding any other provision of this chapter, the Committee shall grant an exemption for any agency action if the Secretary of Defense finds that such exemption is necessary for reasons of national security.

(k) Exemption decision not considered major Federal action; environmental impact statement

An exemption decision by the Committee under this section shall not be a major Federal action for purposes of the National Environmental Policy Act of 1969 [> 42 U.S.C.A. S 4321 et seq.]: Provided, That an environmental impact statement which discusses the impacts upon endangered species or threatened species or their critical habitats shall have been previously prepared with respect to any agency action exempted by such order.

(l) Committee order granting exemption; cost of mitigation and enhancement measures; report by applicant to Council on Environmental Quality

(1) If the Committee determines under subsection (h) of this section that an exemption should be granted with respect to any agency action, the Committee shall issue an order granting the exemption and specifying the mitigation and enhancement measures established pursuant to subsection (h) of this section which shall be carried out and paid for by the exemption applicant in implementing the agency action. All necessary mitigation and enhancement measures shall be authorized prior to the implementing of the agency action and funded concurrently with all other project features.

(2) The applicant receiving such exemption shall include the costs of such mitigation and enhancement measures within the overall costs of continuing the proposed action. Notwithstanding the preceding sentence the costs of such measures shall not be treated as project costs for the purpose of computing benefit-cost or other ratios for the proposed action. Any applicant may request the Secretary to carry out such mitigation and enhancement measures. The costs incurred by the Secretary in carrying out any such measures shall be paid by the applicant receiving the exemption. No later than one year after the granting of an exemption, the exemption applicant shall submit to the Council on Environmental Quality a report describing its compliance with the mitigation and enhancement measures prescribed by this section. Such a report shall be submitted annually until all such mitigation and enhancement measures have been completed. Notice of the public availability of such reports shall be published in the Federal Register by the Council on Environmental Quality.

(m) Notice requirement for citizen suits not applicable

The 60-day notice requirement of section 1540(g) of this title shall not apply with respect to review of any final determination of the Committee under subsection (h) of this section granting an exemption from the requirements of subsection (a) (2) of this section.

(n) Judicial review

Any person, as defined by section 1532(13) of this title, may obtain judicial review, under chapter 7 of Title 5, of any decision of the Endangered Species Committee under subsection (h) of this section in the United States Court of Appeals for (1) any circuit wherein the agency action concerned will be, or is being, carried out, or (2) in any case in which the agency action will be, or is being, carried out outside of any circuit, the District of Columbia, by filing in such court within 90 days after the date of issuance of the decision, a written petition for review. A copy of such petition shall be transmitted by the clerk of the court to the Committee and the Committee shall file in the court the record in the proceeding, as provided in section 2112, of Title 28. Attorneys designated by the Endangered Species Committee may appear for, and represent the Committee in any action for review under this subsection.

(o) Exemption as providing exception on taking of endangered species

Notwithstanding sections 1533(d) and 1538(a)(1)(B) and (C) of this title, sections 1371 and 1372 of this title, or any regulation promulgated to implement any such section—
(1) any action for which an exemption is granted under subsection (h) of this section shall not be considered to be a taking of any endangered species or threatened species with respect to any activity which is necessary to carry out such action; and
(2) any taking that is in compliance with the terms and conditions specified in a written statement provided under subsection (b)(4)(iv) of this section shall not be considered to be a prohibited taking of the species concerned.

(p) Exemptions in Presidentially declared disaster areas

In any area which has been declared by the President to be a major disaster area under the Disaster Relief and Emergency Assistance Act [> 42 U.S.C.A. S 5121 et seq.], the President is authorized to make the determinations required by subsections (g) and (h) of this section for any project for the repair or replacement of a public facility substantially as it existed prior to the disaster under section 405 or 406 of the Disaster Relief and Emergency Assistance Act [> 42 U.S.C.A. SS 5171 or > 5172], and which the President determines (1) is necessary to prevent the recurrence of such a natural disaster and to reduce the potential loss of human life, and (2) to involve an emergency situation which does not allow the ordinary procedures of this section to be followed. Notwithstanding any other provision of this section, the Committee shall accept the determinations of the President under this subsection.

(ESA § 8)
§ 1537. International cooperation

(a) Financial assistance

As a demonstration of the commitment of the United States to the worldwide protection of endangered species and threatened species, the President may, subject to the provisions of section 1306 of Title 31, use foreign currencies accruing to the United States Government under the Agricultural Trade Development and Assistance Act of 1954 [> 7 U.S.C.A. S 1691 et seq.] or any other law to provide to any foreign country (with its consent) assistance in the development and management of programs in that country which the Secretary determines to be necessary or useful for the conservation of any endangered species or threatened species listed by the Secretary pursuant to section 1533 of this title. The President shall provide assistance (which includes, but is not limited to, the acquisition, by lease or otherwise, of lands, waters, or interests therein) to foreign countries under this section under such terms and conditions as he deems appropriate. Whenever foreign currencies are available for the provision of assistance under this section, such currencies shall be used in preference to funds appropriated under the authority of section 1542 of this title.

(b) Encouragement of foreign programs

In order to carry out further the provisions of this chapter, the Secretary, through the Secretary of State, shall encourage —
(1) foreign countries to provide for the conservation of fish or wildlife and plants including endangered species and threatened species listed pursuant to section 1533 of this title;
(2) the entering into of bilateral or multilateral agreements with foreign countries to provide for such conservation; and
(3) foreign persons who directly or indirectly take fish or wildlife or plants in foreign countries or on the high seas for importation into the United States for commercial or other purposes to develop and carry out with such assistance as he may provide, conservation practices designed to enhance such fish or wildlife or plants and their habitat.

(c) Personnel

After consultation with the Secretary of State, the Secretary may —
(1) assign or otherwise make available any officer or employee of his department for the purpose of cooperating with foreign countries and international organizations in developing personnel resources and programs which promote the conservation of fish or wildlife or plants; and

(2) conduct or provide financial assistance for the educational training of foreign personnel, in this country or abroad, in fish, wildlife, or plant management, research and law enforcement and to render professional assistance abroad in such matters.

(d) Investigations

After consultation with the Secretary of State and the Secretary of the Treasury, as appropriate, the Secretary may conduct or cause to be conducted such law enforcement investigations and research abroad as he deems necessary to carry out the purposes of this chapter.

(ESA § 8A)
§ 1537a. Convention implementation

(a) Management Authority and Scientific Authority

The Secretary of the Interior (hereinafter in this section referred to as the "Secretary") is designated as the Management Authority and the Scientific Authority for purposes of the Convention and the respective functions of each such Authority shall be carried out through the United States Fish and Wildlife Service.

(b) Management Authority functions

The Secretary shall do all things necessary and appropriate to carry out the functions of the Management Authority under the Convention.

(c) Scientific Authority functions; determinations

(1) The Secretary shall do all things necessary and appropriate to carry out the functions of the Scientific Authority under the Convention.
(2) The Secretary shall base the determinations and advice given by him under Article IV of the Convention with respect to wildlife upon the best available biological information derived from professionally accepted wildlife management practices; but is not required to make, or require any State to make, estimates of population size in making such determinations or giving such advice.

(d) Reservations by the United States under Convention

If the United States votes against including any species in Appendix I or II of the Convention and does not enter a reservation pursuant to paragraph (3) of Article XV of the Convention with respect to that species, the

Secretary of State, before the 90th day after the last day on which such a reservation could be entered, shall submit to the Committee on Merchant Marine and Fisheries of the House of Representatives, and to the Committee on the Environment and Public Works of the Senate, a written report setting forth the reasons why such a reservation was not entered.

(e) Wildlife Preservation in Western Hemisphere

(1) The Secretary of the Interior (hereinafter in this subsection referred to as the "Secretary"), in cooperation with the Secretary of State, shall act on behalf of, and represent, the United States in all regards as required by the Convention on Nature Protection and Wildlife Preservation in the Western Hemisphere (56 Stat. 1354, T.S. 982, hereinafter in this subsection referred to as the "Western Convention"). In the discharge of these responsibilities, the Secretary and the Secretary of State shall consult with the Secretary of Agriculture, the Secretary of Commerce, and the heads of other agencies with respect to matters relating to or affecting their areas of responsibility.

(2) The Secretary and the Secretary of State shall, in cooperation with the contracting parties to the Western Convention and, to the extent feasible and appropriate, with the participation of State agencies, take such steps as are necessary to implement the Western Convention. Such steps shall include, but not be limited to —

(A) cooperation with contracting parties and international organizations for the purpose of developing personnel resources and programs that will facilitate implementation of the Western Convention;

(B) identification of those species of birds that migrate between the United States and other contracting parties, and the habitats upon which those species depend, and the implementation of cooperative measures to ensure that such species will not become endangered or threatened; and

(C) identification of measures that are necessary and appropriate to implement those provisions of the Western Convention which address the protection of wild plants.

(3) No later than September 30, 1985, the Secretary and the Secretary of State shall submit a report to Congress describing those steps taken in accordance with the requirements of this subsection and identifying the principal remaining actions yet necessary for comprehensive and effective implementation of the Western Convention.

(4) The provisions of this subsection shall not be construed as affecting the authority, jurisdiction, or responsibility of the several States to manage, control, or regulate resident fish or wildlife under State law or regulations.

(ESA § 9)
§ 1538. Prohibited acts

(a) Generally

(1) Except as provided in sections 1535(g)(2) and 1539 of this title, with respect to any endangered species of fish or wildlife listed pursuant to section 1533 of this title it is unlawful for any person subject to the jurisdiction of the United States to—
(A) import any such species into, or export any such species from the United States;
(B) take any such species within the United States or the territorial sea of the United States;
(C) take any such species upon the high seas;
(D) possess, sell, deliver, carry, transport, or ship, by any means whatsoever, any such species taken in violation of subparagraphs (B) and (C);
(E) deliver, receive, carry, transport, or ship in interstate or foreign commerce, by any means whatsoever and in the course of a commercial activity, any such species;
(F) sell or offer for sale in interstate or foreign commerce any such species; or
(G) violate any regulation pertaining to such species or to any threatened species of fish or wildlife listed pursuant to section 1533 of this title and promulgated by the Secretary pursuant to authority provided by this chapter.
(2) Except as provided in sections 1535(g)(2) and 1539 of this title, with respect to any endangered species of plants listed pursuant to section 1533 of this title, it is unlawful for any person subject to the jurisdiction of the United States to—
(A) import any such species into, or export any such species from, the United States;
(B) remove and reduce to possession any such species from areas under Federal jurisdiction; maliciously damage or destroy any such species on any such area; or remove, cut, dig up, or damage or destroy any such species on any other area in knowing violation of any law or regulation of any State or in the course of any violation of a State criminal trespass law;
(C) deliver, receive, carry, transport, or ship in interstate or foreign commerce, by any means whatsoever and in the course of a commercial activity, any such species;
(D) sell or offer for sale in interstate or foreign commerce any such species; or
(E) violate any regulation pertaining to such species or to any threatened species of plants listed pursuant to section 1533 of this title and promulgated by the Secretary pursuant to authority provided by this

chapter.

(b) Species held in captivity or controlled environment

(1) The provisions of subsections (a)(1)(A) and (a)(1)(G) of this section shall not apply to any fish or wildlife which was held in captivity or in a controlled environment on (A) December 28, 1973, or (B) the date of the publication in the Federal Register of a final regulation adding such fish or wildlife species to any list published pursuant to subsection (c) of section 1533 of this title: Provided, That such holding and any subsequent holding or use of the fish or wildlife was not in the course of a commercial activity. With respect to any act prohibited by subsections (a)(1)(A) and (a)(1)(G) of this section which occurs after a period of 180 days from (i) December 28, 1973, or (ii) the date of publication in the Federal Register of a final regulation adding such fish or wildlife species to any list published pursuant to subsection (c) of section 1533 of this title, there shall be a rebuttable presumption that the fish or wildlife involved in such act is not entitled to the exemption contained in this subsection.

(2)(A) The provisions of subsection (a) (1) of this section shall not apply to—

(i) any raptor legally held in captivity or in a controlled environment on November 10, 1978; or

(ii) any progeny of any raptor described in clause (i);

until such time as any such raptor or progeny is intentionally returned to a wild state.

(B) Any person holding any raptor or progeny described in subparagraph (A) must be able to demonstrate that the raptor or progeny does, in fact, qualify under the provisions of this paragraph, and shall maintain and submit to the Secretary, on request, such inventories, documentation, and records as the Secretary may by regulation require as being reasonably appropriate to carry out the purposes of this paragraph. Such requirements shall not unnecessarily duplicate the requirements of other rules and regulations promulgated by the Secretary.

(c) Violation of Convention

(1) It is unlawful for any person subject to the jurisdiction of the United States to engage in any trade in any specimens contrary to the provisions of the Convention, or to possess any specimens traded contrary to the provisions of the Convention, including the definitions of terms in article I thereof.

(2) Any importation into the United States of fish or wildlife shall, if—

(A) such fish or wildlife is not an endangered species listed pursuant to section 1533 of this title but is listed in Appendix II to the Convention,

(B) the taking and exportation of such fish or wildlife is not contrary to the provisions of the Convention and all other applicable requirements of the Convention have been satisfied,

(C) the applicable requirements of subsections (d), (e), and (f) of this section have been satisfied, and

(D) such importation is not made in the course of a commercial activity, be presumed to be an importation not in violation of any provision of this chapter or any regulation issued pursuant to this chapter.

(d) Imports and exports

(1) In general

It is unlawful for any person, without first having obtained permission from the Secretary, to engage in business —

(A) as an importer or exporter of fish or wildlife (other than shellfish and fishery products which (i) are not listed pursuant to section 1533 of this title as endangered species or threatened species, and (ii) are imported for purposes of human or animal consumption or taken in waters under the jurisdiction of the United States or on the high seas for recreational purposes) or plants; or

(B) as an importer or exporter of any amount of raw or worked African elephant ivory.

(2) Requirements

Any person required to obtain permission under paragraph (1) of this subsection shall —

(A) keep such records as will fully and correctly disclose each importation or exportation of fish, wildlife, plants, or African elephant ivory made by him and the subsequent disposition made by him with respect to such fish, wildlife, plants, or ivory;

(B) at all reasonable times upon notice by a duly authorized representative of the Secretary, afford such representative access to his place of business, an opportunity to examine his inventory of imported fish, wildlife, plants, or African elephant ivory and the records required to be kept under subparagraph (A) of this paragraph, and to copy such records; and

(C) file such reports as the Secretary may require.

(3) Regulations

The Secretary shall prescribe such regulations as are necessary and appropriate to carry out the purposes of this subsection.

(4) Restriction on consideration of value or amount of African elephant ivory imported or exported

In granting permission under this subsection for importation or exportation of African elephant ivory, the Secretary shall not vary the requirements for obtaining such permission on the basis of the value or amount of ivory imported or exported under such permission.

(e) Reports

It is unlawful for any person importing or exporting fish or wildlife (other than shellfish and fishery products which (1) are not listed pursuant to section 1533 of this title as endangered or threatened species, and (2) are imported for purposes of human or animal consumption or taken in waters under the jurisdiction of the United States or on the high seas for recreational purposes) or plants to fail to file any declaration or report as the Secretary deems necessary to facilitate enforcement of this chapter or to meet the obligations of the Convention.

(f) Designation of ports

(1) It is unlawful for any person subject to the jurisdiction of the United States to import into or export from the United States any fish or wildlife (other than shellfish and fishery products which (A) are not listed pursuant to section 1533 of this title as endangered species or threatened species, and (B) are imported for purposes of human or animal consumption or taken in waters under the jurisdiction of the United States or on the high seas for recreational purposes) or plants, except at a port or ports designated by the Secretary of the Interior. For the purpose of facilitating enforcement of this chapter and reducing the costs thereof, the Secretary of the Interior, with approval of the Secretary of the Treasury and after notice and opportunity for public hearing, may, by regulation, designate ports and change such designations. The Secretary of the Interior, under such terms and conditions as he may prescribe, may permit the importation or exportation at nondesignated ports in the interest of the health or safety of the fish or wildlife or plants, or for other reasons if, in his discretion, he deems it appropriate and consistent with the purpose of this subsection.
(2) Any port designated by the Secretary of the Interior under the authority of section 668cc-4(d) of this title, shall, if such designation is in effect on December 27, 1973, be deemed to be a port designated by the Secretary under paragraph (1) of this subsection until such time as the Secretary otherwise provides.

(g) Violations

It is unlawful for any person subject to the jurisdiction of the United States to attempt to commit, solicit another to commit, or cause to be committed, any offense defined in this section.

(ESA § 10)
§ 1539. Exceptions

(a) Permits

(1) The Secretary may permit, under such terms and conditions as he shall prescribe —
(A) any act otherwise prohibited by section 1538 of this title for scientific purposes or to enhance the propagation or survival of the affected species, including, but not limited to, acts necessary for the establishment and maintenance of experimental populations pursuant to subsection (j) of this section; or
(B) any taking otherwise prohibited by section 1538(a)(1)(B) of this title if such taking is incidental to, and not the purpose of, the carrying out of an otherwise lawful activity.
(2)(A) No permit may be issued by the Secretary authorizing any taking referred to in paragraph (1)(B) unless the applicant therefor submits to the Secretary a conservation plan that specifies —
(i) the impact which will likely result from such taking;
(ii) what steps the applicant will take to minimize and mitigate such impacts, and the funding that will be available to implement such steps;
(iii) what alternative actions to such taking the applicant considered and the reasons why such alternatives are not being utilized; and
(iv) such other measures that the Secretary may require as being necessary or appropriate for purposes of the plan.
(B) If the Secretary finds, after opportunity for public comment, with respect to a permit application and the related conservation plan that—
(i) the taking will be incidental;
(ii) the applicant will, to the maximum extent practicable, minimize and mitigate the impacts of such taking;
(iii) the applicant will ensure that adequate funding for the plan will be provided;
(iv) the taking will not appreciably reduce the likelihood of the survival and recovery of the species in the wild; and
(v) the measures, if any, required under subparagraph (A)(iv) will be met;

and he has received such other assurances as he may require that the plan will be implemented, the Secretary shall issue the permit. The permit shall contain such terms and conditions as the Secretary deems necessary or appropriate to carry out the purposes of this paragraph, including, but not limited to, such reporting requirements as the Secretary deems necessary for determining whether such terms and conditions are being complied with.

(C) The Secretary shall revoke a permit issued under this paragraph if he finds that the permittee is not complying with the terms and conditions of the permit.

(b) Hardship exemptions

(1) If any person enters into a contract with respect to a species of fish or wildlife or plant before the date of the publication in the Federal Register of notice of consideration of that species as an endangered species and the subsequent listing of that species as an endangered species pursuant to section 1533 of this title will cause undue economic hardship to such person under the contract, the Secretary, in order to minimize such hardship, may exempt such person from the application of section 1538(a) of this title to the extent the Secretary deems appropriate if such person applies to him for such exemption and includes with such application such information as the Secretary may require to prove such hardship; except that (A) no such exemption shall be for a duration of more than one year from the date of publication in the Federal Register of notice of consideration of the species concerned, or shall apply to a quantity of fish or wildlife or plants in excess of that specified by the Secretary; (B) the one-year period for those species of fish or wildlife listed by the Secretary as endangered prior to December 28, 1973 shall expire in accordance with the terms of section 668cc-3 of this title; and (C) no such exemption may be granted for the importation or exportation of a specimen listed in Appendix I of the Convention which is to be used in a commercial activity.

(2) As used in this subsection, the term "undue economic hardship" shall include, but not be limited to:

(A) substantial economic loss resulting from inability caused by this chapter to perform contracts with respect to species of fish and wildlife entered into prior to the date of publication in the Federal Register of a notice of consideration of such species as an endangered species;

(B) substantial economic loss to persons who, for the year prior to the notice of consideration of such species as an endangered species, derived a substantial portion of their income from the lawful taking of any listed species, which taking would be made unlawful under this chapter; or

(C) curtailment of subsistence taking made unlawful under this chapter by persons (i) not reasonably able to secure other sources of subsistence; and (ii) dependent to a substantial extent upon hunting and fishing for subsistence; and (iii) who must engage in such curtailed taking for subsistence purposes.

(3) The Secretary may make further requirements for a showing of undue economic hardship as he deems fit. Exceptions granted under this section may be limited by the Secretary in his discretion as to time, area, or other factor of applicability.

(c) Notice and review

The Secretary shall publish notice in the Federal Register of each application for an exemption or permit which is made under this section. Each notice shall invite the submission from interested parties, within thirty days after the date of the notice, of written data, views, or arguments with respect to the application; except that such thirty-day period may be waived by the Secretary in an emergency situation where the health or life of an endangered animal is threatened and no reasonable alternative is available to the applicant, but notice of any such waiver shall be published by the Secretary in the Federal Register within ten days following the issuance of the exemption or permit. Information received by the Secretary as a part of any application shall be available to the public as a matter of public record at every stage of the proceeding.

(d) Permit and exemption policy

The Secretary may grant exceptions under subsections (a)(1)(A) and (b) of this section only if he finds and publishes his finding in the Federal Register that (1) such exceptions were applied for in good faith, (2) if granted and exercised will not operate to the disadvantage of such endangered species, and (3) will be consistent with the purposes and policy set forth in section 1531 of this title.

(e) Alaska natives

(1) Except as provided in paragraph (4) of this subsection the provisions of this chapter shall not apply with respect to the taking of any endangered species or threatened species, or the importation of any such species taken pursuant to this section, by —
(A) any Indian, Aleut, or Eskimo who is an Alaskan Native who resides in Alaska; or
(B) any non-native permanent resident of an Alaskan native village;

if such taking is primarily for subsistence purposes. Non-edible byproducts of species taken pursuant to this section may be sold in interstate commerce when made into authentic native articles of handicrafts and clothing; except that the provisions of this subsection shall not apply to any non-native resident of an Alaskan native village found by the Secretary to be not primarily dependent upon the taking of fish and wildlife for consumption or for the creation and sale of authentic native articles of handicrafts and clothing.

(2) Any taking under this subsection may not be accomplished in a wasteful manner.

(3) As used in this subsection —

(i) The term "subsistence" includes selling any edible portion of fish or wildlife in native villages and towns in Alaska for native consumption within native villages or towns; and

(ii) The term "authentic native articles of handicrafts and clothing" means items composed wholly or in some significant respect of natural materials, and which are produced, decorated, or fashioned in the exercise of traditional native handicrafts without the use of pantographs, multiple carvers, or other mass copying devices. Traditional native handicrafts include, but are not limited to, weaving, carving, stitching, sewing, lacing, beading, drawing, and painting.

(4) Notwithstanding the provisions of paragraph (1) of this subsection, whenever the Secretary determines that any species of fish or wildlife which is subject to taking under the provisions of this subsection is an endangered species or threatened species, and that such taking materially and negatively affects the threatened or endangered species, he may prescribe regulations upon the taking of such species by any such Indian, Aleut, Eskimo, or non-Native Alaskan resident of an Alaskan native village. Such regulations may be established with reference to species, geographical description of the area included, the season for taking, or any other factors related to the reason for establishing such regulations and consistent with the policy of this chapter. Such regulations shall be prescribed after a notice and hearings in the affected judicial districts of Alaska and as otherwise required by section 1373 of this title, and shall be removed as soon as the Secretary determines that the need for their impositions has disappeared.

(f) Pre-Act endangered species parts exemption; application and certification; regulation; validity of sales contract; separability; renewal of exemption; expiration of renewal certification

(1) As used in this subsection —

(A) The term "pre-Act endangered species part" means —

(i) any sperm whale oil, including derivatives thereof, which was lawfully held within the United States on December 28, 1973, in the course of a commercial activity; or

(ii) any finished scrimshaw product, if such product or the raw material for such product was lawfully held within the United States on December 28, 1973, in the course of a commercial activity.

(B) The term "scrimshaw product" means any art form which involves the substantial etching or engraving of designs upon, or the substantial carving of figures, patterns, or designs from, any bone or tooth of any marine mammal of the order Cetacea. For purposes of this subsection, polishing or the adding of minor superficial markings does not constitute substantial etching, engraving, or carving.

(2) The Secretary, pursuant to the provisions of this subsection, may exempt, if such exemption is not in violation of the Convention, any pre-Act endangered species part from one or more of the following prohibitions:

(A) The prohibition on exportation from the United States set forth in section 1538(a)(1)(A) of this title.

(B) Any prohibition set forth in section 1538(a)(1)(E) or (F) of this title.

(3) Any person seeking an exemption described in paragraph (2) of this subsection shall make application therefor to the Secretary in such form and manner as he shall prescribe, but no such application may be considered by the Secretary unless the application —

(A) is received by the Secretary before the close of the one-year period beginning on the date on which regulations promulgated by the Secretary to carry out this subsection first take effect;

(B) contains a complete and detailed inventory of all pre-Act endangered species parts for which the applicant seeks exemption;

(C) is accompanied by such documentation as the Secretary may require to prove that any endangered species part or product claimed by the applicant to be a pre-Act endangered species part is in fact such a part; and

(D) contains such other information as the Secretary deems necessary and appropriate to carry out the purposes of this subsection.

(4) If the Secretary approves any application for exemption made under this subsection, he shall issue to the applicant a certificate of exemption which shall specify —

(A) any prohibition in section 1538(a) of this title which is exempted;

(B) the pre-Act endangered species parts to which the exemption applies;

(C) the period of time during which the exemption is in effect, but no exemption made under this subsection shall have force and effect after the close of the three-year period beginning on the date of issuance of the certificate unless such exemption is renewed under paragraph (8); and

(D) any term or condition prescribed pursuant to paragraph (5)(A) or (B), or both, which the Secretary deems necessary or appropriate.

(5) The Secretary shall prescribe such regulations as he deems necessary and appropriate to carry out the purposes of this subsection. Such regulations may set forth —

(A) terms and conditions which may be imposed on applicants for exemptions under this subsection (including, but not limited to, requirements that applicants register inventories, keep complete sales records, permit duly authorized agents of the Secretary to inspect such inventories and records, and periodically file appropriate reports with the Secretary); and

(B) terms and conditions which may be imposed on any subsequent purchaser of any pre-Act endangered species part covered by an exemption granted under this subsection;

to insure that any such part so exempted is adequately accounted for and not disposed of contrary to the provisions of this chapter. No regulation prescribed by the Secretary to carry out the purposes of this subsection shall be subject to section 1533(f)(2)(A)(i) of this title.

(6)(A) Any contract for the sale of pre-Act endangered species parts which is entered into by the Administrator of General Services prior to the effective date of this subsection and pursuant to the notice published in the Federal Register on January 9, 1973, shall not be rendered invalid by virtue of the fact that fulfillment of such contract may be prohibited under section 1538(a)(1)(F) of this title.

(B) In the event that this paragraph is held invalid, the validity of the remainder of this chapter, including the remainder of this subsection, shall not be affected.

(7) Nothing in this subsection shall be construed to —

(A) exonerate any person from any act committed in violation of paragraphs (1)(A), (1)(E), or (1)(F) of section 1538(a) of this title prior to July 12, 1976; or

(B) immunize any person from prosecution for any such act.

(8)(A) (i) Any valid certificate of exemption which was renewed after October 13, 1982, and was in effect on March 31, 1988, shall be deemed to be renewed for a six-month period beginning on October 7, 1988. Any person holding such a certificate may apply to the Secretary for one additional renewal of such certificate for a period not to exceed 5 years beginning on October 7, 1988.

(B) If the Secretary approves any application for renewal of an exemption under this paragraph, he shall issue to the applicant a certificate of renewal of such exemption which shall provide that all terms, conditions, prohibitions, and other regulations made applicable by the previous certificate shall remain in effect during the period of the renewal.

(C) No exemption or renewal of such exemption made under this subsection shall have force and effect after the expiration date of the certificate of renewal of such exemption issued under this paragraph.

(D) No person may, after January 31, 1984, sell or offer for sale in interstate or foreign commerce, any pre-Act finished scrimshaw product unless such person holds a valid certificate of exemption issued by the Secretary under this subsection, and unless such product or the raw material for such product was held by such person on October 13, 1982.

(9) Repealed. Pub.L. 100-478, Title I, S 1011(d), Oct. 7, 1988, 102 Stat. 2314.

(g) Burden of proof

In connection with any action alleging a violation of section 1538 of this title, any person claiming the benefit of any exemption or permit under this chapter shall have the burden of proving that the exemption or permit is applicable, has been granted, and was valid and in force at the time of the alleged violation.

(h) Certain antique articles; importation; port designation; application for return of articles

(1) Sections 1533(d) and 1538(a) and (c) of this title do not apply to any article which —
(A) is not less than 100 years of age;
(B) is composed in whole or in part of any endangered species or threatened species listed under section 1533 of this title;
(C) has not been repaired or modified with any part of any such species on or after December 28, 1973; and
(D) is entered at a port designated under paragraph (3).
(2) Any person who wishes to import an article under the exception provided by this subsection shall submit to the customs officer concerned at the time of entry of the article such documentation as the Secretary of the Treasury, after consultation with the Secretary of the Interior, shall by regulation require as being necessary to establish that the article meets the requirements set forth in paragraph (1)(A), (B), and (C).
(3) The Secretary of the Treasury, after consultation with the Secretary of the Interior, shall designate one port within each customs region at which articles described in paragraph (1)(A), (B), and (C) must be entered into the customs territory of the United States.
(4) Any person who imported, after December 27, 1973, and on or before November 10, 1978, any article described in paragraph (1) which —
(A) was not repaired or modified after the date of importation with any part of any endangered species or threatened species listed under section 1533 of this title;
(B) was forfeited to the United States before November 10, 1978, or is subject to forfeiture to the United States on such date of enactment, pursuant to the assessment of a civil penalty under section 1540 of this title; and
(C) is in the custody of the United States on November 10, 1978;

may, before the close of the one-year period beginning on November 10, 1978, make application to the Secretary for return of the article. Application shall be made in such form and manner, and contain such documentation, as the Secretary prescribes. If on the basis of any such application which is timely filed, the Secretary is satisfied that the requirements of this paragraph are met with respect to the article concerned, the Secretary shall return the article to the applicant and the importation of such article shall, on and after the date of return, be deemed to be a lawful importation under this chapter.

(i) Noncommercial transshipments

Any importation into the United States of fish or wildlife shall, if—

(1) such fish or wildlife was lawfully taken and exported from the country of origin and country of reexport, if any;

(2) such fish or wildlife is in transit or transshipment through any place subject to the jurisdiction of the United States en route to a country where such fish or wildlife may be lawfully imported and received;

(3) the exporter or owner of such fish or wildlife gave explicit instructions not to ship such fish or wildlife through any place subject to the jurisdiction of the United States, or did all that could have reasonably been done to prevent transshipment, and the circumstances leading to the transshipment were beyond the exporter's or owner's control;

(4) the applicable requirements of the Convention have been satisfied; and

(5) such importation is not made in the course of a commercial activity,

be an importation not in violation of any provision of this chapter or any regulation issued pursuant to this chapter while such fish or wildlife remains in the control of the United States Customs Service.

(j) Experimental populations

(1) For purposes of this subsection, the term "experimental population" means any population (including any offspring arising solely therefrom) authorized by the Secretary for release under paragraph (2), but only when, and at such times as, the population is wholly separate geographically from nonexperimental populations of the same species.

(2)(A) The Secretary may authorize the release (and the related transportation) of any population (including eggs, propagules, or individuals) of an endangered species or a threatened species outside the current range of such species if the Secretary determines that such release will further the conservation of such species.

(B) Before authorizing the release of any population under subparagraph (A), the Secretary shall by regulation identify the population and determine, on the basis of the best available information, whether or not such population is essential to the continued existence of an endangered species or a threatened species.

(C) For the purposes of this chapter, each member of an experimental population shall be treated as a threatened species; except that—

(i) solely for purposes of section 1536 of this title (other than subsection (a)(1) thereof), an experimental population determined under subparagraph (B) to be not essential to the continued existence of a species shall be treated, except when it occurs in an area within the National Wildlife Refuge System or the National Park System, as a species proposed to be listed under

(ii) critical habitat shall not be designated under this chapter for any experimental population determined under subparagraph (B) to be not essential to the continued existence of a species.

(3) The Secretary, with respect to populations of endangered species or threatened species that the Secretary authorized, before October 13, 1982, for release in geographical areas separate from the other populations of such species, shall determine by regulation which of such populations are an experimental population for the purposes of this subsection and whether or not each is essential to the continued existence of an endangered species or a threatened species.

(ESA § 11)
§ 1540. Penalties and enforcement

(a) Civil penalties

(1) Any person who knowingly violates, and any person engaged in business as an importer or exporter of fish, wildlife, or plants who violates, any provision of this chapter, or any provision of any permit or certificate issued hereunder, or of any regulation issued in order to implement subsection (a)(1)(A), (B), (C), (D), (E), or (F), (a)(2)(A), (B), (C), or (D), (c), (d) (other than regulation relating to recordkeeping or filing of reports), (f) or (g) of section 1538 of this title, may be assessed a civil penalty by the Secretary of not more than $25,000 for each violation. Any person who knowingly violates, and any person engaged in business as an importer or exporter of fish, wildlife, or plants who violates, any provision of any other regulation issued under this chapter may be assessed a civil penalty by the Secretary of not more than $12,000 for each such violation. Any person who otherwise violates any provision of this chapter, or any regulation, permit, or certificate issued hereunder, may be assessed a civil penalty by the Secretary of not more than $500 for each such violation. No penalty may be assessed under this subsection unless such person is given notice and opportunity for a hearing with respect to such violation. Each violation shall be a separate offense. Any such civil penalty may be remitted or mitigated by the Secretary. Upon any failure to pay a penalty assessed under this subsection, the Secretary may request the Attorney General to institute a civil action in a district court of the United States for any district in which such person is found, resides, or transacts business to collect the penalty and such court shall have jurisdiction to hear and decide any such action. The court shall hear such action on the record made before the Secretary and shall sustain his action if it is supported by substantial evidence on the record considered as a whole.

(2) Hearings held during proceedings for the assessment of civil penalties authorized by paragraph (1) of this subsection shall be conducted in

accordance with section 554 of Title 5. The Secretary may issue subpoenas for the attendance and testimony of witnesses and the production of relevant papers, books, and documents, and administer oaths. Witnesses summoned shall be paid the same fees and mileage that are paid to witnesses in the courts of the United States. In case of contumacy or refusal to obey a subpena served upon any person pursuant to this paragraph, the district court of the United States for any district in which such person is found or resides or transacts business, upon application by the United States and after notice to such person, shall have jurisdiction to issue an order requiring such person to appear and give testimony before the Secretary or to appear and produce documents before the Secretary, or both, and any failure to obey such order of the court may be punished by such court as a contempt thereof.

(3) Notwithstanding any other provision of this chapter, no civil penalty shall be imposed if it can be shown by a preponderance of the evidence that the defendant committed an act based on a good faith belief that he was acting to protect himself or herself, a member of his or her family, or any other individual from bodily harm, from any endangered or threatened species.

(b) Criminal violations

(1) Any person who knowingly violates any provision of this chapter, of any permit or certificate issued hereunder, or of any regulation issued in order to implement subsection (a)(1)(A), (B), (C), (D), (E), or (F); (a)(2)(A), (B), (C), or (D), (c), (d) (other than a regulation relating to recordkeeping, or filing of reports), (f), or (g) of section 1538 of this title shall, upon conviction, be fined not more than $50,000 or imprisoned for not more than one year, or both. Any person who knowingly violates any provision of any other regulation issued under this chapter shall, upon conviction, be fined not more than $25,000 or imprisoned for not more than six months, or both.

(2) The head of any Federal agency which has issued a lease, license, permit, or other agreement authorizing a person to import or export fish, wildlife, or plants, or to operate a quarantine station for imported wildlife, or authorizing the use of Federal lands, including grazing of domestic livestock, to any person who is convicted of a criminal violation of this chapter or any regulation, permit, or certificate issued hereunder may immediately modify, suspend, or revoke each lease, license, permit or other agreement. The Secretary shall also suspend for a period of up to one year, or cancel, any Federal hunting or fishing permits or stamps issued to any person who is convicted of a criminal violation of any provision of this chapter or any regulation, permit, or certificate issued hereunder. The United States shall not be liable for the payments of any compensation, reimbursement, or damages in connection with the modification, suspension, or revocation of any leases, licenses, permits, stamps, or other

suspension, or revocation of any leases, licenses, permits, stamps, or other agreements pursuant to this section.

(3) Notwithstanding any other provision of this chapter, it shall be a defense to prosecution under this subsection if the defendant committed the offense based on a good faith belief that he was acting to protect himself or herself, a member of his or her family, or any other individual, from bodily harm from any endangered or threatened species.

(c) District court jurisdiction

The several district courts of the United States, including the courts enumerated in section 460 of Title 28, shall have jurisdiction over any actions arising under this chapter. For the purpose of this chapter, American Samoa shall be included within the judicial district of the District Court of the United States for the District of Hawaii.

(d) Rewards and incidental expenses

The Secretary or the Secretary of the Treasury shall pay, from sums received as penalties, fines, or forfeitures of property for any violation of this chapter or any regulation issued hereunder (1) a reward to any person who furnishes information which leads to an arrest, a criminal conviction, civil penalty assessment, or forfeiture of property for any violation of this chapter or any regulation issued hereunder, and (2) the reasonable and necessary costs incurred by any person in providing temporary care for any fish, wildlife, or plant pending the disposition of any civil or criminal proceeding alleging a violation of this chapter with respect to that fish, wildlife, or plant. The amount of the reward, if any, is to be designated by the Secretary or the Secretary of the Treasury, as appropriate. Any officer or employee of the United States or any State or local government who furnishes information or renders service in the performance of his official duties is ineligible for payment under this subsection. Whenever the balance of sums received under this section and section 3375(d) of this title, as penalties or fines, or from forfeitures of property, exceed $500,000, the Secretary of the Treasury shall deposit an amount equal to such excess balance in the cooperative endangered species conservation fund established under section 1535(i) of this title.

(e) Enforcement

(1) The provisions of this chapter and any regulations or permits issued pursuant thereto shall be enforced by the Secretary, the Secretary of the Treasury, or the Secretary of the Department in which the Coast Guard is operating, or all such Secretaries. Each such Secretary may utilize by agreement, with or without reimbursement, the personnel, services, and

facilities of any other Federal agency or any State agency for purposes of enforcing this chapter.

(2) The judges of the district courts of the United States and the United States magistrate judges may, within their respective jurisdictions, upon proper oath or affirmation showing probable cause, issue such warrants or other process as may be required for enforcement of this chapter and any regulation issued thereunder.

(3) Any person authorized by the Secretary, the Secretary of the Treasury, or the Secretary of the Department in which the Coast Guard is operating, to enforce this chapter may detain for inspection and inspect any package, crate, or other container, including its contents, and all accompanying documents, upon importation or exportation. Such person may make arrests without a warrant for any violation of this chapter if he has reasonable grounds to believe that the person to be arrested is committing the violation in his presence or view, and may execute and serve any arrest warrant, search warrant, or other warrant or civil or criminal process issued by any officer or court of competent jurisdiction for enforcement of this chapter. Such person so authorized may search and seize, with or without a warrant, as authorized by law. Any fish, wildlife, property, or item so seized shall be held by any person authorized by the Secretary, the Secretary of the Treasury, or the Secretary of the Department in which the Coast Guard is operating pending disposition of civil or criminal proceedings, or the institution of an action in rem for forfeiture of such fish, wildlife, property, or item pursuant to paragraph (4) of this subsection; except that the Secretary may, in lieu of holding such fish, wildlife, property, or item, permit the owner or consignee to post a bond or other surety satisfactory to the Secretary, but upon forfeiture of any such property to the United States, or the abandonment or waiver of any claim to any such property, it shall be disposed of (other than by sale to the general public) by the Secretary in such a manner, consistent with the purposes of this chapter, as the Secretary shall by regulation prescribe.

(4)(A) All fish or wildlife or plants taken, possessed, sold, purchased, offered for sale or purchase, transported, delivered, received, carried, shipped, exported, or imported contrary to the provisions of this chapter, any regulation made pursuant thereto, or any permit or certificate issued hereunder shall be subject to forfeiture to the United States.

(B) All guns, traps, nets, and other equipment, vessels, vehicles, aircraft, and other means of transportation used to aid the taking, possessing, selling, purchasing, offering for sale or purchase, transporting, delivering, receiving, carrying, shipping, exporting, or importing of any fish or wildlife or plants in violation of this chapter, any regulation made pursuant thereto, or any permit or certificate issued thereunder shall be subject to forfeiture to the United States upon conviction of a criminal violation pursuant to subsection (b)(1) of this section.

(5) All provisions of law relating to the seizure, forfeiture, and

condemnation of a vessel for violation of the customs laws, the disposition of such vessel or the proceeds from the sale thereof, and the remission or mitigation of such forfeiture, shall apply to the seizures and forfeitures incurred, or alleged to have been incurred, under the provisions of this chapter, insofar as such provisions of law are applicable and not inconsistent with the provisions of this chapter; except that all powers, rights, and duties conferred or imposed by the customs laws upon any officer or employee of the Treasury Department shall, for the purposes of this chapter, be exercised or performed by the Secretary or by such persons as he may designate.

(6) The Attorney General of the United States may seek to enjoin any person who is alleged to be in violation of any provision of this chapter or regulation issued under authority thereof.

(f) Regulations

The Secretary, the Secretary of the Treasury, and the Secretary of the Department in which the Coast Guard is operating, are authorized to promulgate such regulations as may be appropriate to enforce this chapter, and charge reasonable fees for expenses to the Government connected with permits or certificates authorized by this chapter including processing applications and reasonable inspections, and with the transfer, board, handling, or storage of fish or wildlife or plants and evidentiary items seized and forfeited under this chapter. All such fees collected pursuant to this subsection shall be deposited in the Treasury to the credit of the appropriation which is current and chargeable for the cost of furnishing the services. Appropriated funds may be expended pending reimbursement from parties in interest.

(g) Citizen suits

(1) Except as provided in paragraph (2) of this subsection any person may commence a civil suit on his own behalf—

(A) to enjoin any person, including the United States and any other governmental instrumentality or agency (to the extent permitted by the eleventh amendment to the Constitution), who is alleged to be in violation of any provision of this chapter or regulation issued under the authority thereof; or

(B) to compel the Secretary to apply, pursuant to section 1535(g)(2)(B)(ii) of this title, the prohibitions set forth in or authorized pursuant to section 1533(d) or 1538(a)(1)(B) of this title with respect to the taking of any resident endangered species or threatened species within any State; or

(C) against the Secretary where there is alleged a failure of the Secretary to perform any act or duty under section 1533 of this title which is not discretionary with the Secretary.

The district courts shall have jurisdiction, without regard to the amount in controversy or the citizenship of the parties, to enforce any such provision or regulation, or to order the Secretary to perform such act or duty, as the case may be. In any civil suit commenced under subparagraph (B) the district court shall compel the Secretary to apply the prohibition sought if the court finds that the allegation that an emergency exists is supported by substantial evidence.

(2)(A) No action may be commenced under subparagraph (1)(A) of this section—

(i) prior to sixty days after written notice of the violation has been given to the Secretary, and to any alleged violator of any such provision or regulation;

(ii) if the Secretary has commenced action to impose a penalty pursuant to subsection (a) of this section; or

(iii) if the United States has commenced and is diligently prosecuting a criminal action in a court of the United States or a State to redress a violation of any such provision or regulation.

(B) No action may be commenced under subparagraph (1)(B) of this section—

(i) prior to sixty days after written notice has been given to the Secretary setting forth the reasons why an emergency is thought to exist with respect to an endangered species or a threatened species in the State concerned; or

(ii) if the Secretary has commenced and is diligently prosecuting action under section 1535(g)(2)(B)(ii) of this title to determine whether any such emergency exists.

(C) No action may be commenced under subparagraph (1) (C) of this section prior to sixty days after written notice has been given to the Secretary; except that such action may be brought immediately after such notification in

the case of an action under this section respecting an emergency posing a significant risk to the well-being of any species of fish or wildlife or plants.

(3)(A) Any suit under this subsection may be brought in the judicial district in which the violation occurs.

(B) In any such suit under this subsection in which the United States is not a party, the Attorney General, at the request of the Secretary, may intervene on behalf of the United States as a matter of right.

(4) The court, in issuing any final order in any suit brought pursuant to paragraph (1) of this subsection, may award costs of litigation (including reasonable attorney and expert witness fees) to any party, whenever the court determines such award is appropriate.

(5) The injunctive relief provided by this subsection shall not restrict any right which any person (or class of persons) may have under any statute or common law to seek enforcement of any standard or limitation or to seek any other relief (including relief against the Secretary or a State agency).

(h) Coordination with other laws

The Secretary of Agriculture and the Secretary shall provide for appropriate coordination of the administration of this chapter with the administration of the animal quarantine laws (> 21 U.S.C. 101 to > 105, > 111 to > 135b, and > 612 to > 614) and section 306 of the Tariff Act of 1930 (> 19 U.S.C. 1306). Nothing in this chapter or any amendment made by this Act shall be construed as superseding or limiting in any manner the functions of the Secretary of Agriculture under any other law relating to prohibited or restricted importations or possession of animals and other articles and no proceeding or determination under this chapter shall preclude any proceeding or be considered determinative of any issue of fact or law in any proceeding under any Act administered by the Secretary of Agriculture. Nothing in this chapter shall be construed as superseding or limiting in any manner the functions and responsibilities of the Secretary of the Treasury under the Tariff Act of 1930 [> 19 U.S.C.A. S 1202 et seq.], including, without limitation, section 527 of that Act (> 19 U.S.C. 1527), relating to the importation of wildlife taken, killed, possessed, or exported to the United States in violation of the laws or regulations of a foreign country.

(ESA § 12)
§ 1541. Endangered plants

The Secretary of the Smithsonian Institution, in conjunction with other affected agencies, is authorized and directed to review (1) species of plants which are now or may become endangered or threatened and (2) methods of adequately conserving such species, and to report to Congress, within one year after December 28, 1973, the results of such review including recommendations for new legislation or the amendment of existing legislation.

ESA § 15)
§ 1542. Authorization of appropriations

(a) In general

Except as provided in subsections (b), (c), and (d) of this section, there are authorized to be appropriated —
(1) not to exceed $35,000,000 for fiscal year 1988, $36,500,000 for fiscal year 1989, $38,000,000 for fiscal year 1990, $39,500,000 for fiscal year 1991, and $41,500,000 for fiscal year 1992 to enable the Department of the Interior to carry out such functions and responsibilities as it may have been given

under this chapter;

(2) not to exceed $5,750,000 for fiscal year 1988, $6,250,000 for each of fiscal years 1989 and 1990, and $6,750,000 for each of fiscal years 1991 and 1992 to enable the Department of Commerce to carry out such functions and responsibilities as it may have been given under this chapter; and

(3) not to exceed $2,200,000 for fiscal year 1988, $2,400,000 for each of fiscal years 1989 and 1990, and $2,600,000 for each of fiscal years 1991 and 1992, to enable the Department of Agriculture to carry out its functions and responsibilities with respect to the enforcement of this chapter and the Convention which pertain to the importation or exportation of plants.

(b) Exemptions

There are authorized to be appropriated to the Secretary to assist him and the Endangered Species Committee in carrying out their functions under sections 1536(e), (g), and (h) of this title not to exceed $600,000 for each of fiscal years 1988, 1989, 1990, 1991, and 1992.

(c) Convention implementation

There are authorized to be appropriated to the Department of the Interior for purposes of carrying out section 1537a(e) of this title not to exceed $400,000 for each of fiscal years 1988, 1989, and 1990, and $500,000 for each of fiscal years 1991 and 1992, and such sums shall remain available until expended.

(d) Redesignated (c)

(ESA § 17)
§ 1543. Construction with Marine Mammal Protection Act of 1972

Except as otherwise provided in this chapter, no provision of this chapter shall take precedence over any more restrictive conflicting provision of the Marine Mammal Protection Act of 1972 [> 16 U.S.C.A. S 1361 et seq.].

(ESA § 18)
§ 1544. Annual cost analysis by Fish and Wildlife Service

On or before January 15, 1990, and each January 15 thereafter, the Secretary of the Interior, acting through the Fish and Wildlife Service, shall submit to the Congress an annual report covering the preceding fiscal year which shall contain—

(1) an accounting on a species by species basis of all reasonably identifiable

Federal expenditures made primarily for the conservation of endangered or threatened species pursuant to this chapter; and

(2) an accounting on a species by species basis of all reasonably identifiable expenditures made primarily for the conservation of endangered or threatened species pursuant to this chapter by States receiving grants under section 1535 of this title.

BIBLIOGRAPHY

I. FURTHER READING BY CHAPTER

Chapter One

Babbitt, Bruce, The Endangered Species Act and Takings: A Call for Innovation Within the Terms of the Act, 24 *Envtl. L.* 355 (1994).

Bean, Michael. *The Evolution of National Wildlife Law* (1997).

Flippen, John. The Nixon Administration, Timber, and the Call of the Wild, 19 *Envtl. Hist. Rev.* 37 (1995).

Graf, William. *Wilderness Preservation and the Sagebrush Rebellions* (1990).

——. *Beauty, Health, and Permanence* (1987).

Hays, Samuel. *Conservation and the Gospel of Efficiency* (1959).

Meltz, Robert. Where the Wild Things Are: The Endangered Species Act and Private Property, 24 *Envtl. L.* 369 (1994).

Reiger, John. *American Sportsmen and the Origins of Conservation* (1975).

Sher, Victor M. Travels with Strix: The Spotted Owl's Journey Through The Federal Courts, 14 *Pub. Land L. Rev.* 41 (1993).

Tober, James. *Who Owns the Wildlife?* (1982).

Trefethen, James. *An American Crusade for Wildlife* (1975).

Yaffee, Steven. *The Wisdom of the Spotted Owl* (1994).

Chapter Two

Bertelson, III, Richard W. Note, Danger for the Endangered Species Act?: Catron County Board of Commissioners, New Mexico v. United States Fish and Wildlife Service, 12 *J. Nat. Resources & Envtl. L.* 167 (1996-1997).

Division of Endangered Species, U.S. Fish and Wildlife Service, *Endangered Species Listing Handbook: Procedural Guidance for the Preparation and Processing of Rules and Notices Pursuant to the Endangered Species Act* (4th ed. 1994).

Ecological Society of America Ad Hoc Committee on Endangered Species, Strengthening the Use of Science in Achieving the Goals of the Endangered Species Act: An Assessment by the Ecological Society of America, 6(1) *Ecological Applications* 1 (1996).

Emery, Jean M. Environmental Impact Statements and Critical Habitat: Does NEPA apply to the Designation of Critical Habitat under the Endangered Species Act?, 8 *Ariz. St. L.J.* 973 (1996).

Houck, Oliver. The Endangered Species Act and Its Implementation by the U.S. Departments of Interior and Commerce, 64 *U. Colo. L. Rev.* 278 (1993).

Mann, Charles C. & Plummer, Mark L. *Noah's Choice: The Future of the Endangered Species Act* (1995).

McDonald, Jack. Critical Habitat Designation Under the Endangered Species Act: A Road to Recovery?, 28 *Envtl. L.* 671 (1998).

McMillan, Margaret. *Effects of the Moratorium on Listings Under the Endangered Species Act, Endangered Species Update,* Vol. 13 No. 1, 1996.

Meltz, Robert. Where the Wild Things Are: the Endangered Species Act and Private Property, 24 *Envtl. L.* 369 (1994).

National Research Council, *Science and the Endangered Species Act* (1995).

National Wilderness Institute, *Going Broke?: Costs of the Endangered Species Act as Revealed in Endangered Species Recovery Plans* (1994).

Ruhl, J. B. Section 7(A)(1) of the "New" Endangered Species Act: Rediscovering and Redefining the Untapped Power of Federal Agencies' Duty to Conserve Species, 25 *Envtl. L.* 1107 (1995).

Salzman, James. Evolution and Application of Critical Habitat Under the Endangered Species Act, 14 *Harv. Envtl. L. Rev.* 311 (1990).

Slaton, Jeffrey B. Natural Resources Defense Council v. United States Department of Interior: Making Critical Habitat Critical?, 21-FEB *Environs Envtl. L. & Pol'y J.* 75 (1998).

U.S. Fish and Wildlife Service & National Marine Fisheries Service, *Endangered Species Petition Management Guidance* (1996).

Zellmer, Sandi B. Indian Lands as Critical Habitat for Indian Nations and Endangered Species: Tribal Survival and Sovereignty Come First, 43 *S.D. L. Rev.* 381 (1998).

Chapter Three

Daugherty, Steven A. Threatened Owls and Endangered Salmon: Implementing the Consultation Requirements of the Endangered Species Act, 14 *Pub. Land L. Rev.* 203 (1993).

Des Rosiers, Jared. The Exemption Process under the Endangered Species Act: How the "God Squad" Works and Why, 66 *Notre Dame L. Rev.* 825 (1991).

Erdheim, Eric. The Wake of the Snail Darter: Insuring the Effectiveness of Section 7 of the Endangered Species Act, 9 *Ecology L.Q.* 629 (1981).

Freeman, Deborah L. & Sower, Carmen M. Against the Flow: Emerging Conflicts Between Endangered Species Protection and Water Use, 40 *Rocky Mtn. Min. L. Inst.* 23-1 (1994).

Houck, Oliver A. The Endangered Species Act and Its Implementation by the U.S. Departments of Interior and Commerce, 64 *U. Colo. L. Rev.* 278 (1993).

Hudson, Eric. Note, The National Park Service Organic Act and Section 7(A)(1) of the Endangered Species Act: Prioritizing Recreation and Endangered Species Preservation in the National Parks, 22 *Vt. L. Rev.* 953 (1998).

Kopf, Jeffrey S. Steamrolling Section 7(D) of the Endangered Species Act: How Sunk Costs Undermine Environmental Regulation, 23 *B.C. Envtl. Aff. L. Rev.* 393 (1996).

Patlis, Jason. Biodiversity, Ecosystems, and Endangered Species, in *Biodiversity and the Law* 43 (William J. Snape III ed., 1996).

Ruhl, J. B. Section 7(A)(1) of the "New" Endangered Species Act: Rediscovering and Redefining the Untapped Power of Federal Agencies' Duty to Conserve Species, 25 *Envtl. L.* 1107 (1995).

Schmidt, Brian A. Note, Reconciling Section 7 of the Endangered Species Act with Native American Water Rights, 18 *Stan. Envtl. L.J.* 109 (1999).

Steiger, John W. The Consultation Provision of Section 7(A)(2) of the Endangered Species Act and its Application to Delegable Federal Programs, 21 *Ecology L.Q.* 243 (1994).

U.S. Fish and Wildlife Service and National Marine Fisheries Service, *Endangered Species Consultation Handbook* (1998).

Chapter Four

Babbitt, Bruce. ESA & Private Property: The Endangered Species and "Takings": A Call for Innovation within the Terms of the Act, 24 *Envtl. L.* 355 (1994).

Batt, Kevin D. Above All, Do No Harm: Sweet Home and Section Nine of the Endangered Species Act, 75 *B.U. L. Rev.* 1177 (1995).

Causey, Inga Haagenson. The Reintroduction of the Wolf in Yellowstone: Has the Program Fatally Wounded the Very Species it Sought to Protect?, 11 *Tul. Envtl. L.J.* 461 (1998).

Cheever, Frederico M. An Introduction to the Prohibition Against Takings in Section 9 of the Endangered Species Act of 1973: Learning to Live With a Powerful Species Preservation Law, 62 *U. Colo. L. Rev.* 109 (1991).

Cribb, Steven. Endangered Species Act, Section 10(J): Special Rules to Reestablish the Mexican Wolf to its Historic Range in the American Southwest, 21-FEB *Environs Envtl. L. & Pol'y J.* 49 (1998).

Davison, Steven G. Alteration of Wildlife Habitat as a Prohibited Taking Under the Endangered Species Act, 10 *J. Land Use & Envtl. L.* 155 (1995).

Goldman-Carter, Janice. Federal Conservation of Threatened Species: By Administrative Discretion or Legislative Standard?, 11 *B.C. Envtl. Aff. L. Rev.* 63 (1983).

Halleland, Keith J. Sierra Club v. Clark: The Government Cries Wolf, 11 *Wm. Mitchell L. Rev.* 969 (1985).

Houck, Oliver A. The Endangered Species Act and Its Implementation by the U.S. Departments of Interior and Commerce, 64 *U. Colo. L. Rev.* 277 (1993).

Mueller, Tara L. Babbitt v. Sweet Home Chapter of Communities: When Is Habitat Modification a Take? (Part II of a Two-Part Article), 3 *Hastings W.-N.W. J. Envtl. L. & Pol'y* 333 (1996).

Murray, Paula C. Private Takings of Endangered Species as Public Nuisance: Lucas v. South Carolina Coastal Council and the Endangered Species Act, 12 *UCLA J. Envtl. L. & Pol'y* 119 (1993).

Nagel, Stacy. The Taking of the Delhisands Flower-Loving Fly: A Commerce Clause Challenge to the Application of Section 9(A)(1) of the Endangered Species Act, 5 *Mo. Envtl. L. & Pol'y Rev.* 143 (1998).

Nagle, John Copeland & Landrith, III, George C. *The Meaning of the Prohibition on Taking an Endangered Species* (National Legal Center for the Public Interest 1998).

Powell, Frona M. Defining Harm Under the Endangered Species Act: Implications of Babbitt v. Sweet Home, 33 *Am. Bus. L.J.* 131 (1995).

Quarles, Steven P. et al., Sweet Home and the Narrowing of Wildlife "Take" Under Section 9 of the Endangered Species Act, 26 *Envtl. L. Rep.* 10003 (1996).

Shaheen, Susan. The Endangered Species Act: Inadequate Species Protection in the Wake of the Destruction of Private Property Rights, 55 *Ohio St. L.J.* 453 (1994).

Thompson, Jr., Barton H. The Endangered Species Act: A Case Study in Takings and Incentives, 49 *Stan. L. Rev.* 305 (1997).

U.S. General Accounting Office, *Endangered Species: Information on Species Protection on Nonfederal Lands* (1994).

Yuen, Diane S. L. Casenote. Babbitt v. Sweet Home: Will the Endangered Species Act Survive? 18 *U. Haw. L. Rev.* 909 (1996).

Chapter Five

Barry, Donald J. Keynote Speech, Opportunity in the Face of Danger: The Pragmatic Development of Habitat Conservation Plans, 4 *Hastings W.-N.W. J. Envtl. L. & Pol'y* 129 (1998).

Baur, Donald C. and Donovan, Karen L. The No Surprises Policy: Contracts 101 Meets the Endangered Species Act, 27 *Envtl. L.* 767 (1997).

Bean, Michael J. et al., *Reconciling Conflicts Under the Endangered Species Act: The Habitat Conservation Planning Experience* (World Wildlife Fund 1991).

Beatley, Timothy. *Habitat Conservation Planning: Endangered Species and Urban Growth* (1994).

Bosselman, Fred P. The Statutory and Constitutional Mandate for a No Surprises Policy, 24 *Ecology L.Q.* 707 (1997).

Defenders of Wildlife, *Frayed Safety Nets: Conservation Planning Under the Endangered Species Act* (1998).

Derry, Amy C. Note, No Surprises After Winstar: Contractual Certainty and Habitat Conservation Planning Under the Endangered Species Act, 17 *Va. Envtl. L.J.* 357 (1998).

Fisher, Eric. Habitat Conservation Planning Under the Endangered Species Act: No Surprises & the Quest for Certainty, 67 *U. Colo. L. Rev.* 371 (1996).

Hall, Daniel A. Using Habitat Conservation Plans to Implement the Endangered Species Act in Pacific Coast Forests: Common Problems and Promising Precedents, 27 *Envtl. L.* 803 (1997).

Jasny, Michael. *Natural Resources Defense Council, Leap of Faith* (1997).

Jester, Jennifer. Habitat Conservation Plans Under Section 10 of the Endangered Species Act: The Alabama Beach Mouse and the Unfulfilled Mandate of Species Recovery, 26 *B.C. Envtl. Aff. L. Rev.* 131 (1998).

Kaiser, Jocelyn. Endangered Species: When a Habitat Is Not a Home, *Science*, June 13, 1997, at 1636.

Kareiva, Peter, et al. National Center for Ecological Analysis and Synthesis & American Institute of Biological Sciences, Using Science in Habitat Conservation Plans (1999) (visited Aug. 13, 1998) <http://www.nceas.ucsb.edu>.

Kostyack, John. Reshaping Habitat Conservation Plans for Species Recovery: An Introduction to a Series of Articles on Habitat Conservation Plans, 27 *Envtl. L.* 755 (1997).

Lin, Albert C. Participants' Experiences with Habitat Conservation Plans and Suggestions for Streamlining the Process, 23 *Ecology L.Q.* 369 (1996).

Mann, Charles & Plummer, Mark. Qualified Thumbs Up for Habitat Plan Science, *Science*, Dec. 17, 1997, at 2052.

Manson, Craig. Species and Habitat Conservation: Natural Communities Conservation Planning: California's New Ecosystem Approach to Biodiversity, 24 *Envtl. L.* 603 (1994).

Marsh, Lindell L. & Thornton, Robert D. *The San Bruno Mountain Habitat Conservation Plan, in Managing Land Use Conflicts* 114 (David J. Brower and Daniel S. Carol, eds, 1994).

Marsh, Lindell L. Conservation Planning Under the Endangered Species Act: A New Paradigm for Conserving Biological Diversity, 8 *Tul. Envtl. L.J.* 97, 110 (1994).

Minette, Mary & Cullinan, Tim. *A Citizen's Guide to Habitat Conservation Plans* (1997).

National Audubon Society, *Report of the National Audubon Society Task Force on Habitat Conservation Plans* (1997).

National Wildlife Federation, Regional Habitat Conservation Plan Summaries (visited May 4, 1998) <http://www.igc.apc.org/nwf/endangered/hcp/plnsum.html>.

Noss, R. F. et al. *The Science of Conservation Planning: Habitat Conservation Planning Under the Endangered Species Act* (Island Press 1997).

Phelps, Martha. Candidate Conservation Agreements Under the Endangered Species Act: Prospects and Perils of an Administrative Experiment, 25 *B.C. Envtl. L. Rev.* 175 (1997).

Ruhl, J. B. Regional Habitat Conservation Planning Under the Endangered Species Act: Pushing the Legal and Practical Limits of Species Protection, 44 *Sw. L.J.* 1393 (1991).

——. How to Kill Endangered Species, Legally: The Nuts and Bolts of Endangered Species Act "HCP" Permits for Real Estate Development, 5 *Envtl. Law.* 345 (1999).

Sheldon, Karin P. Habitat Conservation Planning: Addressing the Achilles Heel of the Endangered Species Act, 6 *N.Y.U. Envtl. L.J.* 279 (1998).

Shilling, Fraser. Do Habitat Conservation Plans Protect Endangered Species. *Science*, June 13, 1997, at 1662.

Sohn, David & Cohen, Madeline. From Smokestacks to Species: Extending the Tradable Permit Approach from Air Pollution to Habitat Conservation, 15 *Stan. Envtl. L.J.* 405, 409 (1996).

Special Issue, Habitat Conservation Planning, *Endangered Species Update*, Jul.-Aug. 1997.

Tasso, Jon P. Habitat Conservation Plans as Recovery Vehicles: JumpStarting the Endangered Species Act, 16 *UCLA J. Envtl. L. & Pol'y* 297 (1997-1998).

Taylor, Melinda E. Promoting Recovery or Hedging a Bet Against Extinction: Austin, Texas's Risky Approach to Ensuring Endangered Species' Survival in the Texas Hill Country, 24 *Envtl. L.* 581 (1994).

Thompson, Jr., Barton H. The Endangered Species Act: A Case Study in Takings and Incentives. 49 *Stan. L. Rev.* 305, 318 (1997).

Thornton, Robert D. The Endangered Species Act: Searching for Consensus and Predictability: Habitat Conservation Planning Under the Endangered Species Act of 1973, 21 *Envtl. L.* 605 (1991).

U.S. Fish and Wildlife Service & National Marine Fisheries Service, *Habitat Conservation Planning Handbook* (1997).

United States Fish and Wildlife Service, Habitat Conservation Plans and the Incidental Take Permitting Process (visited May 23, 1999) <http://www.fws.gov/r9endspp/hcp/hcpplan.html>.

U.S. General Accounting Office, *Endangered Species: Information on Species Protection on Non-Federal Lands* (1994).

Woodrow Wilson School of Public and International Affairs Policy Task Force, *Too Hot to Handle? Hot Spots, Habitat Conservation Plans, and the Endangered Species Act* (Princeton University 1997).

Younger, Christine L. Environmental Groups Say "No Surprises Is No Good," 11-7-96 *WLN* 11897.

Chapter Six

Alagappan, Meena. The United States' Enforcement of the Convention on International Trade in Endangered Species of Wild Fauna and Flora, 10 *Nw. J. Int'l L. & Bus.* 541 (1990).

Andrew, Dale & Steinfatt, Karsten. *Experience with the Use of Trade Measures in the Convention on International Trade in Endangered Species (CITES)* (OECD 1997).

Brooks, Jennifer Zoe. A Survey of the Court Enforcement of International Wildlife Trade Regulations Under United States Law, 17 *Wm. & Mary J. Envtl. L.* 145 (1993).

Cadeddu, Marlo Pfister. Note, Turtles in the Soup? An Analysis of the GATT Challenge to the United States Endangered Species Act Section 609 Shrimp Harvesting Nation Certification Program for the Conservation of Sea Turtles, 11 *Geo. Int'l Envtl. L. Rev.* 179 (1998).

Cheung, Julie. Implementation and Enforcement of CITES: An Assessment of Tiger and Rhinoceros Conservation Policy in Asia, 5 *Pac. Rim L. & Pol'y J.* 125 (1995).

Environmental Resources Management, *Study on How to Improve the Effectiveness of the Convention on International Trade in Endangered Species of Wild Fauna and Flora,* Reference 3717 (1996).

Favre, David S. Debate within the CITES Community: What Direction for the Future?, 33 *Nat. Resources J.* 875 (1993).

——. The Risk Of Extinction: A Risk Analysis of the Endangered Species Act as Compared to CITES, 6 *N.Y.U. Envtl. L.J.* 341 (1998).

Hara, Mafaniso. *International Trade in Ivory from the African Elephant: Issues Surrounding the CITES Ban and SACWM's Chances of Overturning it* (Centre for Southern African Studies 1997).

Harland, David. *Killing: International Law and the African Elephant* (1994).

Hill, Kevin D. The Convention on International Trade in Endangered Species: Fifteen Years Later, 13 *Loy. L.A. Int'l & Comp. L.J.* 231 (1990).

International Wildlife Trade: A CITES Sourcebook (Ginette Hemley ed., World Wildlife Fund & Island Press 1994).

Jenks, Daniel T. The Convention on Biological Diversity — An Efficient Framework for the Preservation of Life on Earth?, 15 *Nw. J. Int'l L. & Bus.* 636 (1995).

Master, Julie B. Note, International Trade Trumps Domestic Environmental Protection: Dolphins and Sea Turtles are "Sacrificed on the Altar of Free Trade," 12 *Temp. Int'l & Comp. L.J.* 423 (1998).

Patel, Shennie. Note, The Convention on International Trade in Endangered Species: Enforcement and the Last Unicorn, 18 *Hous. J. Int'l L.* 157 (1995).

Rogers, Kathleen & Moore, James A. Revitalizing the Convention on Nature Protection and Wild Life Preservation in the Western Hemisphere: Might Awakening a Visionary but "Sleeping" Treaty Be the Key to Preserving Biodiversity and Threatened Natural Areas in the Americas?, 36 *Harv. Int'l L.J.* 465 (1995).

Schwab, Michael J. Lujan v. Defenders of Wildlife: The Need for a Uniform Approach to Extraterritoriality, 19 *Brook. J. Int'l L.* 1009 (1993).

Wijnstekers, Willem. *International Fund for Animal Welfare, The Evolution of CITES: A Reference to the Convention on International Trade in Endangered Species of Wild Fauna and Flora* (Secretariat of the CITES 3d rev. ed. 1992).

Chapter Seven

Barney, Deanne M. Notes, The Supreme Court Gives an Endangered Act New Life: Bennett v. Spear and its Effect on Endangered Species Act Reform, 76 *N.C. L. Rev.* 1889 (1998).

Chaudhari, Preeti S. Bennett v. Spear: Lions, Tigers and Bears Beware; The Decline of Environmental Protection, 18 *N. Ill. U. L. Rev.* 553 (1998).

Christensen, Ronald K. Supreme Court Expands Standing Under the Endangered Species Act, 18 *J. Land Resources & Envtl. L.* 146 (1998).

Dobson, R. Margaret. Note, Endangered Species Act: Standing to Sue. Bennett v. Spear, 117 S. Ct. 1154 (1997), 20 *U. Ark. Little Rock L.J.* 1003 (1998).

Feldman, Murray D. Bennett v. Spear: Supreme Court Confirms Standing to Challenge Excessive Government Regulation Under Endangered Species Act, *Advocate,* June 1997, at 20.

Pham, Brandon L. The Federal Endangered Species Act: Is Judicial Review Available to Safeguard Against Agency Decisions Not to En-force? 13 *UCLA J. Envtl. L. & Pol'y* 329 (1994/1995).

Reimer, Monica. Competitive Injury as a Basis for Standing in Endangered Species Act Cases, 9 *Tul. Envtl. L.J.* 109 (1995).

Smith, Arthur D. Programmatic Consultation Under the Endangered Species Act: An Anatomy of the Salmon Habitat Litigation, 11 *J. Envtl. L. & Lit.* 247 (1996).

Sunstein, Cass. What's Standing After Lujan? Of Citizen Suits, "Injuries," and Article III, 91 *Mich. L. Rev.* 163 (1992).

II. OTHER ENDANGERED SPECIES READING

Ackerman, Diane. *The Rarest of the Rare: Vanishing Animals, Timeless Worlds* (Random House 1995).

Alvarez, Ken. *Twilight of the Panther: Biology, Bureaucracy, and Failure in an Endangered Species Program* (Myakka River Pub. 1993).

Balancing on the Brink of Extinction: The Endangered Species Act and Lessons for the Future (Kathryn A. Kohm ed., Island Press 1991).

Baldauf, Craig Robert. Searching for a Place to Call Home: Courts, Congress, and Common Killers Conspire to Drive Endangered Species into Extinction, 30 *Wake Forest L. Rev.* 847 (1995).

Balog, James. *Survivors: A New Vision of Endangered Wildlife* (H.N. Abrams 1990).

Beacham's Guide to International Endangered Species (Walton Beacham & Kirk H. Beetz eds., Vol. 1-2, Beacham Pub. 1998).

Bean, Michael J. & Rowland, Melanie J. *The Evolution of National Wildlife Law* (3rd ed., Environmental Defense Fund & World Wildlife Fund, U.S. 1997).

Bean, Michael J. Endangered Species Act and Private Land: Four Lessons Learned from the Past Quarter Century, 28 *Envtl. L. Rep.* 10701 (1998).

Bergoffen, Marty. *Endangered Species Act Reauthorization: A Biocentric Approach* (Elissa C. Lichtenstein ed., American Bar Association 1995).

Biodiversity Protection: Implementation and Reform of the Endangered Species Act (University of Colorado Natural Resources Law Center 1996).

Bogert, Laurence Michael. That's My Story and I'm Stickin' to It: Is the "Best Available" Science Any Available Science Under the Endangered Species Act?, 31 *Idaho L. Rev.* 85 (1994).

Brown, Jacqueline Lesley. Preserving Species: The Endangered Species Act Versus Ecosystem Management Regime, Ecological and Political Considerations, and Recommendations for Reform, 12 *J. Envtl. L. & Litig.* 151 (1997).

Center for Wildlife Law & Defenders of Wildlife, *State Endangered Species Acts: Past, Present, and Future* (Defenders of Wildlife & Center for Wildlife Law 1998).

Cheever, Federico. The Road to Recovery: A New Way of Thinking About the Endangered Species Act, 23 *Ecology L.Q.* 1 (1996).

Clark, Tim W. *Averting Extinction: Reconstructing Endangered Species Recovery* (Yale University Press 1997).

Coleman, Warren T. Legal Barriers to the Restoration of Aquatic Systems and the Utilization of Adaptive Management, 23 *Vt. L. Rev.* 177 (1998).

Coursey, Don L. The Revealed Demand for a Public Good: Evidence from Endangered and Threatened Species, 6 *N.Y.U. Envtl. L.J.* 411 (1998).

Craig, Barbara. The Federal Endangered Species Act, 38-OCT *Advocate* (Idaho) 12 (1995).

Defenders of Wildlife, Biodiversity and the Law (William J. Snape III ed., Island Press 1996).

Delaney, J., et al., *Land Use Practice and Forms: Handling the Land Use Case* (2nd ed. 1998).

Diner, David N. The Army and the Endangered Species Act: Who's Endangering Whom? 143 *Mil. L. Rev.* 161 (1994).

Doremus, Holly. Preserving Citizen Participation in the Era of Reinvention: The Endangered Species Act Example, 25 *Ecology L.Q.* 707 (1999).

———. Restoring Endangered Species: The Importance of Being Wild, 23 *Harv. Envtl. L. Rev.* 1 (1999).

Drozdowski, James. Note, Saving an Endangered Act: The Case for a Biodiversity Approach to ESA Conservation Efforts, 45 *Case W. Res. L. Rev.* 553 (1995).

The Endangered Species Act: A Commitment Worth Keeping. (The Wilderness Society for the Endangered Species Coalition 1992).

Endangered Species Act Conference, December 11-12, 1997, San Francisco, California (CLE International, Denver, Colo. 1997).

Endangered Species Recovery: Finding the Lessons, Improving the Process (Tim W. Clark et al., eds., Island Press 1994).

Melissa K. Estes, The Effect of the Federal Endangered Species Act on State Water Rights, 22 *Envtl. L.* 1027 (1992).

Fischer, Hank. *Building Economic Incentives into the Endangered Species Act* (Wendy E. Hudson ed., Defenders of Wildlife, 3rd ed. 1994).

Flournoy, Alyson C. Beyond the "Spotted Owl Problem": Learning From the Old-Growth Controversy, 17 *Harv. Envtl. L. Rev.* 261 (1993).

Frank, Andrew G. Reforming the Endangered Species Act: Voluntary Conservation Agreements, Government Conservation and Incentives for Private Action, 22 *Colum. J. Envtl. L.* 137 (1997).

Gidari, Albert. The Economy of Nature, Private Property, and the Endangered Species Act, 6 *Fordham Envtl. L.J.* 661 (1995).

Green, Blaine I. The Endangered Species Act and Fifth Amendment Takings: Constitutional Limits of Species Protection 15 *Yale J. on Reg.* 329 (1998).

Grierson, Kevin W. The Concept of Species and the Endangered Species Act, 11 *Va. Envtl. L.J.* 463 (1992).

Hill, Kevin D. The Endangered Species Act: What Do We Mean By Species?, 20 *B.C. Envtl. Aff. L. Rev.* 239 (1993).

Houck, Oliver A. The Endangered Species Act and Its Implementation by the U.S. Departments of Interior and Commerce, 64 *U. Colo. L. Rev.* 277 (1993).

———. Why Do We Protect Endangered Species, and What Does that Say About Whether Restrictions on Private Property to Protect Them Constitute "Takings"?, 80 *Iowa L. Rev.* 297 (1995).

———. Symposium on Clinton's New Land Policies: Reflections on the Endangered Species Act, 25 *Envtl.L.* 689 (1995).

Jackson, Thomas C. Lessons from the Endangered Species Wars, 12-FALL *Nat. Resources & Envt* 105 (1997).

Keiter, Robert B. Beyond the Boundary Line: Constructing a Law of Ecosystem Management, 65 *U. Colo. L. Rev.* 293 (1994).

Kirchheim, Diana. The Endangered Species Act: Does "Endangered" Refer to Species, Private Property Rights, the Act Itself, or All of the Above?, 22 *Seattle U. L. Rev.* 803 (1999).

Kunich, John Charles. The Fallacy of Deathbed Conservation Under the Endangered Species Act, 24 *Envtl. L.* 501 (1994).

Lambert, Thomas & Smith, Robert J. *The Endangered Species Act: Time for a Change* (Center for the Study of American Business, Washington University No. 119 1994).

Littell, Richard. *Endangered and Other Protected Species: Federal Law and Regulation* (Bureau of National Affairs 1992).

Losos, Elizabeth Claire. *Taxpayers' Double Burden: Federal Resource Subsidies and Endangered Species* (Wilderness Society & Environmental Defense Fund 1993).

Mann, Charles C. & Plummer, Mark L. *Noah's Choice: The Future of Endangered Species* (Knopf 1995).

Mann, Joe. Student Article, Making Sense of the Endangered Species Act: a Human-Centered Justification, 7 *N.Y.U. Envtl. L.J.* 246 (1999).

Meyer, Stephen M. The Economic Impact of the Endangered Species Act on the Housing and Real Estate Markets, 6 *N.Y.U. Envtl. L.J.* 450 (1998).

Miller, Brian, et al., *Prairie Night: Black-footed Ferrets and the Recovery of Endangered Species* (Smithsonian Institution Press 1996).

Moore, Michael R., et al., *Endangered Species and Irrigated Agriculture: Water Resource Competition in Western River Systems* (U.S. Dept. of Agriculture, Economic Research Service; ERS-NASS 1995).

Moulton, Michael P. & Sanderson, James. *Wildlife Issues in a Changing World* (St. Lucie Press 1997).

Mueller, Tara L. *Guide to the Federal and California Endangered Species Laws* (Planning and Conservation League Foundation 1994 & Supp. 1995 & Supp. 1996).

National Research Council, *Science and the Endangered Species Act* (1995).

O'Keefe, Kelly A. A "New American Land Ethic": Utilizing the Endangered Species Act to Settle Land Use Disputes, 21 *Fla. St. U. L. Rev.* 1031 (1994).

Parenteau, Patrick A. Who's Taking What? Property Rights, Endangered Species, and the Constitution, 6 *Fordham Envtl. L.J.* 619 (1995).

——. Rearranging the Deck Chairs: Endangered Species Act Reforms in an Era of Mass Extinction, 22 *Wm. & Mary Envtl. L. & Pol'y Rev.* 227 (1998).

Patliss, Jason M. Biodiversity, Ecosystems and Species: Where Does the Endangered Species Act Fit in?, 8 *Tul. Envtl. L.J.* 33 (1994).

——. Recovery, Conservation, and Survival Under the Endangered Species Act: Recovering Species, Conserving Resources, and Saving the Law, 17 *Pub. Land & Resources L. Rev.* 55 (1996).

Plater, Zygmunt J. B. The Embattled Social Utilities of the Endangered Species Act—A Noah Presumption and Caution Against Putting Gasmasks on the Canaries in the Coalmine, 27 *Envtl. L.* 845 (1997).

Private Property and the Endangered Species Act: Saving Habitats, Protecting Homes (Jason F. Shogren ed., University of Texas Press 1998).

Reference Book of Policies and Guidance for Implementing the Endangered Species Act (ESA) (Office of Protected Resources, U.S. Dept. of Commerce 1996).

Rockwell, A. Kimberly. The Fifth Amendment Implications of Including Habitat Modification in the Definition of Harm to Endangered Species (Babbitt v. Sweet Home Chapter of Communities for a Great Oregon, 115 S.Ct. 2407 (1995)), 11 *J. Land Use & Envtl. L.* 573 (1996).

Ruhl, J. B. Thinking of Environmental Law as a Complex Adaptive System: How to Clean up the Environment by Making a Mess of Environmental Law, 34 *Hous. L. Rev.* 933 (1997).

——. While the Cat's Asleep: The Making of the "New" ESA, 12-*WTR Nat. Resources & Env't* 187 (1998).

——. Who Needs Congress? An Agenda for Administrative Reform of the Endangered Species Act, 6 *N.Y.U. Envtl. L.J.* 367 (1998).

Sherry, Clifford J. *Endangered Species: A Reference Handbook* (ABC-CLIO 1998).

Shoemaker, Alan H. et al. *AZA Manual of Federal Wildlife Regulations* (American Zoo and Aquarium Association 1994).

Simon, Noel. *World Conservation Monitoring Centre, Nature in Danger: Threatened Habitats and Species* (Oxford University Press 1995).

Smith, Andrew A. et al. The Endangered Species Act at Twenty: An Analytical Survey of Federal Endangered Species Protection, 33 *Nat. Resources J.* 1027 (1993).

Souder, Jon A. Chasing Armadillos Down Yellow Lines: Economics in the Endangered Species Act, 33 *Nat. Resources J.* 1095 (1993).

Species Survival in Fragmented Landscapes (Josef Settele ed., Kluwer Academic 1996).

Stearns, Beverly Peterson & Stearns, Stephen C. *Watching, from the Edge of Extinction* (Yale University Press 1999).

Thompson, Jr., Barton H. People or Prairie Chickens: The Uncertain Search for Optimal Biodiversity, 51 *Stan. L. Rev.* 1127 (1999).

———. The Endangered Species Act: A Case Study in Takings and Incentives, 50 *Stan. L. Rev.* 305 (1997).

Tobias, Michael. *Nature's Keepers: On the Front Lines of the Fight to Save Wildlife in America* (John Wiley 1998).

Vaughan, Ray. State of Extinction: The Case of the Alabama Sturgeon and Ways Opponents of the Endangered Species Act Thwart Protection for Rare Species, 46 *Ala. L. Rev.* 569 (1995).

Villareal, Gavin R. Note, One Leg to Stand on: The Treaty Power and Congressional Authority for the Endangered Species Act After United States v. Lopez, 76 *Tex. L. Rev.* 1125 (1998).

Wilcove, David, The Promise and the Disappointment of the Endangered Species Act, 6 *N.Y.U. Envtl. L.J.* 275 (1998).

———, et al. *Environmental Defense Fund, Toward a More Effective Endangered Species Act for Private Land* (1996).

Wilcove, David Samuel. *The Condor's Shadow: The Loss and Recovery of Wildlife in America* (W. H. Freeman and Co. 1999).

Wildlife Conservation Society, Saving Wildlife: A Century of Conservation (Donald Goddard & Sam Swope eds., Harry N. Abrams 1995).

Winter, Kimberley K. The Endangered Species Act Under Attack: Could Conservation Easements Help Save the ESA?, 13 *N. Ill. U. L. Rev.* 371 (1993).

Wood, Mary Christina. Reclaiming the Natural Rivers: The Endangered Species Act as Applied to Endangered River Ecosystems, 40 *Ariz. L. Rev.* 197 (1998).

Zedler, Joy B. Adaptive Management of Coastal Ecosystems Designed to Support Endangered Species, 24 *Ecology L.Q.* 735 (1997).

INDEX

action agency, 84, 86-96, 100-101
Ad Hoc Committee on
    Endangered Species of the
    Ecological Society of
    America, 53
Administrative Procedure Act,
    28, 42-44, 50, 52, 54, 102, 205,
    213
    arbitrary and capricious
    standard, 54
Administrator of National
    Oceanic and Atmospheric
    Administration, 22
Administrator of the EPA, 22
Africa leopards, 200
African elephant, 184-187, 200
Agricultural Trade
    Development and Assistance
    Act of 1954, 175
Alabama beach mouse, 152
Alameda whipsnake, 40-42
Alaska, 14, 32
Alaskan bald eagle, 32
Alaskan brown bear, 189
American alligator, 189
American Forest & Paper Ass'n
    v. U.S.E.P.A., 100, 210
American Rivers v. National
    Marine Fisheries Service, 213
amoeba, 34
Anti-Deficiency Act, 163
Argali sheep, 200
Argentina, 174, 195, 197

Babbitt v. Sweet Home, 29, 107,
    109-110

Babbitt, Bruce, 28-29, 121, 133
bacteria, 34
Baker, Howard, 21
Balcones Canyonlands
    Conservation Plans, 144
    Regional HCP, 157
bald eagle, 1, 32, 35, 37, 58, 124,
    133, 135, 145, 214
Bald Eagle Protection Act, 17,
    126
Bennett v. Spear, 204-206, 209,
    213
bigleaf mahogany, 184
biodiversity, 1-2, 4-5, 8, 78, 125,
    174
biological assessment, 68, 84, 86-
    88, 90-91, 97, 101
biological opinion, 84, 89-97,
    100, 103, 206, 213
bison, 7, 15-16
bluefin tuna, 7
blue-tailed mole skink, 134
bobcat, 181, 189-190
Bolivia, 184, 195
Botswana, 186
Brazil, 184, 195, 197
brown pelican, 145
Bruneau Hot Springs snail, 50-
    52
Building Industry Association
    of Southern California v.
    Babbitt, 49, 51
bull trout, 48-49
Bureau of Fisheries, 17
Bureau of Land Management
    (BLM), 27, 48, 85

Sabertooth tiger, 2
Safe Harbor agreements, 168-170
sagebrush rebellion, 24
San Bruno Mountain HCP, 133, 135, 144, 155-157, 163
San Diego HCP, 144-145
San Joaquin kit fox, 144
sand skink, 134
Saudi Arabia, 181
Save the Yaak Committee v. Block, 211
scarlet macaw, 180
sea otter, 5-6
sea turtle, 6, 211
Seattle Audubon Society v. Espy, 210
Secretary of Agriculture, 16, 22, 102
Secretary of the Army, 22, 102
Secretary of the Interior, 17, 22, 24, 28-29, 68, 100, 102, 196, 211
Section 4, 26-27, 31, 39-40, 42-43, 46, 56-59, 64, 66-68, 71-73, 75-76, 115-116, 197, 200, 202, 212
Section 7, 12, 22-23, 27-28, 46, 59, 60, 67-68, 75-86, 88, 90-91, 97-100, 102-103, 104, 117, 127, 128-131, 133, 135, 146, 166, 173, 198-199, 207-208, 212-213
  action agency, 86-87
  action area, 86
  applicable agency actions, 86
  biological assessments, 87-88
    environmental impact statement (EIS) as sufficient, 88
  biological opinion, 91-93
    conservation recommendations, 94-95

consultation history, 92
cumulative effects, 93
description of proposed action, 92
effects of the action, 93
environmental baseline, 93
incidental take statement, 94
literature cited, 95
reasonable and prudent alternatives, 91, 93-94
reinitiation notice, 95
required content, 91-92
status of species, 92
commitment of resources, 97
conferences regarding proposed species, 88-89
consultation requirements, 85
  coordinated actions, 85
  ecosystem protection, 85
  programmatic actions, 85
critical habitat, 99
  jeopardy standard, 99
early consultation for federal permittees, 95-96
  preliminary biological opinion, 96
emergency consultation, 96-97
exemptions, 100-102
  ex parte contact, 102
  Gray Rocks Dam, 101
  Oregon timber sales, 101
  Tellico Dam, 101
expert agency, 86-87
formal consultation, 89-95
  initiation, 89-90
  timeframes, 90-91
incidental take statements
  required contents, 129-130
informal consultation, 87
judicial review, 102-103
major components, 78-79
procedural overview, 84